Praise for From Corporate Globalization to Glob

"This is a book that not only experts, but also concerned citizens should read. With outstanding clarity the author shows the enormous degree to which conventional economics is alien to the real world. If economics were a science, economists would behave like scientists. That is; if a theory proves to be wrong, the scientist immediately starts searching for an alternative. This is exactly what conventional economists never do. No matter how disastrous an economic situation may be, the answer is always 'more of the same.' Thatcher's TINA (There is no alternative) is the most dramatic case that has done so much damage to the world. But an additional value of the book is the true alternatives for a New Economy that the author brilliantly offers. After reading the book, one feels that, after all, a better world is possible."

— Manfred Max-Neef, Universidad Austral de Chile.

"We all know something is fundamentally wrong in our world, wrong in a way that requires a deep transformation in our thinking and behaviour. Tom Webb offers a path to another future, one based on co-operation and respect for the whole of creation. A lovely book."

— Maude Barlow, National Chairperson of the Council of Canadians and winner of the 2005 Right Livelihood Award.

"A book not to miss. Provocative, radical, incisive — Tom Webb never fails to nail the issues."

— Dame Pauline Green,
past president of the International Co-operative Alliance.

"Tom Webb is a passionate visionary and he is surely right in the core claim of this important book, that the world needs co-operation now more than ever."

— Edward Mayo, Secretary General of Co-operatives UK.

"The journey this book offers asks the reader to pack two items: a belief that we can build a healthier and more equitable world, and a willingness to be of open mind and heart to drive the innovation and creativity that diverse thinking creates."

— Kathy Bardswick, President and CEO of the Co-operators.

"The market system that triumphs over most of the Earth today is a clear danger to the health of many life forms, including human societies. In describing his lifelong commitment to co-operatives as an alternative approach to production, Tom Webb offers hope for movement toward a realistic alternative economic/social system. This books offers practical, experience-based information on how to understand the co-operative movement and how to help it expand its influence."

— Dr. Neva R. Goodwin, Co-Director, Global Development and Environment Institute, Tufts University.

"This will be a very useful book for those who want to know about co-operation but also for those inside co-operation who wonder how to fix up the problems that co-operatives sometimes face. We particularly agree on the book's premise, that co-operation is based on an anthropological assumption that is opposite to that of the mainstream, namely the 'innate goodness of people' who practice the 'golden rule' of reciprocity. Those people must have appropriate institutions to express that golden rule and not be constrained into egoistic structures."

—Dr. Stefano Zamagni and Dr. Vera Negri, University of Bologna.

"Many voices are calling for wide-ranging changes to our economic, social and political systems. They are driven by concerns about rising inequality, the destruction of nature, and the undermining of democracy resulting from increasing global corporate power. Tom Webb's important contribution stands out from the crowd because of his impassioned, informed and inspiring advocacy of the co-operative business model as an essential feature of any successful alternative to the current system of ailing capitalism and its dependence on endless economic growth."

— Peter A. Victor,
author of *Managing Without Growth: Slower by Design, Not Disaster.*

"Tom Webb delivers a collection of reflections about humanity in disconnect with its economic life. His unwavering trust in people and co-operation come through in every chapter, as does the sorrow in witnessing our civilization melt away at our collective fingertips. A mix between observation and hope, the book is a legacy of a true visionary co-operator who, by stating the obvious, always points out to everything we, humans, take for granted."

— Sonja Novković, Saint Mary's University.

From Corporate Globalization to

GLOBAL
CO-OPERATION

From Corporate Globalization to

GLOBAL CO-OPERATION

We Owe It to Our Grandchildren

J. TOM WEBB

FERNWOOD PUBLISHING
HALIFAX & WINNIPEG

Editing: Brenda Conroy
Cover design: John van der Woude, inspired by a drawing by the author
Photos: CanStock
Printed and bound in Canada

Published by Fernwood Publishing
32 Oceanvista Lane, Black Point, Nova Scotia, B0J 1B0
and 748 Broadway Avenue, Winnipeg, Manitoba, R3G 0X3

www.fernwoodpublishing.ca

Fernwood Publishing Company Limited gratefully acknowledges the financial support of the Government of Canada through the Canada Book Fund, the Manitoba Department of Culture, Heritage and Tourism under the Manitoba Publishers Marketing Assistance Program and the Province of Manitoba, through the Book Publishing Tax Credit, for our publishing program. We are pleased to work in partnership with the Province of Nova Scotia to develop and promote our creative industries for the benefit of all Nova Scotians. We acknowledge the support of the Canada Council for the Arts, which last year invested $153 million to bring the arts to Canadians throughout the country.

Library and Archives Canada Cataloguing in Publication

Webb, Tom, 1946-, author
From corporate globalization to global co-operation:
we owe it to our grandchildren / Tom Webb.

Includes bibliographical references and index.
Issued in print and electronic formats.
ISBN 978-1-55266-872-6 (paperback).--ISBN 978-1-55266-874-0
(kindle).--ISBN 978-1-55266-873-3 (epub)

1. Cooperative societies. 2. Social entrepreneurship.
3. Capitalism. 4. Globalization. I. Title.

HD2963.W42 2016   334   C2016-903193-4
C2016-903194-2

Contents

I dedicate this book to those, except for whom,
it would never have been written:
Marion, for her love and support
My parents, whose love and values nurtured my spirit
My beloved children and grandchildren and future
generations, who deserve a better world

ACKNOWLEDGEMENTS

This book was written in the hope that its ideas will help make this a better world. At my age, I have little to gain from these ideas, but I know that the shape of the world that is unfolding will be of immense importance to our children and grandchildren and future generations. As a species, we are spiritually bound to generations past and to come. Their dreams and hopes are connected to us. In a healthy society, we live for ourselves and for them. The book is written for us but also very much for them.

My parents left me a better world than the one they grew up in, amidst World War I, the Great Depression and World War II. They instilled in our family strong values and ethical reflection. I hope we have done the same for our children, but I fear the world we are leaving them is not improved, but seriously diminished. My belief that there can be a better world began with my parents and family. My brother, Jim, who served as a Jesuit priest in Jamaica for more than twenty years, also had a powerful influence on my thinking. He had a deep commitment to social justice and lived out a preferential option for the poor, day by day. His focus on education, justice, co-operative development and peace was evident not only in what he preached but in the way he lived, and in his deep love for the people of Jamaica. He dedicated his life to making a better world.

The ideas expressed in the book owe a great deal to the inspiration of Dr. Sidney Pobihushchy, long time co-operative activist and thinker, academic, volunteer and friend. I first met Sid at a worker co-operative conference in 1981 where I gave a talk. He told me he was very impressed by my talk and asked me to join him for dinner. By the time we finished desert he had raised eight questions he thought I should "reflect about," given my speech. Feeling a bit chastened and defensive, I retired to my hotel room to lick my wounds. I reread the speech. He was right about every point, had raised them in the order in which they had occurred, and did it all without notes. It was brilliant! We had breakfast the next morning. Sid challenged people to think clearly about co-operation, and like Moses Coady, Jimmy Tompkins and Don Jose Arizmendiarretia, he left you with books and papers to read and prodded you until you read them. Then he prodded you more until he was sure you were thinking critically about the ideas. I hope this book is worth at least a bit of the time he spent prodding me. I was enormously pleased when Saint Mary's University in Halifax, Nova Scotia, awarded him an honorary degree. Sid's death was a great loss to the cause of co-operation.

I had the good fortune in the late 1980s to work with Glenn Haddrell and the Co-operative Housing Foundation of Canada. Glenn had a deep co-operative spirit and a profound commitment to the values of co-operation. His leadership style was one that celebrated giving others the opportunity to be their best. While he was a key leader in the development of co-operative housing in Canada, his mind applied co-operation to every aspect of life with a keen intelligence. He enthusiastically organized study visits to centres of worker co-operation in England, France and Spain. Glenn was at once a gentle but spirited co-operator who questioned and pushed whenever the activities of co-operatives strayed from the spirit of co-operation. He remains an inspiration and a valued friend.

Working on the Co-operative Management Education (CME) program at Saint Mary's University gave me the opportunity to think about how managing a co-operative is profoundly different. It is different from managing other forms of organization — like investor-owned businesses, social enterprises or government departments. I am deeply grateful to Dr. John Chamard, whose faith in building a master's level degree program in co-operative management was instrumental in making it happen. John, the chair of the Management Department, led the push to bring the program to Saint Mary's. He was a clear thinker and deeply anti-bureaucratic. His fine mind, well-earned credibility and deeply held values played a strong role in creating the CME program. At John's request, one of the songs sung at his funeral was Peter, Paul and Mary's "If I Had a Hammer." John had a well-used hammer.

The program would have struggled with many issues had not Saint Mary's been led by its visionary president, Dr. Colin Dodds. I was moved and delighted when he served as a co-host of the International Co-operative Summit and the Imagine 2012 International Conference on Co-operative Economics, held in Quebec City, Canada, in October 2012. He cleared obstacles out of the way and was unceasingly encouraging. Also crucial was the support and work of Dr. Sonja Novković, and Drs. Larry and Judy Haiven. Their presence as part of the co-operative management team, building the rational case for the program and teaching in it, were powerful supports. I am also deeply grateful to the administrative work of Cathy Mason, who made things happen even when it should not have been possible. Intelligent administrative effort is irreplaceable, and Cathy provided it.

The CME program had the freedom to engage some of the finest available academics from around the globe who researched and wrote about co-operative management. I learned a great deal as they developed their courses for the program, and I am profoundly grateful to them: Dr. Stephen Dutcher from University of New Brunswick brought not only his deep knowledge of co-operatives but an approach to learning co-operatively that shaped the program; Alan Robb, a co-operative accounting pioneer, taught co-operative accounting at Canterbury University in New Zealand; Daniel Cote of the Haut Études Commercial in Montreal brought years of research on co-operative identity; Dr. E.G. Nadeau from University of Wisconsin taught about innovation in co-operatives; Dr. Tommy Singleton from Alabama developed our first accounting course; Dr. Gregory Fleet from University of New Brunswick brought years of experience in digital technology to bear on co-operation; Georgina Whyatt from Oxford Brookes University in the U.K. taught about how to market the co-operative advantage; Dr. Daphne Rixon from the Saint Mary's Accounting Department shifted much of her research to co-operatives and became executive director of the Centre of Excellence in Accounting and Reporting for Co-operatives (CEARC); Jim Smith, an experienced co-operative accountant from Virginia, brought his depth of experience in working with co-operatives in the United States.

I am grateful as well to the Canadian Institute of Chartered Accountants and its successor organization, Chartered Professional Accountants of Canada, which provided generous support, and the National Society of Co-operative Accountants in the U.S. Both were open to and supportive of new ideas. Promoting new ideas around what to account for in co-operatives played a central role in the CME program. Working on the CME program facilitated my exposure to dozens of co-operative scholars from around the world. I have benefited from their work and analysis. I fear that much of their knowledge and critical thinking shaped my thought without my being fully able to give them credit for their ideas. I hope I do their thinking the justice it deserves.

Dennis Deters of the Co-operators Insurance championed the CME program and ensured that the program had both strong financial support and enrolment from his organization and other co-operatives. Dennis cared about developing a co-operative way to manage and placed great value on challenging people to develop the capacity for critical analysis. When, from time to time, we taught ideas he did not agree with, he valued them because they stimulated thought. Dennis's thoughtful commitment to the ideas and values of co-operation made him another logical recipient of a Saint Mary's University honorary degree.

I am also enormously grateful to the many fine co-operative managers who enrolled in the program. Almost everyone who taught in the program sponta- neously remarked that it is the quality of students that makes faculty value the opportunity to teach in it. The high calibre of the online group discussions and of student papers is impressive and a source of great hope for the future. There is much depth in the leadership of the co-operative movement, and our graduates are poised and able to make impressive contributions. I want to name them all, but with more than ninety graduates to date, space does not permit me to do that. I look forward to the day when a thousand networked CME graduates around the globe become key drivers of global co-operation.

In many ways the conceptual framework for this book came from Imagine 2012: The International Conference on Co-operative Economics. I am enormously grateful to Sonja Novković and Cathy Mason who organized the conference with me and to the presenters: Thomas Homer-Dixon, Neva Goodwin, Vera Negri-Zamagni, John Fullerton, William Rees, Peter Victor, Ronald Colman, Stefano Zamagni, Manfred Max-Neef, Richard Wilkinson, David Erdal, Avner Ben-Ner and Claudia Sanchez Bajo. I am also grateful to Dr. Barbara Allen who assisted in putting together our tribute to the thought of Dr. Elinor Ostrom, who had agreed to speak at the conference but sadly died a couple of months before. Dr. Ostrom's work on how to regulate the commons earned her the Economics Prize in Memory of Alfred Nobel. Together the presenters demonstrated there is a powerful and deep body of clear economic thought that fits with the values of co-operation. They proved that we can move beyond destructive neoclassical economic ideology.

I am also grateful to Robert H. Burlton, former CEO of Oxford Swindon and Gloucester and Midcounties Co-operatives, chair of the Co-operative Group, Co-operative Financial Services and Co-operatives U.K. and president of the 1999 U.K. Co-operative Congress. Bob is an innovative thinker and supportive of others breaking new ground. His dedication to and support of the CME program was superlative. Bob provided me with an understanding of the co-operative movement in the U.K., and introduced me to many inspiring and supportive co-operative leaders, like Dame Pauline Green, who just concluded her term as president of the International Co-operative Alliance; Peter Couchman, with the Plunkett Foundation; and Ben Reid, the current innovative CEO of Midcounties Co-operative.

I owe much to co-operative leaders who run so many fine co-operative businesses in Canada, the United States and the United Kingdom, who had faith in the idea that managing a co-operative was different and so generously supported the development of the Saint Mary's University program. The Co-operative Bank and the Co-operative Group, in the pre Peter Marks era, showed brilliant leadership. Vivian Woodell and the U.K. Phone Co-op, as well as the Scottish Organization of Agricultural Societies (SOAS), were inspiring supporters. The whole network of food co-operatives in the United States is impressive, and the Consumer Co-operative Management Association (CCMA) conferences led by Dr. Ann Hoyt lifted my spirits every time I had the privilege to attend. Doing a workshop or making a speech at

CCMA conferences demanded thoughtful preparation and always resulted in my learning more than I was able to give.

I had the immense good fortune to be involved with outstanding co-operators from around the globe: Jane Livingston, Terry Appleby, Sean Doyle, Russell Wasson and Paul Hazen in the U.S.; Jesus Herrasti, Mikel Lezamiz and Fred Freundilch in Mondragon in the Basque Country of Spain; Ian Reid, Girol Karacaoglu and Ramsey Margolis in New Zealand; Kathy Bardswick and Dennis Deters from The Co-operators in Canada; Don Kinnersley, Rowan Dowland, Trent Bartlett and Tim Mazzarol in Australia; and Monique Leroux and her colleagues at Desjardins who so generously supported the Imagine 2012 International Conference on Co-operative Economics; Tamara Vrooman from VanCity, a credit union that inspires people around the world; Geoff Southwood with United Farmers of Alberta; and dozens of others who equally deserve mention.

I am grateful to Sheng Hong, who took on the task of tracking down permissions and high resolution copies of many of the graphs and figures in the book. She did not always meet with co-operation but she stuck to the task with intelligence and perseverance.

I would also like to express my appreciation to Fernwood Publishing. Errol Sharpe has encouraged the idea for this book from the beginning and gave valuable feedback. Beverley Rach has steered it through a process of making it better. Brenda Conroy did a superb editing job. Nancy Malek and Curran Faris have provided great support in marketing and promotion. The Fernwood experience has been very positive indeed.

Finally, I would be remiss if I did not highlight the contribution of my family. My children have all been a source of reflection and my growth as a person. Thank you Coady, Syntoya, Amber, Matthew and in a special way, Tara, who built the index to the book and did a perceptive and thoughtful cover to cover edit. Tara's husband Andrew also provided valuable and helpful editorial comments. My wife and partner Marion has stood with me, for better or for worse, for almost fifty years. Of all the choices I have made in my life she was and remains the very best. The values of co-operation are in her DNA. She not only ensured I had the comfort of a safe and empowering home base, but has proved an intelligent and thoughtful editor, especially for this book. She seems to know when my words do not capture my ideas and refuses to let unclear passages slide by, often when I am impatient to move on. Her support endured even when the book impinged on our precious time together.

I am blessed.

SEARCHING FOR A BETTER WORLD

This book is not about economics or politics or society. It is about where they all meet. It is not value free. The vision that drives it is the search for a better world. The motivation for writing it is grounded in a growing apprehension about the capitalism-driven trends of the last fifty years, a profound belief in the general goodness of humanity and a sense of realistic optimism. It is a set of reflections about the human condition and how we might better organize our thinking, structures and processes to enhance human dignity. Intuitively and rationally, I have come to the conclusion that the ideas, principles and values of co-operation offer the best opportunity to enhance human dignity. My bias is that co-operation is more important and healthier than competition; that forgiveness is better than revenge; that giving and sharing produce a greater sense of personal wellbeing than getting and hoarding; and that love produces a better world. If these things are true, we should base our actions and organizations and our economic, social and political systems on co-operation, forgiveness, giving, sharing and nurturing love. We have not done so.

I come by these ideas as a result of growing up in a particular family, community, culture and religious tradition. Others can and have reached similar ideas from other families, communities and faith traditions. One of the beautiful characteristics of co-operation and co-operatives is that they provide a comfortable organizational framework to peoples of differing religious beliefs, languages and cultures from all over the globe.

The book begins with an uncomfortable exploration of the trends that offer the greatest threat to our world. It is not a pessimist's view. If we cannot face the problems, we cannot solve them. Chapters 2 and 3 focus on the intellectual thinking and organizational form that drive the key trends. Chapter 4 explores the foundations of co-operation, not simply as an organizational form, but as a driving force in the evolution of life on our planet. It looks at the purpose, values and principles of co-operative organizations and the organizational flexibility they offer humanity. Chapter 5 examines how co-operatives can help us remediate global trends based on organizational characteristics and past performance. Chapter 6 is an uncompromising look at how co-operatives and co-operators need to improve their performance if they are to make the kind of contribution they should in facing global trends and creating a better world. Chapter 7 looks at the kind of public policies that would support a gradual shift to a co-operative economy. Chapter 8 presents some conclusions about what is possible.

BASIC ASSUMPTIONS UNDERLYING CO-OPERATION

I once received a memo from the CEO of a co-operative. He let me know in no uncertain terms that he believed that workers (likely including me) in our co-operative were abusing their expense claims. He indicated he would be taking action to end the abuse by personally reviewing ten claims each month. Anyone found making a questionable claim would be dealt with. What a difficult job that manager had! He could have sent out a request for help with the expectation that workers would respond and help him meet the target. Instead, he made it clear that he thought the workers were untrustworthy. His message was: "You will co-operate only because I am looking over your shoulder and will punish you." If you hold that view, how can you manage a co-operative? Why would you want to? If you held that view you would never choose the co-operative way of organizing a business.

The CEO's effort failed. Expense claims went up. He simply misjudged human nature. Research shows that the solutions developed by groups are almost invariably superior to individual solutions. Co-operation harnesses the creativity of groups and brings out the best in each person.

My own belief in the innate goodness of people is deeply rooted in the way my parents and many others treated me as a child. It comes from the idea planted early that all creation, including us, reflects a good and beautiful creator. The idea has also been reinforced by observation. For the most part, when people are given the choice between good and evil, they choose good. In the mid 1980s I visited the Haitian *batays* (villages) in the Dominican Republic. In the village of Santa Maria there was a woman, completely crippled, who lived alone in a tiny hut. Her one-room home was made of mud and sticks with a banana leaf roof and a mud floor. All the homes in the *batay* were the same, except most were a bit bigger and housed more people. She had no relatives and we asked who looked after her. "People in the village" was the response. These people earned only about $2 (Cdn) a day for eight to ten hours of backbreaking work. While many in the village suffered from malnutrition, she did not. I have encountered human meanness too. There is a lot less of it, but meanness makes the news while most kindness does not.

The United Nations Universal Declaration of Human Rights begins with the following phrase: "Whereas, recognition of the inherent dignity and of the equal and inalienable rights of all members of the human family is the foundation of freedom, justice and peace in the world." It is around this concept of dignity that all thinking about human society must revolve. Whatever erodes this dignity is to be shunned and whatever enhances it must be nurtured. For me this is the meaning of the words of the Christian prayer, "Thy will be done on earth as it is in heaven." The goodness of people in every corner of our planet shows in the beliefs they have evolved independently from each other. If we believe people are good and have dignity and worth then we wish to treat them as we ourselves wish to be treated. I have often marvelled at how thinkers and mystics from varied traditions think similar thoughts. Out of the religions of the world come the following examples:

> Islam: "Not one of you truly believes until you wish for others what you wish for yourself." The Prophet Muhammad, Hadith
>
> Buddhism:" Treat not others in ways that you yourself would find hurtful." Udana-Varga 5.18
>
> Judaism: "What is hateful to you, do not do to your neighbor. This is the whole Torah; all the rest is commentary." Hillel, Talmud, Shabbat 31a
>
> Taoism: "Regard thy neighbor's gain as your own gain and your neighbor's loss as your own loss." T'ai Shang Kan Ying P'ien, 213–218
>
> Sikhism: "I am a stranger to no one and no one is a stranger to me. Indeed I am a friend to all." Guru Granth Shaib, page 1299
>
> Confucianism: "One word sums up the basis of all good conduct … loving kindness. Do not do to others what you do not want done to yourself." Confucius, Analects 15:23

The beauty and complexity of human, plant and animal life and the intricacy of interrelationships among living organisms in our world are awe inspiring. Creation is humbling. Seeing creation as one, beautiful and good, all at the same time, is a powerful aid to understanding the ecology of our earth. That makes all the more incredible the way we destroy that creation and put human society at risk. To work against creation, or to subdue it, will ultimately lead to our own destruction, for we are enmeshed in it. The dignity of people and the dignity of creation are sides of the same coin.

Another part of my heritage is the great value that I place upon community. Outside of community, it is almost impossible for people to find any profound meaning in life. The dignity of each individual is not diminished by the paradoxically social nature of our species. The process of human development is the process of becoming fully individual and perfecting our uniqueness. In the words of M. Scott Peck:

> We are beckoned toward that self-sufficiency, that wholeness, required for independent thought and action. But all this is only one side of the story.... Yet the reality is that we are inevitably social creatures who desperately need each other, not merely for sustenance, not merely for company, but for any meaning to our lives whatsoever.[1]

Peck goes on to confront the cult of "rugged individualism," which is the plague of our time.

> Thus the problem — indeed the total failure — of the "ethic" of rugged individualism is that it runs with only one side of this paradox, it incorporates only one half of our humanity. It recognizes that we are called to individuation, power and wholeness. But it denies entirely the other part of the human story: that we can never fully get there and that we are, of necessity in our uniqueness, weak and imperfect creatures who need each other.[2]

It is in community that we test our worth and derive our meaning. It is in service, not in taking, that we become all we can be. What this all describes is the reality of our interdependence, which has been commented upon by many outstanding thinkers. Dr. Elise Boulding expressed it well when she said: "It is hard for true individuality to flourish in a milieu that lacks attentive others who can mirror back the growth of one's individuality over time."[3] Desmond Tutu put it clearly in a speech in Toronto: "We are placed on earth to discover that we are made for togetherness, for interdependence, for complementarity."[4]

Another fundamental assumption of co-operation is justice. Justice is not to be confused with charity. Charity has to do with sharing what we have with those who have suffered misfortune. When there is an earthquake we give to protect the lives and dignity of those who have suffered. It is charitable to give to the poor through food banks. Charity, especially this latter charity, carries with it a risk — it can be done to make the giver feel good or even superior. Carried to its extreme, a charitable gift could even become an evil action if the givers intend to use it to boost their reputation and power in society. Charity can also be used to give donors control over recipients, completely subverting any semblance of "doing good."

Food banks exist, after all, because our society functions in such a way as to permit some to be wealthy beyond reason while others lack access to even the most basic necessities. In a society characterized by justice, each person would have the dignity that comes from being able to contribute, and no one would lack the basic necessities of life. Not having the ability to contribute to society erodes our sense of meaning, demeans our spirits and diminishes our will to live. Not having the basic necessities of life degrades us and for many means malnutrition, disability and death. A society which is increasingly characterized by the widespread degradation of human dignity in these ways is becoming less civilized.

There is another aspect of justice that seems important. The discussion of justice makes some rich and powerful people, and even some middle-income people, uncomfortable. Dom Helder Camara, a former Brazilian archbishop, captured this discomfort about justice when he said: "When I feed the poor they call me a saint. When I ask why they are poor they call me a communist." Those of us who are among the less than 10 percent of the world's population who own cars, risk discomfort when we contemplate why we have a car while billions starve and lack water and shelter. Charity offers no hope in confronting the problems which face our world. At best charity can buy some time if our world is in the process of becoming more just. Alas, our world is becoming less just. So is my country.

Finally, there is the question of judgement. Deeply imbedded in my psyche is a red warning light which comes on when I find myself judging people. If people are inherently good, then how can I judge them to be otherwise? Time has taught me how little I know about anyone else. At times, I scarcely know why I do what I do, and I am puzzled by my own actions. How could I ever know enough to judge others? On the other hand, structures and actions are not only candidates for judgement but must be judged. A respect for human dignity and a love for creation demands judgement of actions and structures, not people. We know too that we are not always correct, and our fallibility demands an openness to reconsider.

When I think of my five children, I feel a profound sense of joy. When I look at the major trends sweeping our world, my joy is tempered with sadness. Co-operation is not a panacea, but the structures of co-operation offer great hope. They nurture human dignity better than most business structures. They are more open to ecological action because of their community ownership base. They free the human spirit and allow us to act on a range of goals and aspirations. They give us freedom to build a better world.

NOTES
1   Peck 1987: 54–55.
2   Peck 1987: 56.
3   Boulding 1978: 5.
4   Tutu 2000.

Chapter 1

A WORLD
OF OMINOUS
UNCERTAINTY

We live in a world turned inside out. It is the age of economics, of capitalist economics, as opposed to the age of reality. In the real world human society exists as part of the natural world. Human society has cultural, social and economic aspects. The economy is embedded in human society (see Figure 1-1). We are dependent on the natural world for our very existence. In destroying the natural world, we are undermining the viability of our own existence. We need clean air to breathe, clean water to drink, food that will nourish our bodies and natural spaces to nourish our spirits. If we render the planet uninhabitable for a large portion of life, we may well be among the forms of life that perish. Some of us might survive in a natural world much less hospitable to life, but it will be a remnant and the human economy will be a remnant as well.

The same is true of human society. We need a healthy functioning society to have a healthy functioning economy. Most people would agree that a healthy society is one with healthy functioning families and communities. In the inside-out, economy-driven world, families and communities are expendable. Consider the commonly accepted statement: "People have to go where the jobs are." The logic is that we should tear apart families and communities if it is "profitable." In the inside-out world it is increasingly accepted that "jobs" are short-term or part-time or contract. Such work insecurity makes family and community life increasingly unstable, but it is convenient and profitable to our corporations. A healthy society is one in which families are able to provide themselves with food, clothing, shelter, health care and education — the basics of comfortable life — and still have some time for leisure with family and friends. In a world whose purpose is to serve the economy, low wages are profitable and wealth moves to where they may be obtained.

Alas, we are living in an inside-out world where many of our leaders tell us we must destroy nature to fuel the economy. Most public policy decisions are made in line with this belief, as demonstrated by the appalling inability of our economic leaders and their political followers with regard to climate change. Faced with overwhelming scientific evidence and analysis, almost all economic and political leaders around the globe respond at best by doing nothing, and at worst, as in Canada, by cutting research, silencing scientists and destroying libraries or making them inaccessible, and reducing the available information for decision making. Many of the super-rich use their economic resources to deny and distort science or to sow as much confusion as possible so they can continue with business as usual. Others are simply silent, being too occupied generating wealth from the destruction of the planet. The wellbeing of future generations, their health and their ability to earn a living and sustain their communities are being sacrificed for the next quarter's profits.

Figure 1-1 shows the place of human society in "right-side-out" and "inside-out" thinking. Common sense tells us that the economy is a part of human society, not the reverse. It is people who create the economy, not the economy which creates people. Yet there are spokespersons for the inside-out view of the world, who deny that society even exists. In neoclassical austerity economics, society exists but only as a subset of the economy — something to be manipulated to make the economy healthy. We are told that spending on education, health care and the elderly must be cut if we are to improve the economy, even if it has a deleterious effect on society. Austerity policies were in full force during the infamous World Bank/International Monetary Fund sponsored structural adjustment period. For

Figure 1-1 Losing Touch with Reality

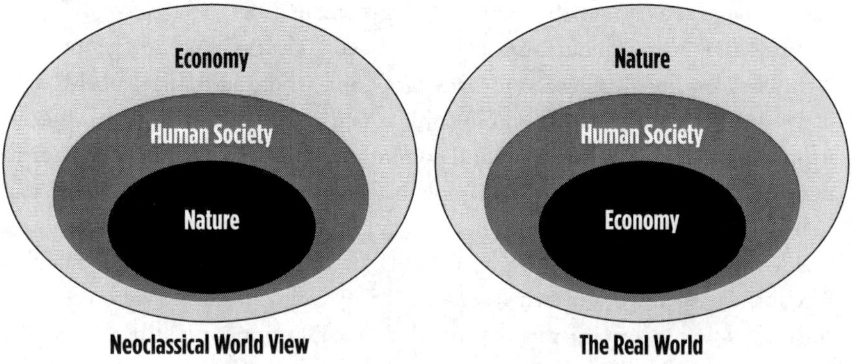

Neoclassical World View   The Real World

example, in the late 1980s the child-to-staff ratio in the main orphanage in Kingston, Jamaica, doubled, supposedly so that Jamaica could build a healthy economy following WB/IMF rules. The real reason was to ensure that loans made by rich world banks would be paid. Children were very seldom picked up or cared for properly, causing anguish to the staff charged with looking after them and terrible damage to the children. The Jamaican economy did not improve, and the children, when adults, will be an enormous burden to Jamaican society. But the economy exists as a part of human society. To the extent we destroy human society we destroy the possibility of a healthy economy.

INTERRELATED GLOBAL ISSUES

This chapter looks at the powerful trends sweeping our world. These interrelated global issues include growing inequality, massive environmental problems, an addiction to infinite growth in a finite world and growing economic instability. The driving force shaping these issues is capitalism and its latest attempt at self-serving justification, neoclassical economics, which is largely supported and financed by it. Interwoven with these issues are symptoms that include an inability to shift from non-renewable energy sourcing, food insecurity, financialization of the economy, corporate concentration, corporate globalization, increasing urbanization and the explosion of urban slums, degradation of the oceans and collapse of the fish resources, fresh water pollution, natural resources depletion, the technology explosion fuelling the rate of change, declining resilience and a robotic revolution.

None of these trends exists in isolation. For example, food security and oil are interdependent. Rising energy prices drive up food prices since more and more of the world's food comes from larger and larger corporations using petroleum-based fertilizers and pesticides and petroleum-dependent farm equipment. On the other hand, if OPEC countries drop the price of oil, it will temporarily lower food prices and accelerate the use of oil. This will lead to a more rapid depletion of oil supplies, rapid oil price hikes and higher food prices. In other words, any change in energy use or price will impact food.

Corporate concentration drives urbanization. Escalating fossil fuel use drives climate change. Climate change drives economic instability and shifts the use of resources from meeting needs to disaster recovery. The trends interact, and in a capitalist setting they are mutually reinforcing. Multiple trends interacting makes it difficult to understand cause and effect. The impacts of multiple issues on each other are sometimes nearly invisible and other times clear but difficult to measure. For example, what is the connection between energy use and volcanoes? If fossil fuel consumption drives global warming, which in turn melts huge ice sheets in Greenland, reducing pressure on the earth's crust and triggering a volcanic eruption, can we be sure what role global warming played? Would the volcano have erupted anyway? The science says there is a link, but how big a link? Unknown. Margaret Chan, with the World Health Organization, tells us: "For public health, climate change is the defining issue for the 21st century."[1] The issues are connected. If we don't understand the connections it can kill us, our children and/or our grandchildren.

Let me end this introduction to trends with a caution. Halfway through this you may find yourself getting depressed. Why should you read on? Imagine you lived in a neighbourhood where children were being hit by cars. Every day, when you learned of some new tragedy you said to your partner in life, "I don't want to talk about it — it is simply too depressing. Let's focus on something positive." What if everyone in the neighbourhood did the same? Logic tells us children would continue to be hit by cars. A true cause for depression would be lacking the courage to examine reality and face it. I sometimes refer to it tongue in cheek as the "curse of positive thinking." If we do not have the courage to examine our unpleasant realities, then there is little hope for our children and grandchildren. Hope grows out of courage. Without courage there can be no real hope.

ECOLOGICAL OVERSHOOT

The simple reality is that the global economy is in ecological overshoot. The concept of "ecological footprint" was developed in 1996.[2] It is a measure of the land, air, water and natural resources required to produce the goods and services we consume and the waste we produce annually. As of 2008, humanity was using 1.5 times the resources each year that the natural world can provide on a sustainable basis. What this means is that the available fresh water supply is shrinking, fisheries and forest resources are in decline, and pollution and waste are piling up faster than nature can absorb them. According to William Rees, global overshoot day in 2012, the day by which we used a whole year's worth of sustainable resources, was August 22. "In effect for the duration of 2012, the growth and maintenance of the human enterprise will be funded by unsustainably depleting the Earth's limited 'natural capital', polluting ecosystems and otherwise degrading global life support functions."[3]

ENVIRONMENTAL DESTRUCTION AND EXTINCTIONS

For 650 million years there has been life on this planet. Over time life evolves, creating ever-increasing variety and complexity. Simple life forms become more complex. The varieties of butterflies and animals and fish and reptiles — all multiply. The number of species on the planet increases with time until something interferes. Fossil records show steady increases and then sudden catastrophic declines. But

Figure 1-2 Extinction – 650 Million Years Ago to Present

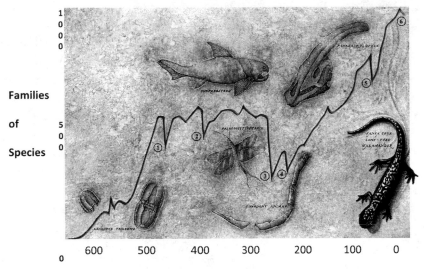

Source: Morell 1999: 49.

after each massive die-off the number of species begins again to increase. Science tells us the die-offs of species were caused by events like large volcanic eruptions or asteroids colliding with earth. The dust or volcanic ash thrown up obscured the sun, reducing the sunlight reaching the surface of the planet. The result was years of reduced plant growth and with it the food supply upon which many species depended, resulting in their extinction. Mass extinctions have occurred five times over the past 650 million year history of the planet.

Today we are in the beginning of the sixth mass extinction. Figure 1-2 illustrates the history of life on the earth.[4] The numbered dots represent catastrophic events resulting in a massive die-off of species. The first five were the result of natural events, but the sixth catastrophe is the impact of our economy. Our economic activity is literally rendering the planet unfit for life.

DESTRUCTIVE ENERGY SOURCING AND USE

As life evolved over millions of years in a natural cycle of birth and death, layers of dead plant life became buried under billions of tons of sediment, creating vast storehouses of fossil fuels, which our clever species figured out how to use to keep us warm, cook food, create new materials and run machines. It is a finite resource. Once depleted it will be irreplaceable. Some uses for fossil fuels will be more difficult than others to find replacements for. There may be even more important uses yet to be discovered. The main criteria for their use now is whether they generate profits and how fast. We are desperately clinging to non-renewable fuel use. Figure

1-3 graphs the long-term relationship between oil and humanity. It is clear we will need to adopt new energy sources. The only question is whether we will do so in a controlled and planned way or wait until we are sliding down the oil supply decline out of control. Little investment, except in a few countries, like Germany and China, is being made in research or development of renewable energy sources.

As we gallop toward the depletion of our fossil fuels, the cost of remaining supplies will escalate, not in a straight line but rather in an erratic pattern dictated by speculative markets and geopolitical scheming and oil wars (see Figure 1-4). This erratic economic behaviour will have important consequences for food security, transportation and a host of other issues.

Figure 1-3: Long-Term View of Historical Oil Use

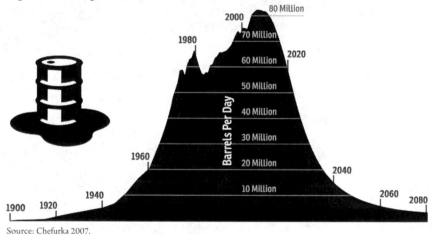

Source: Chefurka 2007.

Figure 1-4: World Oil Prices 1946 – 2018

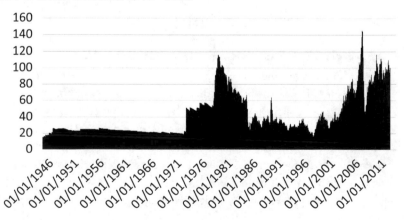

Historical monthly WTI crude oil prices per barrel back to 1948. Data is adjusted for inflation using the headline CPI. Source: Macrotrends <http://www.macro-trends.net/chart/1369/crude-oil-price-history-chart>.

CLIMATE CHANGE

The indiscriminate use of fossil fuels is pumping greenhouse gases into our atmosphere at a rate that is resulting in a rapid increase in global warming.[5] This is a trend denied only by ignorance, wilful ignorance or knowing the facts but denying they exist. The latter is often accompanied by attempts to confuse using "cigarette company science," funded by those who put their short-term profits ahead of the wellbeing of future generations. Climate change is, unless contained by a sharp reduction in greenhouse gases, an accelerating process. As the climate warms, ice caps and glaciers shrink and permafrost thaws. The resulting exposed rock and water absorb solar energy previously reflected back into space, and thawed permafrost releases trapped methane, further increasing greenhouse gases and speeding capture of energy by our atmosphere.

Climate change will produce a wide variety of effects around the world, including a rise in ocean levels, inundating coastal cities; changing ocean temperatures and currents; a shift in spawning and reproductive patterns of fish; changing ocean acidity; increasing moisture in the air, producing storms of increased intensity and frequency; accelerating desertification in arid areas; and changes in what crops may be grown where. Already, insurance companies around the globe are recognizing the increasing claims from weather disasters (see Figure 1-5). Annual insured losses between 1990 and 2000 averaged $23.5 billion a year, but for the period between 2001 and 2014, this figure more than doubled, to $47.1 billion.[6]

Figure 1-5 Human-Caused Disasters and Natural Catastrophes

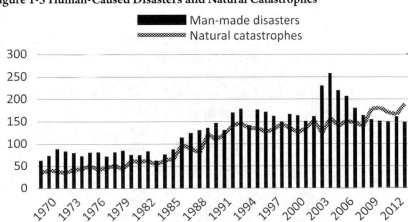

Source: Swiss Re 2015.

These disasters are far more serious for the 80 percent of the population sharing less than 15 percent of global income. Some changes in a region may be positive (the possibility of new crops) and some will be negative (flooded coastal cities and damage by more frequent and more massive storms). At best there will be significant economic adjustments and at worst enormous economic damage. In the name of short-term profits we are leaving a huge environmental time bomb for our children. It is even worse to leave our grandchildren an environmental debt enormously larger than the financial debt required to solve environmental problems.

FRESH WATER DEPLETION AND POLLUTION

The demand for fresh water is spiralling. Mineral and oil sands production are polluting fresh water at an ever-increasing rate as low cost sources of these non-renewable resources are depleted. For decades, the number of acres of cropland being irrigated increased every year, but now that trend has slowed and in more and more areas is declining. Water is being turned into a commodity more expensive than oil, and significant sources are being privatized on a user-pay basis, with a growing gap between rich and poor. Some of the world's largest multinational companies are bottling millions of litres of water for sale in the midst of droughts and shortages for family consumption and agriculture. Fossil aquifers[7] are being depleted around the globe using electric and diesel pumps. Deserts are growing. This represents a dual process which on the one hand passes the problems associated with pollution on to society but on the other hand converts the water, needed by rich and poor alike for daily survival, from a public good into a source of private gain. The result is growing water insecurity especially for those in the bottom 80 percent of the population.

As easily obtained fossil fuel energy is depleted, new costlier energy sources like oil recovery from Canada's tar sands and hydrocarbons obtained by "fracking" are becoming a growing part of energy use. Both tar sands oil and fracking energy products use enormous amounts of water and produce massive amounts of polluted water. In the Amazon there is ongoing logging and clearing of forests to grow sugarcane and soybeans, for ethanol fuel and cattle feed, and mainly for export. These crops use great quantities of water. More crucially, this disrupts the so called "flying rivers" of moisture collected by warm air moving over the tropical forests, with the result that areas downwind experience drought. Again, short-term gain for a few comes at the expense of future generations.

DEGRADATION OF THE OCEANS

Seventy percent of our planet is covered with oceans. With our new ability for space travel we have dubbed our home the blue planet. And yet we are having a devastating impact on these vast spaces. The dead zones in the ocean caused by oxygen depletion fuelled by fertilizers are growing. In them, huge algae blooms deplete oxygen to the point where little or no life exists. Stocks of many species have collapsed from over-fishing and from environmental shifts, such as changing water temperatures in spawning grounds. Off the shores of Atlantic Canada, codfish that in the 1600s were so numerous they could be caught in baskets lowered over the side of a boat, are depleted to the point where the stocks have not recovered even after a more than twenty-year moratorium on commercial fishing.

Earth's oceans are increasingly home to floating beds, or "gyres," of discarded plastic, which are deadly to many fish and ocean mammals (see Figure 1-6). An estimated eight million tons of plastic waste a year make their way into the world's oceans, enough to line up five filled grocery bags of garbage for every foot of the world's coastlines.[8] Micro plastic bits, ingested by and toxic to many forms of sealife, are found in increasing concentrations in the oceans as a result of the failure of humanity to control its plastic wastes. These toxic wastes are the product of business practices where it is regarded as efficient to "externalize" the costs as part of the profit maximization process.[9]

Figure 1-6 Ocean Gyres[10]

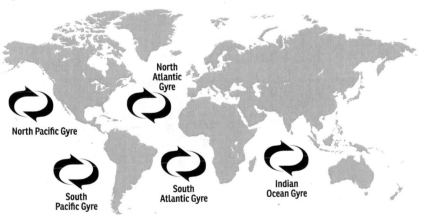

DESTRUCTIVE INEQUALITY

Two leading Italian economists with global stature note a basic truth: "The market system cannot function properly in the long run if a substantial quota of people are unable to participate in it for lack of purchasing power. We are all aware of countries that have regressed miserably because, in spite of having considerable natural and human capital, they are unsuccessful in properly applying the rule of equity."[11]

In the mid-1990s the United Nations Global Development Report showed that the distribution of wealth around the world had reached incredible levels. Figure 1-7 shows that, in 1996, the richest 20 percent of the world's people received 82.7 percent of the world's income. The remaining 80 percent shared just 17.3 percent and the poorest 20 percent obtained only 1.4 percent. The gap between the rich countries and the poor countries was growing, as was the gap between rich and poor individuals worldwide. It was not possible to make any moral or rational justification for this massive inequality in 1996, and since then the situation has worsened. Now the richest 20 percent have more than 87 percent of the world's wealth. This may be regarded as a "trickle down theory" failure or perhaps the genesis for a new data-based theory, the "trickle up reality."[12]

Since 1996, the population of the world has grown; global economic productivity has increased; the gap between some of the poor countries and the rich countries has slightly narrowed; the incomes of the very rich have grown enormously even during the 2008 Great Recession (see Figure 1-8); and the gap between the rich

Figure 1-7: The Global Champagne Glass Economy

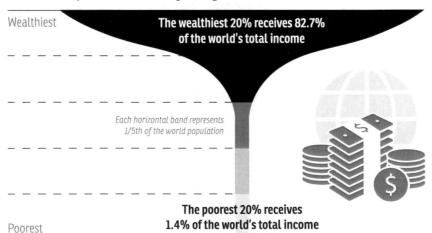

DISTRIBUTION OF WORLD INCOME
World's Population Classified by Income   Source: UNDP Development Report 1996

Wealthiest

The wealthiest 20% receives 82.7% of the world's total income

Each horizontal band represents 1/5th of the world population

The poorest 20% receives 1.4% of the world's total income

Poorest

Source: Graphic by John van der Would, developed for the author based on UNDP statistics from 1996.

and poor within both rich countries and poor countries has widened. A 2014 report by Oxfam indicates that the richest 1% have almost 50 percent of the world's wealth.[13] It might well be argued that this incredible inequality represents the most glaring evil in our world.

In recent years growing attention is being paid to the share of the world's wealth going to the extremely rich. "In the United States the share of national income going to the top 1 percent has doubled from 1980 going from 10 to 20 percent. For the top 0.01 percent it has quadrupled." This is not confined to the United States or indeed to the rich countries. In the U.K. inequality is rapidly returning to levels not seen since the time of Charles Dickens. In China the top 10 percent now take home nearly 60 percent of the income (see Figure 1-9). This economy will dominate the global economy in the not too distant future. What happens to it is important.

Globally the incomes of the top 1 percent have increased 60 percent in twenty years. Following the financial crisis, the process has accelerated, with the top 1 percent further increasing their share of income."[14] Even more startling is the inequality of wealth. "The wealth of 1 percent of the world's richest people is equivalent to a total of US$110 trillion — sixty-five times the total wealth of the poorer half of the world's population. In the last twenty-five years, wealth has been increasingly

Figure 1-8 — Distribution of Average Income Growth During Expansions, U.S., 1949–2012

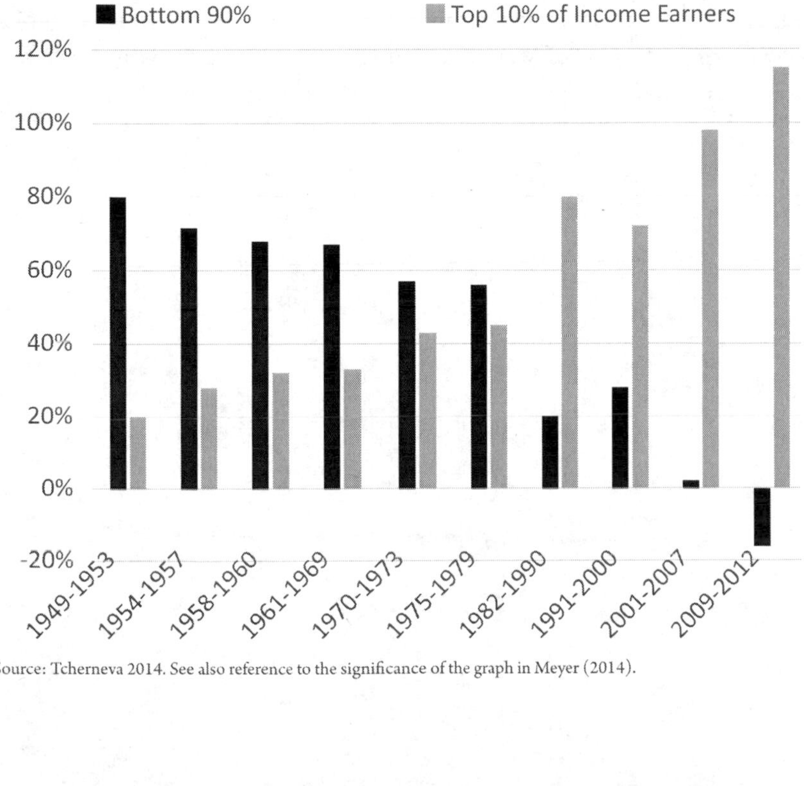

Source: Tcherneva 2014. See also reference to the significance of the graph in Meyer (2014).

concentrated in the hands of a few, leading to a tiny elite owning 46 percent of the world's wealth."[15]

The reason for this wealth concentration lies not just in government policies to focus our economies on the desires of capital owners but also on the extensive use by the super-rich of tax havens. These are financial institutions in countries other than the home country of the wealthy individual where money can be hidden to avoid paying taxes. Gabriel Zucman estimates that just under 10 percent of the world's wealth is hidden in tax havens and that the loss of tax revenue is around U.S.$200 billion annually.[16] Tax havens serve the rich in two ways: they protect their wealth and they weaken the ability of governments to protect their citizens.

An important aspect of the income gap is the increasing ability of corporate CEOs, with the acquiescence of boards controlled by the super-rich, to reward themselves, even when their results are disastrous. Witness the $60 million a year given to the CEO of Lehman Brothers Bank in the seven years leading up to its collapse. During a period of dismal economic performance CEOs continued to be paid many times what the performance of the companies they controlled seem to warrant. Based on data from the Organization for Economic Co-operation and Development, the American Federation of Labour reports the average Canadian CEO made 206 times more ($8.7 million a year) than the average Canadian worker ($42,253), and the average American CEO made a staggering 354 times more (over $12 million a year) than the average worker ($34,645) in the U.S.[17] With millions of gallons of toxic sludge pouring into salmon rivers in British Columbia, oil disasters in the Gulf of Mexico, sourcing from Bangladesh sweatshops where thousands of workers died, and the millions who died in the aftermath of the 2008

Figure 1-9: China's Rising Income Inequality

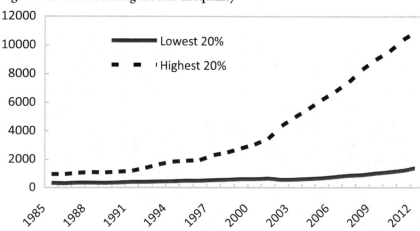

Source: Talley 2015.

financial mismanagement, it is not possible to imagine any justification for these obscene salary gaps.

> You might have heard about recent reports stating that global inequality is decreasing. This is a nice example of constructing the comparison according to the result you would like to see. Yes, inequality between countries has declined but the most important comparison is what is happening to inequality within countries, as this tells you how the distribution system that is under direct political control works. And if you look at this you can only shake your head in disbelief.[18]

The cost of inequality is staggering. In their seminal book, *Spirit Level*, Richard Wilkinson and Kate Pickett enumerate the following impacts as income inequality within a country grows:

- life expectancy decreases;
- math and literacy skills decline;
- infant mortality rises;
- child wellbeing declines;
- homicides increase;
- imprisonment rates increase;
- teenage births increase;
- trust among the population declines;
- obesity increases;
- mental illness increases;
- drug and alcohol addictions increase; and
- social mobility, the likelihood poor people can improve their lot in life, declines.

This is an appalling price to pay for having an economy organized to only serve capital. It is interesting to note that the United States, which imagines itself as the land where anyone can reach the top, has one of the lowest levels of social mobility in the world. This is a product of successful capitalism, whose purpose, after all, is to maximize the return to those who own capital. In perhaps the ultimate comment on the present economic system, Wilkinson and Pickett show that greater equality benefits both rich and poor. If greater equality also benefits the rich, it would seem capitalism renders the rich unable to understand how to look after their own best interests.

FOOD INSECURITY

In the latter half of the twentieth century it had begun to look as if humanity had conquered the problem of feeding the world's population. The agricultural Green Revolution, combining new crop varieties, mechanized farm production, effective petroleum based pesticides and fertilizers, was producing global surpluses in spite of rising populations. Alas, a series of food-linked problems emerged. Income inequality is linked to population growth and as inequality grows family size grows. Income inequality results in a double-edged food security challenge. Growing income inequality means the poor simply cannot purchase the food they need and the global population grows faster.

As noted above there is a direct link between the cost of food produced by mechanized fossil fuel powered agriculture, and the cost of energy.[19] In addition, as energy prices rise, the demand for biofuels rises, re-purposing land from food production to energy production. The agrifood business globally is becoming more and more concentrated in fewer and fewer hands.[20] Analysts suggest that within a decade or two, ten to fifteen huge global corporations will control more than 70–80 percent of the world's food supply. As early as 1995 the top eleven global food corporations were referred to as the "global food cartel," noting that very little food moves anywhere around the globe without their involvement.[21] History has shown that corporate concentration, even on much smaller scales, produces market and price controls, and there are no effective global controls on oligopoly price manipulation. It is also evident that as large corporations seek land it is the lowest income people who suffer with a negative impact on income equality. "What we have learned from the biofuel land grab, is it is always the hungriest, the poorest, the most marginalized who suffer the most. In the end, they get pushed off their land and thrown into poverty as they can't afford the price of food."[22] The bottom line is that the purpose of mega food corporations is not the production of food but maximization of returns to investors.

Concern over the loss of arable land has been rising over the past fifty years. The dust bowl of the Great Depression represented not just a period of dramatically reduced production but a long-term loss of arable and quality farm land. In 1984 the Canadian Senate held extensive hearings and produced a significant report on soil loss and degradation. The report had little impact. Soil erosion remains a serious threat to human society. Humans obtain more than 90 percent of their food from land-based production. Each year about ten million hectares of cropland are lost due to soil erosion, with more than 3.7 billion people malnourished in the world. Overall, soil is being lost from land areas ten (U.S.) to forty (China) times faster than the rate of soil renewal, imperiling future human food security and environmental quality. Between 1961 and 2002 alone, arable land decreased from 0.42

Mechanical erosion of the soil

hectares per person to just 0.23.[23] Some new proposals for carbon capture, such as BECCS (bio-energy with carbon capture and storage), will increase the use of land for non-food production. Urban growth, with most cities located on or around prime agricultural land, is anticipated to continue its explosive expansion. Almost 30 percent of global soil degradation is due to industrialization, which is closely related to urban growth, and 35 percent is due to over grazing.[24]

Another perspective from which to view food security is the declining quality of food. Effort to boost growth rates, pest resistance, climate adaptability and durability for transportation time and handling have all led to declines in the nutritional value of food. The objective of many so called food production improvements has been to improve profitability with little attention to food nutritional quality. Studies over time show consistent drops in the nutritional quality of food. While they vary in detail, reports of decline are consistent, and the problem is a significant trend around the world, led by the industrial countries. A British study of twenty vegetables showed the average calcium content had declined 19 percent, iron 22 percent and potassium 14 percent.[25] Another study concluded that one would have to eat eight oranges today to derive the same amount of vitamin A as our grandparents would have gotten from one. A Kushi Institute study comparing analysis of twelve fresh vegetables showed calcium levels dropped 27 percent from 1975 and 1997, iron 37 percent, vitamin A 21 percent and vitamin C 30 percent.[26]

The nutrients give food taste and our bodies have evolved to associate taste with nutrition. As the nutritional quality has declined in response to the drive for return on capital, the food industry has used sophisticated science to add artificial and so called natural flavours to foods that mimic the taste of nutrients but do not deliver them. This drives up sales and profits but the result is that to get the nutrition we need we have to overeat, and we often overeat foods that do not supply nutrition but mimic the taste of nutrition. This is in addition to cleverly advertised "food like" products loaded with salt, sugar and fat.[27] Obesity and profits are the most important products of the industrial food system.[28]

Food safety is also a growing facet of global concern about food security as more and more inspection and regulation are turned over to the corporations themselves. In addition, committees or organizations, dominated by representatives of the corporations, sett the rules and regulations supposedly designed to protect people. As governments shrink, more and more public policy functions are privatized. This is true in most nations and increasingly at the international level. The so-called free trade agreements are prime international examples. They are negotiated, often in secret with minimal public disclosure, with the involvement of the world's largest corporations. The agreements usually include corporate tribunals, whose deliberations are held in secret, to judge whether national laws and regulations to protect citizens are a free trade violation.

As the portion of the food system from farm to plate is increasingly controlled by mega corporations, worrisome aspects of food security trends accelerate. The combination of increasing income inequality, rising energy costs, loss of arable land, corporate concentration in agribusiness, food safety and quality concerns, and climate change all signal increasing volatility in food security.

URBANIZATION AND SLUMS

As corporate farming drives people off the land and mega corporations seek cheap labour in cities, urbanization has exploded faster than predicted by the Club of Rome in its 1972 report on limits to growth. In 1950, 30 percent of the world's population was urban; by 2014 that number had grown to 54 percent, and by 2050 it is projected to swell to 66 percent. In 1950 there were 86 cities around the world with populations in excess of a million. By 2015 there were more than 500 such cities.[29] International Labour Organization (ILO) research suggests that the formal economy seldom constructs more than 20 percent of the new housing in urban areas of poorer countries. This means that people coming to the cities build their own housing out of whatever materials are at hand, rent from slum landlords or live on the sidewalks.[30] Since 1970, in the poorer countries, slum growth has outpaced urbanization.[31]

Affordable urban slum housing

CORPORATE CONCENTRATION

Increases in global trade and market pressures for corporate growth are driving corporate consolidation. Companies not involved in mergers, acquisitions and market share growth can expect their share values to fall rather than rise. As Apple experienced in 2006, growth and profits are not sufficient to stop a drop in share prices — growth and profits have to rise to match the expectations of market speculators. The growth of international trade has made small corporations weak and forced even the largest corporations to expand through predatory economic activity, mergers and acquisitions. There is less and less room for small and medium firms focused on national or regional markets. All companies, including co-operatives and social enterprises, are open to foreign companies entering their marketplaces with predictable results — the larger the new global player, the greater their ability to engage in predatory activity and use their size and technical and financial resources to destroy small competitors.

For a Canadian example, Nova Scotia has been served for decades by two co-operative dairies. In 2013, Scotsburn Co-operative Dairy, formed in 1900, retreated into ice cream specialities and sold its fluid milk business to global multinational Saputo. Farmer's Co-operative, the province's other dairy, established more than eighty years ago has been forced to merge with another large co-operative dairy, Agropur, in Quebec. The main catalyst driving this change was international trade agreements, which signal the end of the Canadian dairy supply management system. The future of even large successful businesses in the face of mega competition is precarious. If a business is to face large and growing competitors it clearly must grow.

Mergers and acquisitions (M&A) are also driven by the pressure on corporate managers to demonstrate successful growth. This combination of internal and external pressures has led to increasing levels of mergers and acquisitions. Since the 1980s there have been three increasingly global waves of M&A: in the mid-1980s; 1998 to 2000; and 2004 to 2007.[32] The dollar value of corporate mergers and acquisitions amounted to $1.4 trillion during the 1980s, exploded to $11 trillion during the 1990s, and continued at a frenetic pace of $7.6 trillion during 2000–03 (including $3.4 trillion in 2000 alone) — adding up to a combined total of $20 trillion of corporate mergers and acquisitions over the past twenty-five years.[33]

To survive in the global economy businesses must not just be large and efficient but huge and powerful. The long-run problem is that they can then become uncompetitive in the normal sense. They become, as the world saw in the 2008 Great Recession, too big to be allowed to fail. In the aftermath of the financial collapse the bailout of mega corporations amounted to $27 trillion,[34] while millions of people who lost their homes and livelihoods could not be helped. Around the world, deficits incurred to combat the recession are not being paid off with increased corporate taxes but with public austerity programs, paid for by those who could not be helped. The power of governments to check this growing corporate power has waned to the point that governments acting on behalf of "national interests" (read corporations) are now preoccupied in facilitating out-of-control corporate growth through trade agreements and tax cuts.

FINANCIALIZATION AND FINANCIAL INSTABILITY

Financialization of the global economy refers to the increased portion of GDP made up of financial services and the increased importance of financial markets, institutions, elites and motives in economic decision-making. It also refers to the growing scale, profitability and deregulation of the finance industry. Our parents learned in the Great Depression that financial institutions needed to be regulated or they could bring about great harm. During the Regan/Thatcher years, the post-Depression lessons were forgotten for reasons that will be dealt with more fully later. One can only conclude that the lessons of the 2008 Great Recession were not severe enough since, for the most part, the Thatcher/Regan deregulation remains in place.

As Figure 1-10 shows, we are daring to repeat the conditions that produced the Great Depression. Between 1940 and 2000, financial industry income as a share of GNP increased 400 percent.

Financialization of the economy can also be described as transforming the real economy into tradable securities. The result is virtual wealth creation but reduced resiliency. Long-term "real economy" financial needs are converted into short-term speculative tools whose purpose is not to provide finance but to generate quick profits. In addition, hyper-financialization creates one more level of separation between investors and the ethical impacts of their investments. Financial decisions get made by agents for purely short-term financial motives and more and more likely without any understanding of and concern for real world consequences. Many of the traders involved in the 2008 mortgage-backed securities debacle likely did not even understand that the products they were reaping their bonuses from were fraudulent and predatory loans.

The negative impacts and risks of hyper financialization of the economy are explosively compounded by computerized high-speed trading. Speculation is not a new problem; Keynes noted in 1936:

> Speculators may do no harm as bubbles on a steady stream of enterprise. But the position is serious when enterprise becomes the bubble on a whirlpool of speculation. When the capital development of a country becomes a by-product of the activities of a casino, the job is likely to be ill-done. The measure of success attained by Wall Street, regarded as an institution of which the proper social purpose is to direct new investment into the most profitable channels in terms of future yield, cannot be claimed as one of the outstanding triumphs of laissez-faire capitalism.[35]

Figure 1-10 Financialization and Inequality

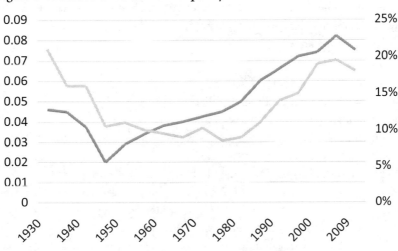

—— Insurance and Finance Incomes as a Portion of the Economy
------ Income Share of Top 20%

Source: Landy 2013.

And Hersh and Erikson point out:

> High-frequency trading is sometimes associated with the phenomenon of "flash crashes," where market prices fall precipitously due to a perfect storm of preprogrammed computer trading. The largest flash crash to date came on May 6, 2010, when the Dow Jones Industrial Average dropped by almost 10 percent from the opening level, and literally billions of dollars in market value disappeared from the stock market in a matter of minutes. Prices rebounded over the next week, though investors were rattled and withdrew $137 billion from the market in the subsequent months. Since then, there have been many more mini flash crashes with no sign of abatement.[36]

In addition a growing portion of market trading is no longer carried out on public stock exchanges but outside of public scrutiny in so-called "dark pools."[37]

Mortgage-backed securities were not a bad thing for everyone. Goldman Sachs, according to reliable reports, made as much as $10 billion "short selling" them.[38] For big market players anticipating market instability, both sharp price rises and price collapses, are very profitable. At its roots, this is what market speculation is all about. They speculate about whether the market will rise or fall. Large pools of capital are increasingly invested and traded by computers based on modest price fluctuations. These modest fluctuations can be created by large pools of capital. If you are very wealthy you can afford to hire the best traders and the best technology. This is not a game for the poorest 90 percent of humanity but perhaps it explains why, in the aftermath of 2008, the rich got richer while many pensioners saw their retirement savings shrink.

ECONOMIC FRAGILITY

If you Google "the next economic collapse" you get 39.2 million results in .39 seconds (March 12, 2015). This is an interesting "confidence index" of dubious meaning. More sobering is the consensus from major conservative sources of financial analysis such as the IMF, the World Bank, the International Institute of Finance and Bloomberg.[39] Their analysis, being neoclassical, is deeply flawed and underestimates the fragility. Let me give an example based on common-sense political economy. The economy of Southern Florida and particularly Miami is fragile if real world rather than neoclassical analysis is used. Real estate development is booming, some of it building flood-proof developments in anticipation of global warming. At some point, perhaps two years from now or perhaps ten, the realization will sink in that large areas simply cannot be realistically protected from storm surges and ocean level rises caused by climate change. Insurance companies, still largely in denial, are beginning to scrutinize potential losses. Inevitably they will refuse to insure properties at any level of premium, triggering a development collapse with profound economic impacts in the U.S. and globally. What will be the impact of this collapse and what will the ripple effect be on other major threatened urban areas such as New York and Boston? Perhaps the trigger will be a development collapse in Osaka, Shanghai, Hong Kong, Ho Chi Minh City, Mumbai or Amsterdam, all mega cities facing enormous threats from rising ocean levels. This is but one source of underrated fragility.

There are other potential flash points for economic collapse. In fragile economies such as Ireland, Portugal, Spain, Italy and Greece, neoclassical austerity programs are potential sources of market panic fueled by speculation. Food shortages can trigger massive unrest especially in rapidly growing urban slums. Energy or water shortages could cause wars. A rise in global unemployment from a robotic revolution could trigger a human revolution. A continuing failure to shift from fossil fuels to renewable energy may make the transition a disaster. Personal debt bubbles required to prop up consumer demand can burst. The list is longer, and as pointed out earlier, the flash point issues are interconnected.

ADDICTION TO GROWTH

As a species we have become addicted to growth. Over the past century the human population tripled, life expectancy doubled and the wealth produced by humans increased more than forty times. "At the same time we are being constrained by what earth systems can tolerate, incomes and wealth are becoming more unequally distributed, the global financial system is faltering, economies are struggling and confidence in political systems to address these problems is in decline."[40] We have fallen into a trap of measuring progress by using a narrow measure of growth: gross national product. If GNP is rising we are told we are doing well. Yet other measures suggest that quality of life actually declines when wealth increases past a certain level. Common sense tells us that as we destroy our environment the quality of life we leave our children declines. As more and more middle and upper level managers experience work weeks of fifty to eighty hours,[41] they clearly have little time for relationships with family or friends. While the fixation on growth is still the dominant trend and clearly in the public policy driver's seat, there is an increasing chorus of informed thought looking for other measures of wellbeing or progress. We return to this more fully in Chapter 2.

DECLINING RESILIENCE

Resilience is the ability to react to and recover from shocks. Thomas Homer-Dixon suggests two notions of resilience: engineering resilience, which puts us back in roughly the same place as when a shock hit, like repairing a clock by taking it apart and putting it back together, replacing a part, but not changing or improving it; and ecological resilience, which allows us to recover but also to improve our ability to survive in the new environment. The trends described in this chapter are shocks requiring ecological resilience. We are a bit like a car speeding down a road that has turned into a four lane then a six lane highway, and the traffic speed has accelerated from 100km/hour to 150km/hour, and the distance between cars has gone from four car lengths to one. It is an accident waiting to happen. One catastrophe, a natural disaster or a terrorist attack, and the system may not be able to deliver.

A drought on the other side of the world results in a price shock here. A banking crisis in Asia causes ripples around the world, and irresponsible mortgages in the U.S. trigger a global recession. A catastrophic storm destroying oil refineries can impact prices globally. Systems become more and more vulnerable to terrorists or targets in war. Computer hacking has the potential to disrupt power, water and transportation systems. The latter two risks make us more vulnerable to real fear and to the politics of fear threatening human liberty in the name of security. Small resilient communities have become tiny parts dependent upon huge, increasingly vulnerable systems.

TECHNOLOGY RESEARCH FOR THE FEW

In the past much of the scientific and social research done around the world was done in universities or by respected and reliable government agencies. As the revenues of governments have shrunk, the funding for research in the public interest has decreased. Funding to university research has also declined. More and more research is being done by corporations, both in-house and through funding research in universities. This is not research in the public interest. Canada, during the Harper years, was an interesting case in point, with the government not only drastically cutting funding for public interest research but muzzling its own scientists and shifting the remaining research funding to what it regarded as commercially valuable. It even crippled its own census, with the result that information useful to analyze or critique government or business became unavailable.[42]

Globally, corporations have moved from being users of publically funded research to controlling research, as they are the primary funders. The resulting technology is commercial. Technology development has shifted from being largely to serve the public to being almost entirely to serve the interests of those holding capital.

In his exploration of technology, Jerry Mander raised profound questions about the power of technology to shape human existence and the importance of having moral and ethical imperatives driving the development of new technologies.[43] We are rapidly moving towards the only consideration in deciding to develop a new technology being whether it generates profits. Political leaders may couch the issue as being about the need to focus on research that will produce jobs in the short run. But the hard truth is that such research is done by very large corporations, and they are wealth creators for the few but are not job creators. As we explore below, robotics are propelling us into a whole new age of technology.

EROSION OF DEMOCRACY

It is easy to understand why political democracy, based on one person one vote, is not treasured by the wealthiest persons in society, who own and control the levers of economic and political power. Democratic governments elected by the whole population and setting the rules of the game for the owners of capital is hardly in the interest of the wealthy elite. Capitalism is inherently inconsistent with democracy. The people want government to regulate the worst abuses of the owners of capital. The owners of capital want to restrict the power of government and be free from regulation.[44] The consistent messages from corporations, corporate leaders and the people who own and control them are that government is inefficient and costs too much; democratic government will not make the tough decisions (by which they mean decisions that will help business but hurt thousands or millions of people) for fear of being defeated at the polls; corporate taxes and taxes on the very rich are too high and are inhibiting their efforts to build a strong economy; the private sector is more efficient; getting government out of their way will unleash this efficiency and grow economic activity; the rising tide of that activity will lift all boats, making everyone wealthier. Sadly, these neoclassical claims bear very little relation to reality in a world where 68 people own 50 percent of the world's wealth[45] and where "the top 100 billionaires added $240 billion to their wealth in 2012 — enough to end world poverty four times over."[46] The rising tide is lifting all billionaires.

This economic power has fuelled the sale of luxury goods — super yachts, villas around the world that are seldom lived in and seldom visited, high end luxury automobiles, etc. - but it has also depressed the sale of everyday necessities to millions of people unable to meet their basic needs. Perhaps much worse, it provides the super-rich with excess billions to spend on political lobbying and corruption of democracy. As Joseph Stiglitz has pointed out, powerful lobbies achieved the relaxed regulation of financial institutions in the United States and caused the 2008 Great Recession.[47] And the gains of the already wealthy during the sharp economic downturn of 2008–10 allowed them to lobby successfully against most of the reforms that might have restored the regulations needed to protect the public. In Canada, between 2012 and 2015, environmental reviews of major corporate projects were curtailed, and the ability of civil society to make submissions to regulatory bodies like the National Energy Board was greatly curtailed. This is corporate pressure in action, reducing democratic access to power.

Except for during the Cold War period, when the wealthiest owners of capital feared a communist revolution, they have generally resisted sharing their wealth or decision-making power with workers. With the collapse of communism, triumphant capitalism, with the theoretical backing of neoclassical economics, has used its power to shape the rules of the game to maximize the elite's share of wealth. The literature on income inequality is huge and unequivocal, showing conclusively that the rich are getting richer and the poor are getting poorer.[48]

EVOLUTION OF WORK

Over centuries, wealth was accumulated by employing large numbers of people at a very low cost, either through slavery or enlisting workers who lacked land and lived in abject poverty. A significant change began with the Industrial Revolution, with machines lowering the need for human labour and increasing production. The use of machines also ensured a large pool of unemployed people needing the jobs that remained. When I was a young man at university, one of the intellectual fashions was speculation about the nature of the "leisure society" that would emerge. This was in the postwar, or Cold War, years. In capitalist countries, faced with the fear of a turn to communism, building a better society was high on the political agenda. Unions were strong (although vilified by those who owned industry), and the forty-hour work week had been established as normal. The questions of the day were: Could we move to a twenty-hour work week? What would the leisure society look like? The growing enormous wealth being produced by human society could be used to create a beautiful new world. We could imagine free health care and education, meaningful work for everyone based on their capacity to contribute, and an end to poverty. Phrases like the "new deal" and the "just society" reflected the optimism.

Some few of us were sceptical. Why, we pondered, would the owners of wealth and industry pass the benefits of growing productivity to the workers? The answer was: "because the wealthy need to keep the population happy and so they will see it as in their own interest to ensure that everyone shares in the good life." Another argument was: "automation produces more jobs requiring more skills and a more and more educated workforce whose education and skills will command even higher pay." There was, before the collapse of communism and the triumph of capitalism, some evidence to support these arguments, even though there was always sharp tension between the owners of capital and the suppliers of work.

Alas, the leisure society was not to be. Triumphant capitalism and its neoclassical explanation have spawned not the leisure society but increasing concentrations of wealth and inequality, with millions of families now needing two jobs to survive with any comfort. Automation has morphed into robotics. We are entering the age when much of the higher paying "educated and skilled" work can be done by robots, and much more will be possible in the near future. Robots will replace doctors and university instructors as well as office workers. As a society we have hardly begun to ponder what will be the outcome of combining triumphant capitalism and robotics.[49] Unless we fundamentally rethink economics and our economy, the result will not be a leisure society but one characterized by unemployment, poverty and bitterness.[50]

More ominous than mere robots, machines are being developed with artificial intelligence — capable of doing not just physical work but of creative thinking independent of humans and at much faster speeds. This has become a major focus of research at Oxford University's Future of Humanity Institute, whose website notes: "Present-day machine learning algorithms (if scaled up to very high levels of intelligence) would not reliably preserve a valued human condition. We therefore face a 'control problem': how to create advanced AI systems that we could deploy without risk of unacceptable side-effects."[51] Who will decide what the goals of such machines will be? What will a world run by emotionless rational machines look and feel like? Already "machine soldiers" are being designed with the ability to make independent decisions on when to kill. Who will design the super artificial intelligence computers capable of deciding the fate of humanity? As democratic governments erode and increasingly serve corporations, it becomes less likely governments will play a meaningful role. That leaves the research, building and design in the hands of those who own and control corporate structures. They will

Figure 1-11 Old Opportunity Distribution in the "Golden Age" of Industrialization

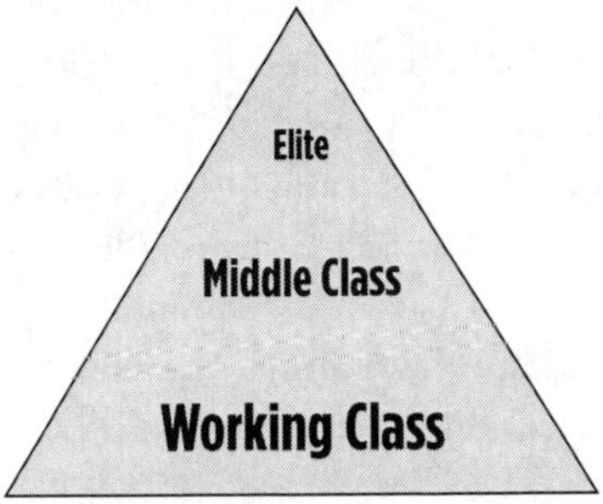

Figure 1-12 Capitalist Economy in the Age of Robotics

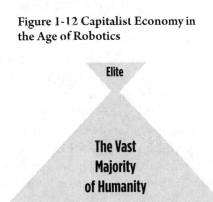

design artificial intelligence for commercial purposes — for profit maximization, wealth concentration and control — as they have done with previous technology. This rivals environmental destruction as the scariest trend of all.

The labour market has evolved and will continue to do so. The old labour market was a pyramid with a few very highly paid jobs at the top, many low-skill jobs at the bottom and a lot of middleskill jobs in between (see Figure 1-11). However, the new labour market is like a distorted hourglass, with relatively few highly skilled jobs at the top, many, many unskilled jobs at the bottom and relatively few jobs in the middle (see Figure 1-12). There are fewer and fewer rewarding well-paying work opportunities and the vast majority of humanity increasingly has very low pay work or is not employed at all. The large, moderately affluent middle class will disappear because, as the range of jobs that can be done by robots expands, the control of labour by capital will grow as fewer jobs will be sought by larger and larger numbers of unemployed. "McJobs" will predominate, and business will always argue that it cannot afford higher minimum wages. In a future robotic economy top managers will continue to earn millions and the returns on capital to the super-rich from investment will increase, while thousands of university graduates will compete with those with little education for low paying, unrewarding positions. This is not a rewarding, exciting future reality for the majority of humanity, but it is the logical outcome of a robotic economy under capitalism. Social unrest will rise sharply. Jobs in the security sector will increase as will the sophistication of their equipment required to protect the status quo.

INTERCONNECTED TRENDS

It is hard to know whether the inequality crisis is worse than the climate change crisis. Or if the erosion of democracy is worse than the sixth extinction of species. Which is the most important to tackle? This is the wrong question. As Naomi Klein so eloquently argues in *This Changes Everything*, we do not need to choose. We need to respond to climate change, income inequality, the extinction of species, eroding democracy and every trend that is undermining our quality of life. These trends are not isolated issues but rather interconnected symptoms.

The environment is not important to the super-wealthy, who control global decision-making. That is not to say that everyone in the wealthiest 10 or 20 percent does not care about environmental issues, poverty and inequality, but simply to recognize that, as a group, they hold global power over economic and political decisions and they are not using that power to solve the world's problems. The world's 2,325 billionaires live sheltered lives.[52] They have retreats in the mountains or by the sea, hundred-foot yachts and gated communities, within which they do not have to live with the destruction their wealth creation is leaving behind.

These interconnected trends are the product of an increasingly dysfunctional economy and economics. What links these trends is capitalism and the investor-owned, capital-driven corporation. Any reasonable, rational reflection on the prospects for our environment and for human society clearly concludes that making the creation of wealth the overriding focus of our economic thinking is a recipe for disaster. What should the central objective of societies be? Should it be the freedom to amass unlimited amounts of capital, or freedom for human beings to live meaningful lives of reasonable comfort in functional communities with functional families in a functional natural environment?

Capitalism has by definition its primary focus on capital. Capitalism is attractive because it is a simple idea: humans are free only if they have unlimited freedom to amass property. This freedom to amass wealth trumps the destruction of the natural world, society, communities and families. It trumps political freedom, freedom of speech, freedom of expression, freedom of thought. That is the essence of capitalism. It is the extreme-right vision of freedom.

Reflecting on the trends documented above, it is obvious that nature and human society are under stress and that we need to rethink how we are meeting our needs. Proponents of capitalism argue that if you protect property rights, energetic individuals will generate wealth which will trickle down to the benefit of all humanity. They argue that unrestricted property rights combined with free markets will solve all problems. Contrary to those ideology-based assertions, growing mountains of evidence demand that we rethink how we live in this world. Chapter 2 explores the economic ideas that have dominated the last thirty five years and their deficiencies. The rest of the book turns its attention to hope.

NOTES

1 Quoted in Rudolph, Gould and Berko (2015).
2 Rees (2014: 87–88).
3 Rees (2014: 87).
4 The big five are not the earth's only extinctions but they have been the most devastating. Each event wiped out at least 17 percent of families of species. A family of species may have dozens or even thousands of species. Climate change caused by catastrophic cosmic impacts is the leading suspect. But scientists agree human activity is the cause of the present sixth great extinction. The first five shown by the red dots were: Ordovician 440 Million years ago — 25 percent loss of species; Devonian 370 million years ago — 19 percent; Permian 250 Million years ago — 54 percent loss of species; Triassic 210 Million years ago — 23 percent; Cretaceous 65 Million years ago — 17 percent; Present period — Quaternary.
5 For an explanation of how carbon dioxide and other greenhouse gases produce climate change, there are numerous reliable sites. For example, see <http://climate.nasa.gov/causes/>.

6   Statistics Portal (n.d.).

7   Fossil Aquifers are large underground reserves of water that were established under past climatic and geological conditions. They can underlie present-day semi-arid environments, providing a key source of groundwater in otherwise water scarce regions.

8   Jambec et al. (2015).

9   "Externalizing costs" refers to the practice of a company generating a cost as a result of its operations, for example dumping pollution into a river, and leaving it to government or the community to pay for the impact on people's health or the environment. For additional information, see One World One Ocean website at <http://www.oneworldoneocean.com> or Mission Blue at <http://mission-blue.org/about/>.

10   Based on a graphic from CBC website (2014). CBC was not able to confirm the source but suggested Ocean Conservancy in New York, which did not respond to email or phone requests for information. Graphic by John van der Would, developed for the author.

11   Bruni and Zamagni (2007: 20).

12   For deep documentation of wealth concentration, see Piketty (2014)

13   Oxfam (2014).

14   Cevik and Correa-Caro (2015). See also Oxfam (2013a).

15   Felicio (2014).

16   Zucman (2015).

17   See Mackensie (2015); *Macleans* (2014); Gavett (2014); AFL-CIO (2014).

18   Meyer (2014).

19   See United Nations (2010).

20   See Frayssinet (2009); De Schutter (2011); Mayer (1997).

21   Freeman (1995).

22   Teresa Anderson, Food Aid, quoted in Fontanilla and Wright (2015).

23   See Global Education Project <http://www.theglobaleducationproject.org/earth/food-and-soil.php>.

24   See: Global Change Program, University of Michigan <http://www.globalchange.umich.edu/globalchange2/current/lectures/land_deg/land_deg.html>.

25   Mayer (1997).

26   For the landmark study see Davis, Epp and Riordan (2004). Also see Mayer (1997); *Scientific American* (2007), Pawlick (2006) and <www.kushiinstitute.org> to suggest only a few sources of information.

27   Moss (2013).

28   Schatzker (2015).

29   <http://www.citypopulation.de/world/Agglomerations.html>.

30   Oberai (1993).

31   Davis (2006).

32   Gaughan (2011).

33   Brock (2005).

34   <http://www.usfederalbailout.com/>.

35   Keynes (1936).

36   Hersh and Erikson (2013).

37   Patterson (2012a and 2012b).

38 Investing Answers website accessed 17 March 2015 <http://www.investinganswers.com/financial-dictionary/real-estate/short-selling-1174>. Damon (2014).

39 *Bloomberg View* (2014); Institute of International Finance (2014); IMF (2015); World Bank (2015).

40 Victor (2014): 102.

41 Deal (2013).

42 While the Liberal government elected in October 2015 has restored the integrity of the census, there is a decade of damage to be undone in terms of public interest research and evidence based decision making.

43 Mander (1991).

44 For a current analysis from Europe see Kowalsky (2015).

45 Elliott (2016).

46 Oxfam (2013a).

47 Stiglitz (2012).

48 See Chapter 1.

49 See Roubini (2015) and Delong (2014).

50 Reich (2015).

51 Future of Humanity Institute <https://www.fhi.ox.ac.uk/research/research-areas/>.

52 Hennesy (2015). In 2014 there were 2,325 billionaires with a total worth of $8.48 trillion. 12.3 percent were women and just under 15 percent of women billionaires worked in non-profit or social organizations.

Chapter 2

DANGEROUS MYTHS OF NEOCLASSICAL ECONOMICS

> Notwithstanding recent financial market nervousness, the global economy remains on track for continued robust growth in 2007 and 2008, although at a somewhat more moderate pace than in 2006. (World Economic Outlook, International Monetary Fund, April 2007: 1)

The IMF statement above underlines the separation between the dominant economic thinking and reality. According to the IMF, the world was on track and the future looked good. That year 1.8 million children starved to death, and more than 5 million were so malnourished they would never lead full normal lives. Yet neoclassical economists told the world that global economic fundamentals were sound. Just a few months later the world plunged into the deepest and most prolonged recession since the Great Depression. What the IMF meant was that, in 2007, for the owners of capital looking for high rates of return, everything was on track. For most of the world's people the global economy was not healthy and about to get much worse.

THE ECONOMICS CONTEXT

We live in the age of capitalism. Our world is controlled not by hereditary elites but by the holders of wealth. As the brief exploration of trends in Chapter 1 demonstrates, the richest 20 percent enjoy more than 85 percent of the world's income. Almost every country around the globe has a super wealthy elite, who own the mega corporations that control the economy and use their economic power to control governments. Governments write the laws that protect them and their corporations. This is true even in those countries that call themselves democratic but that are more accurately described as "quasi" democracies.[1] Over hundreds of years there has always been tension between the welfare of the rich and powerful and the welfare of the rest of humanity. This was true under feudalism and remains true under industrial capitalism. The question is whether it will remain true under the emerging robotic capitalism.

Efforts to make our societies more democratic or to achieve economic reform have tended to be stimulated by economic oppression. The wealthy, and the corporations they own, did not lead the struggle to forbid the use of children in the mines and cotton mills of the 1800s; they resisted. They do not press for increases in minimum wages; they argue against them. They have not led movements to protect the natural world but instead have funded "cigarette company science" to deny facts. Their leadership has focused on amassing wealth rather than on making the world a better place.

A few of the very wealthy have engaged in social justice issues and a considerable number engage in philanthropy.[2] Those among the wealthy who have championed these causes should be held in high regard. Lord Acton suggested long ago: "Power tends to corrupt and absolute power corrupts absolutely. Great men are almost always bad men, even when they exercise influence and not authority."[3] Clearly some people have a higher resistance to corruption than others. There have always been industrialists, like Robert Owen and David Erdal, who struggled to make factories more humane or transferred ownership to their workers, and millionaires and billionaires like Bill Gates, who seems truly determined to give away a large part of his fortune. In general, the exceptions seem to prove Lord Acton's rule rather than undermine it.

"Economics" is derived from the Greek words meaning household customs or laws. As an academic discipline it first emerged as "political economy" in the late eighteenth century and only later as "economics." Its genesis roughly matched the emergence of the Industrial Revolution. The father of political economy is generally regarded as Adam Smith, whose work is often misrepresented by neoclassical economists and neoliberal policymakers. (Neoclassical economics is a distortion of classical economics and neoliberalism is eighteenth-century individualism on steroids.) Smith's seminal book begins: "The annual labour of every nation is the fund which originally supplies it with all the necessaries and conveniences of life which it annually consumes, and which consists always either in the immediate produce of that labour, or in what is purchased from that produce from other nations."[4] Smith's ideas about the moral tone and purpose of economic activity and his description of markets are profoundly different from the modern neoclassical distortions that claim him as their inspiration. While his phrasing is archaic to our ears, his description of the economy is a logical extension of the Greek concept.

The times in which Smith wrote saw the unfolding cruelty and extreme exploitation of the Industrial Revolution. The abuses of industrialization spawned reforms and new ideas in the 1800s. Prominent economists like Alfred Marshall and John Stuart Mill wrote favourably about co-operation as an organizing principle for the economy.

> The form of association, however, which if mankind continues to improve, must be expected in the end to predominate, is not that which can exist between a capitalist as chief, and work-people without a voice in management, but the association of the labourers themselves on terms of equality, collectively owning the capital with which they carry on their operations and working under managers elected by themselves.[5]

The Russian Revolution pushed this strain of thinking in economics into obscurity as capitalism responded to the threat of communism.

Economics is not a science. Like the study of government, it is an art. The economy runs in a certain way because we have set it up to run that way. We can and should measure the impacts and outcomes of economic activity, but we ought not to lose sight of the fact that those outcomes are dependent on human decision-making, not the laws of nature. Physicists endeavour to understand the laws of physics: they do not write them. How a free market capitalist economy works is a result of the laws of governments — not nature. It is governments that decide whether contracts will be honoured or children will work in the mines at age five.[6] It is governments that decide to allow corporations to pollute our air and water, or whether capital flows, or if carbon production is regulated or decided upon by those who own the corporations. It is why the study of political and social economy is vital.

Many of the ideas about how we should order our societies are governed by economic pseudo-science, even when they are absurd when viewed through the lens of common sense or obvious results. For example, we have come to accept as a truism that people must go where the jobs are. Yet, we also know that good societies are not possible if families and communities are destroyed. The economic truism leads to tearing apart families and communities. We know that if we destroy the environment, our ability to provide ourselves with the goods and services we need will be damaged. Yet, both business and governments invoke economics to convince us that the environment must be sacrificed on the altar of the economy. The austerity policies post-2008 have been abject failures in rebuilding economies; yet governments and business tell us government spending must be cut to create a healthy economy.[7] The research and literature on the absolute failure of austerity is much more convincing than the religion-like arguments of neoclassical economists and government policies designed to support investor-driven corporations. Under the austerity program in place in early 2015, Greece can never pay its debts because austerity has crippled its economy. It is ironic that Germany is leading the tough austerity demands on Greece, given that the circumstances in Greece are similar to those imposed on Germany, for different reasons, after World War I. The resulting hopelessness in Germany led to the rise of Hitler.

DEMISE OF COMMUNISM

The brand of communism led by the Soviet Union and the Eastern Bloc countries had its own internal contradictions. Central planning and operating every aspect of the economy to meet the needs of hundreds of millions of people proved to be an impossible task. It concentrated power in fewer and fewer hands, eroded human freedom and required increasingly oppressive state security forces and repression.[8] Lord Acton's observation about power corrupting proved no less true of many communist leaders. The Soviet Union in many ways resembled a colonial power. It became environmentally destructive and proved less and less able to solve the problems it produced. It collapsed because it did not reflect human reality — people are by nature both individualistic and social. It collapsed because excessive power, concentrated in the hands of a tiny elite, corrupts that elite.[9] China's brand of "communism" is evolving as a hybrid between capitalism and communism. It has elements of both socialism and capitalism, including, as noted above, a grow-ing gap between the rich and the poor. It could evolve to have the worst of both communism and capitalism. The same appears to be true in Vietnam, but both countries are experiencing rapid and sustained growth with a level of state control condemned by neoclassical purists. In growth terms, both China and Vietnam are more successful than the Washington Consensus (see below). Cuba presents an interesting example of a socialist state where power is exercised with high level of participation by its people. It is also notable in that the Castro brothers do not live in luxurious villas and levels of corruption are low.[10]

The collapse of communism and the emergence of triumphant capitalism ush-ered in a new aggressive capitalist era with the following characteristics:

- the neoclassical economic justification has been intensified and promoted;
- capital mobility has been used as a lever to stimulate incentives and tax breaks for corporations and the very rich, eroding the capacity of governments to limit the worst excesses of corporations or to reduce the growing inequality between rich and poor; and
- people's organizations and democratic governments have been systematically undermined and denigrated and their functions taken over by investor-owned firms. Government has been systematically attacked by the business community and the media.

FROM MODERATED CAPITALISM TO TRIUMPHANT CAPITALISM

The most enlightened age of capitalism was stimulated by the fear of the wealthy elite that unless they gave in to reforms they might face the threat of communism.[11] During the Cold War, capitalist elites grudgingly moderated the worst tendencies of capitalism to ensure that their publics would be generally supportive. Labour laws gave workers more power to organize and bargain. Social security reforms, like unemployment insurance, old age security and improved welfare programs, were put in place. Programs to increase access to health care were created. The idea of the welfare state emerged, and income inequality modestly improved in the wealthier countries. At the same time capitalist elites nurtured the ideas of neoclassical economics as an intellectual justification. They used their economic power to fund think-tanks and universities to promote ideas that countered communist and socialist thought, including the idea of a welfare state. Capitalist propaganda was created to combat communist propaganda.

The neoclassical economics that emerged with increasing energy after World War II was, and remains, characterized by hyper individualism. Friedrich von Hayek, Ayn Rand and Milton Friedman became the champions of an economics which denied the value of the social nature of humans and celebrated only individual freedom of action, illogically extended to "corporate persons." Workers' collective bargaining and government action in the interest of the whole society were relentlessly attacked. This extremist individualism conveniently justified the existence of the super-rich. They claimed: "Only if the super-rich are allowed to act with complete freedom will there be any progress." The public-policy extension of this was significantly captured by Margaret Thatcher's famous quote:

> "I am homeless, the Government must house me!" and so they are casting their problems on society and who is society? There is no such

thing! There are individual men and women and there are families and no government can do anything except through people and people look to themselves first.[12]

The implication is that individuals are not at the same time social beings, but they are only individuals who should look after their own immediate self-interest.

A key part of this extreme individualist economics is the need for a pool of workers who are not employed and who can be drawn on to replace any worker who resists discipline. The rich and their heirs are not to be part of this pool of available labour. Further, the individuals in that labour pool should not organize to seek fair pay or safe working conditions because that will impinge upon the freedom of those heroic few upon whom the rest must depend. In this economics, the uncertain survival of the unemployed, worried about losing their homes and feeding their families, is a powerful tool in the hands of those for whom the next year's gourmet food and a mansion are assured. This immense difference in wealth and power is what makes competition so attractive to those who possess wealth and power. This way of thinking, with its glorification of predatory behaviour, is offensive to human dignity and any concept of justice. Competition is almost always characterized by many more losers than winners, and most competition is not played out in games for amusement but in struggles to achieve a meaningful life. (We return to this theme in Chapters 4 and 5.)

Much of what is suggested as neoclassical economic policy, if taken seriously, would have one conclude that the economy is an angry god to whom we must offer ongoing sacrifices. If we are to keep the economy functioning we must cut funding to research on environmental issues and to support for immigrants, health care, education and welfare. We must oppose minimum wages, research on social issues, democratic representation, foreign aid and on and on. We cannot afford for government to protect the quality of the air we breathe or the water we drink, nor act to reduce income inequality. We are advised to craft trade agreements that make it less and less possible for governments to act on a growing range of issues lest they be sued by corporations for infringing on corporate rights. Unless corporations are free they will go elsewhere and people will be unemployed. This is because, we are told, there are absolute economic laws similar to the laws of physics, and if they are not observed the world will descend into chaos.

It is useful to explore the link between business models and economics. Neoclassical economics is an attempt to explain the economy assuming that the capitalist, investor-owned business model is clearly the best and perhaps the only business model that makes sense and is capable of generating wealth for humanity's use and progress. Capitalist investor-owned businesses (firms owned by the holders of wealth) and neoclassical economics are inseparable. The former is the way those holding wealth operate, and the latter attempts to explain why it is the best possible and most functional system.

Governments around the world have succumbed to enormous pressure to put in place a framework based on neoclassical economics to enhance the ability of the super-rich and their corporations to act with increasing freedom. In doing so, governments are losing their power to serve the public good. In this framework, the sole role of government is to ensure private gain through "socialism" for the super-rich. For example, the response of governments to the 2008 Great Recession was to bail out the rich and institute austerity for the vast majority to pay for the bailout.

There are many convincing critiques of faltering capitalism and the quasi-religion of neoclassical economics. Neoclassical analysis is crumbling because it cannot explain or predict major economic events, it lacks a basis in common sense, and it is based on beliefs rather than data. This is not to say that neoclassical economics does not gather data. Endless reams of data can be collected on the GNI, GDP and GNP,[13] but their value as measures of progress is minimal. Measuring the ability of the economy to produce wealth for the few is of importance to that few but tells us little about how successful the economy is at meeting human need. Daunting issues for which neoclassical economics offers no solution include environmental crises, real limits to economic growth, growing income inequality, the erosion of democracy, financial instability, resource depletion, galloping urbanization, a looming food crisis, an inability to shift from fossil fuels and more. These issues are interrelated and feed into each other. Perhaps a better name for this particular breed of economics would be "theonomics" where the "god" is capital.

The core belief of capitalism and its neoclassical economics explanation is that the ultimate good will be produced when the increase of wealth is the objective of every structure, decision and process in every society around the globe. It is the focus on wealth and wealth creation that will make a society efficient. A key corollary is the belief that this efficiency is best achieved by unfettered markets and private control of all resources, production and consumption. Everything in the world — animate and inanimate nature, the air we breathe, the water we drink and humanity too — are commodities with a price. The price, including the price of human labour, is determined by "free markets." This theonomics is what we must abandon if we have any compassion for the generations to come.

THE INVISIBLE HAND

Adam Smith's notion of an invisible hand is probably the most overworked idea in economic thought, and the most distorted. The idea as conceived was mentioned three times by Smith, once in *The Wealth of Nations* and twice in *The Theory of Moral Sentiments*. The idea is that a group of individuals, each pursuing their own interests (sellers seeking the highest price and buyers seeking the lowest, assuming quality is constant) will, through these actions, further the public good without actually considering it.

Smith's era was far different from ours. Smith saw the "invisible hand" as being that of the Almighty, guiding humanity toward good. He also saw a significant role for government in regulating economic affairs. He conceived of his idea in a world of community markets, where people knew each other and close to perfect information was possible. It is also possible to restate his description from perhaps an even more plausible perspective: In seeking to co-operate in providing society with the goods and services we need, we each seek to make a particular contribution and exchange with others on a basis which is fair and agreeable to both parties. Finally, Adam Smith was a moral philosopher. It is hard to believe that he would approve of his idea of an invisible hand being used to justify a world where 1 percent owns almost 50 percent of the world's wealth.[14]

The "invisible hand" idea has arguably become the most influential, distorted and abused metaphor in economics. Its use to justify policies supporting dismantling of both the welfare state and regulatory frameworks have led some to speculate as to whether the "invisible hand" of modern times might have just one finger extended. Even at its best, the idea is naïve. In the post-2008 words of a fervent believer: "Those of us who have looked to the self-interest of lending institutions to protect shareholder's equity (myself especially) are in a state of shocked disbelief."[15]

THE MYTH OF FREE MARKETS

Free markets have never existed and never will because corporations and the people who control them would never stand for it. So-called "free trade" agreements protect the rights of corporations to do anything they wish while tying the hands of governments from acting for the public good. "Free trade" agreements are not about human freedom, and not even so much about trade, unless you consider inter-corporate transfers to be about trade. They are about corporate freedom. As an example, Stiglitz points out that new agreements will allow cigarette companies to sue countries, including those growing markets such as China, whose public health warnings result in a loss of profits from sales.[16]

Markets are useful in providing price and supply signals but unless regulated with care are not sufficient. If meeting human need is not profitable to the wealthy, the need will not be met by the corporations they own and control. If a family does not have the money to buy food, they are outside the marketplace and the miracle of the market will leave their plates empty. A student from a low-income family will earn a PhD only with extraordinary effort, amassing great debt or receiving charity, or all three. A wealthy student will obtain one with relative ease. Left unregulated, markets work for the very rich and work imperfectly or not at all for the bottom 80 percent of humanity.

An example of this last point is CEO and senior executive salaries, which as noted earlier, have become obscene. The justification is that these "brilliant" individuals are uniquely equipped to make corporate and economic decisions. Henry Mintzberg, the former dean of Canada's most prestigious business school, commented:

> This is rubbish. Executive bonuses — especially in the form of stock and option grants — represent the most prominent form of legal corruption that has been undermining our large corporations and bringing down the global economy. Get rid of them and we will all be better off for it. ... Too many large corporations today are starved for leadership — true leadership, meaning engaged leadership embedded in concerned management. And the global economy desperately needs renewed enterprise, embedded in the belief that companies are communities.[17]

Economics scholars Michael Todaro and Stephen Smith argue: "A well-functioning market system requires special social, institutional, legal and cultural preconditions.... Fraud, corruption and monopoly do not disappear with a wave of a magical neoclassical wand."[18] They go on to note that a functioning market system would also require, among other things, stable currency, public supervision or operation of natural monopolies and oligopolies, and pubic management of externalities. Many neoclassical economists admit that these requirements are indeed necessary, but make the assumption that all these requirements are met and that we can thus rely on "free markets" to deliver a better world.

Functioning markets, as Adam Smith visualized them, were characterized by all the buyers knowing all the sellers and having close to perfect knowledge of the sellers and their products. His marketplace also assumed a high level of competition between roughly equal producers and sellers. Smith's marketplace bears no resemblance to today's global marketplace. There is no longer any semblance of complete knowledge about products and sellers. The consumer is not king. In the global marketplace the consumer is peasant, and the internet, with its terabytes of unverifiable information, delivers no miracle solutions. Corporate concentration puts information technology into the hands of the corporate management elite on a scale ordinary people, even if well off, cannot match.

Finally, free unregulated market theory is built on the foundation that economic actors almost always make rational decisions based on their self-interest. That rational decision-making can be based on the small percentage of reliable information we can access about the hundreds of complex economic decisions we make every day, is a bizarre assertion. Behavioural economists have documented how much of our decision-making is irrational. We know, thankfully, that our decisions are not just based on self-interest but also on caring, sharing and co-operating. We know that it is possible to only have a small percentage of the information we really need. We know that we often do not act rationally. The case for carefully and thoughtfully developed market regulation is powerful. So, we shall see later, is the case for co-operation in decision-making.[19]

TRICKLE-DOWN THEORY

Trickle-down theory starts with the assertion that human society should be at the service of capital growth and decisions should be in the hands of those who control that wealth. The claim is that this arrangement of society will empower the innovative and the energetic, the doers and shakers, and give them the incentive to produce wealth. The rationale goes that a society which operates in this way will produce vast wealth, which will trickle down to all of humanity. A rising tide of wealth will raise all boats. The only problem is that this theory is that it does not reflect reality. If some wealth does happen to trickle down, it is the result of inefficiency in producing larger returns to capital.

Common sense and wealth inequality measures clearly point to "trickle-up" reality, documented, for example, in the work of French economist Thomas Piketty and colleagues. Examining concentration of wealth and GDP since the beginning of the Industrial Revolution, Piketty shows that, if undisturbed by war or the rise of communism, the rate of growth of concentrated wealth is greater than the growth

And then we told them the wealth would trickle down.

rate of GDP.[20] There is no convincing rebuttal to a decade of careful research. As the events surrounding the 2008 Great Recession show, financial markets have now been perfected so that in times of economic crisis, reality is "geyser-up."

A corollary of the trickle-down myth is that the best way to ensure economic growth and provide jobs for everyone is to provide tax cuts to corporations and the wealthy, who will then invest and spur economic growth. A clear example of this is Canada's Conservative economic development strategy for 2006 to 2015. Tax cut followed tax cut. In spite of a solid system of bank regulation that left Canada relatively undamaged by the 2008 Great Recession, very modest growth has produced an almost jobless recovery. Most of the jobs that have been created are low wage and part-time. So where did the money from tax cuts go? What have corporations done with the money we were told they would invest to create jobs? The answer is that they held on to it. In the early 1990s, cash held by corporations in Canada averaged about 4 percent of GDP. From 1990 to 2012, corporate-held cash almost tripled, to 11 percent of GDP, and the government cut services to make up for the reduction in revenue.[21] With a stagnant economy, Canada's ultra Conservative government adopted the austerity policies that were failing so miserably in Europe. Youth unemployment soared. Despite all evidence to the contrary, the media, including even the publicly owned CBC, consistently awarded the government high marks for economic management.

THE MYTH OF SELF-INTEREST

We are told that people's economic decisions are based on financial self-interest. This is the thinking that drives CEO salaries. If this is true, why do people not base their marriages on financial gain, or their relationships with their neighbours? A marriage based on such motivation, common sense tells us, would likely be short and mean. Neighbours who behave like this would not get along. Very few people behave this way. People are not simple self-interest machines to be plugged into a mathematical model. Human nature, as we explore later, is much more complex; it is a mixture of social and individual. What is meaningful to people is complex.[22] Behavioural economics research tells us that financial motivation is well down on the list of human motivators. For example, the most powerful motivators for workers are workplace autonomy, the opportunity to be the best they can be at what they do, and the opportunity to make the world a better place. Building a workplace around these motivators will produce a much healthier world than one focused on financial gain.[23]

When someone exploits you for their own gain, does it spur you to be kind? When someone goes out of their way to help you, does it spur you to do evil? People are not angels, but most people, most of the time, choose to do good. Violence and revenge produce more violence and revenge. Kindness and forgiveness spawn more kindness and forgiveness. Sharing and caring have always been the most constructive parts of human society. Why then should we build a key element of our society, the economy, on self-interest and greed? How did we end up with an economics that told us to build vital human relationships on self-interest and greed?

WHAT IS PROGRESS?

For neoclassical economics, progress is growth, as measured by GNP. From a capital- or wealth-centred view of the world, this makes absolute sense. From a people-centred viewpoint, that belief is utter nonsense. Using such a simplistic yardstick explains how we miss millions of starving children, social system collapse, the erosion of democracy, and the destruction of the natural world, upon which we all completely depend. Robert Kennedy put it eloquently:

> Yet the gross national product does not allow for the health of our children, the quality of their education or the joy of their play. It does not include the beauty of our poetry or the strength of our marriages, the intelligence of our public debate or the integrity of our public officials. It measures neither our wit nor our courage, neither our wisdom nor our learning, neither our compassion nor our devotion to our country. It measures everything in short, except that which makes life worthwhile.[24]

Yet GNP is almost all our economic and political leaders grasp, and GNP seems to numb the minds of the media. It is the root of our total addiction to mindless growth.

> How can it be that the amazing technologies we keep inventing tend to intensify, not lessen, our pace of work, and make our jobs and lives, less and not more, secure? How can it be in a world of material deprivation, we must worry about industrial over capacity and crises of over production? (How can there be too much stuff, when so many have so little?) Conversely, how can it be that the health of the global economy requires what ecological common sense knows is impossible — ever increasing consumption?[25]

Or as economist Kenneth Boulding, co-founder of general systems theory, put it: "Only a madman or an economist could believe that exponential growth could go on forever in a finite world."[26]

Clearly there is more to human progress than how much "wealth" is created, especially when it is so inequitably distributed. Once, on an economics exam, I was asked to explain GDP.[27] I did so but suggested it was not very important as a measure, pointing out that everyone in my hometown could stop cooking their meals, cleaning their houses, mowing their lawns, walking or driving their cars to get around and looking after their children, and they could pay neighbours to do these things. The GNP would shoot upward. Yet nothing new would be done that had not been done the day before, yet economists from all over the world would come to study this amazing engine of growth. From a GNP perspective this would be great progress. From a human society perspective it is a slide backwards.[28] One might reflect on the growth of the service industries over the past thirty or so years as being this type of growth.

GROWTH DOES NOT EQUAL PROGRESS

The level of inequality within the capitalist economies, democratic and not democratic, is growing. Inequality produces a wide range of social damage for all, rich and poor.[29] In addition, the ability of rising incomes to generate human happiness has an upper limit. For very poor people, their happiness increases as their incomes increase, but, as Figure 2-1 shows, happiness begins to decline as incomes rise beyond a certain point. Research suggests that this decline may be a reflection of a decline in "work-life balance," resulting from efforts to further

Figure 2-1 Relationship between GDP and Life Satisfaction

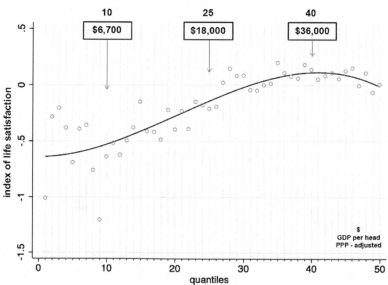

Note: Each point represents the coefficient of an ordered probit regression of life satisfaction on all individuals in the World Values Survey (for the waves 1981–84, 1989–93, 1994–99, 1999–2004, 2005–08) grouped in 50 different quantiles according to the per capita GDP of the country they live in.
Source: Proto and Rusticini 2014, 2013.

increase income. Regardless, if the endless pursuit of wealth destroys our natural environment, produces escalating social costs and fails to deliver happiness, why do our governments and neoclassical economists use mainly measures like GNP, GDP and GNI to measure human progress? Perhaps the only clear explanation is the old saying: "You dance with them that brought you."

"To build a sustainable economy, we need tools of analysis that properly value social, economic and environmental assets, tools that carefully appraise both costs and benefits, and balance them against one another. That's what's known as 'full-cost accounting.'"[30] New measures, called genuine progress indices (GPIs),[31] are emerging but few policymakers use them, and they need more development. A centre of global leadership has emerged in Bhutan, which measures gross national happiness.[32] We need to be able to measure how well our economy meets human need. Is it delivering food, clothing and shelter to everyone in a society? Is it providing education and health care? Does it provide a work life–social life balance? Is it destroying or enhancing nature and the life support ecologies of our planet?

Another dangerous myth is that all technological innovation is progress and all problems can be solved with new technologies. As noted previously, decisions about using new technologies are almost always driven by whether they will generate profit, not by whether they will benefit humanity. The widespread spraying of pesticides or use of PCBs was profitable to some and harmful to nature and billions of people. In a capitalist world there is a panic to rush every new technology lest a competitor get ahead. There will always be pressure to adopt new technologies that will solve problems facing humanity, but many of the technologies we are adopting today with breakneck speed are not like new Ebola drugs, solving urgent problems. Research on problems that are vital to the future of our world and humanity is ignored while we pour millions into the latest commercial or military product, like drones, but spend little on diseases that affect poor people, who would not be able to afford the new drugs produced. We have, for example, only shallow knowledge of how genetically modified organisms will impact us or the natural world. We do know how they will impact the major corporations introducing them. We need to develop much better criteria for assessing technological adoption and return to public funding of research.[33] An economy focused on need will fund research for the health of the planet, not the wealth of the few.

FREE TRADE AND THE LAW OF COMPARATIVE ADVANTAGE

The theory of comparative advantage holds that some countries are more or less efficient than others in the production of certain goods. As a result, wealth and production can be maximized if each country specializes in producing the goods it makes most efficiently. From this, it is argued that free trade will stimulate economic growth, promote greater economic equality and develop each country's strengths. To achieve these desirable outcomes, global markets must be free of government interference and restriction and local self-sufficiency must be abandoned as an inferior policy. This works well "in theory." In reality it works only when a set of impossible conditions are met. It rests on the following same assumptions as free markets:

- It assumes all buyers can have complete and equal knowledge of all sellers and their products. Consider a car. We would know all the sources of all the car's parts, their quality and their price, everywhere in the world, at any given time and therefore be in a position to know which country had the comparative advantage. A huge corporation with immense resources might come close to this achievement, but functional comparative advantage assumes competition, not oligopolies.[34]

- It assumes that a comparative advantage will remain constant over time — that a comparative advantage today will be a comparative advantage next month and next year and the year after. That would be a necessary assumption if we are to have firms in countries around the globe deciding what to produce and invest heavily in people, plants and equipment.

- The advantage must be stable for governments to invest in roads and transportation, schools and hospitals, etc. — all the public infrastructure that would facilitate such production. If this were not so, and comparative advantages were to shift each year or even every five years, the cost to society would be formidable.

- It assumes that the technology of production is fixed and globally available to all countries. This is not reality.

- It assumes that capital rich countries will produce capital intensive products and that less capital endowed countries will produce less capital intensive products. It does not assume that mobile capital will go to poorer countries to seek low wages and weak environmental and working condition regulation. Again, reality is missing.

Should we organize global trade around an "economic law" that is grounded on such assumptions, lacking in common sense and likely to produce chaos? The answer is no, but it is what we have done. That reality is best captured in what is called the Washington Consensus, which dominated global economic thinking in the 1980s and early 1990s.[35] It drew almost exclusively on the neoclassical economic ideas generated out of the Department of Economics at the University of Chicago (often just called the Chicago School), whose graduates had fanned out across the world. The Consensus was a set of ten policies agreed upon by the U.S. government and international financial institutions based in Washington, whose purpose supposedly was to stimulate economic growth worldwide.

The Washington Consensus believers held that a sound economy could only be built on cutting taxation and the size of government, privatizing public services, eliminating all trade barriers, opening capital markets and attracting foreign investment. Any county seeking loans from the IMF had to sign a structural adjustment agreement before getting credit, regardless of the reason they required loans. The human suffering such agreements produced was seen as a minor price for achieving economic health. The problem was they were almost universally disastrous failures.[36]

Structural adjustment agreements were imposed on poor countries and rich countries alike.[37] In dozens of poor countries, public spending was cut on health care, education and social services. State enterprises, profitable or unprofitable, were sold off. Utilities were privatized. Doors were opened to foreign investment. The result was a disaster, especially in poor countries, and is now widely regarded as such, even as most governments continue to follow Washington Consensus policies. The policies did facilitate the emergence of super rich elites in poor countries, exacerbating the gap between rich and poor. The countries experiencing the greatest growth in GDP were those (for example, Korea, Brazil and China) that grew their economies behind protective barriers before opening the doors to trade.

THE TRAGEDY OF THE COMMONS

The tragedy of the commons is an often-cited economic theory put forward by Garrett Hardin in 1968. In it he suggested that individuals acting independently and rationally, according to their own self-interest, will behave contrary to the best interests of the whole group by depleting or polluting some common resource, like a community pasture. The theory was based not on any comprehensive study but on theoretical speculation, stimulated by unfortunate experiences in Victorian England with regard to the use of some unregulated common land. Alas, it has been used by neoclassical economists to claim that the most efficient use of natural resources is to privatize them, let the market regulate them and allow private corporations to make efficient use of them.

Since the 1970s, many publicly owned resources have been privatized. For example, fish stocks around the world have been plundered by fishing boats with advanced sonar technology, in the words of an all too accurate song, "took all where we seldom took any."[38] It is true that overfishing had help from environmental destruction, but corporate abuse of the privatized stocks played the major role. The results of the abuse of Hardin's theorizing might well be called the tragedy of the privates. In contrast, the work for which Elinor Ostrom was awarded the Nobel Prize in economics was based on meticulous data analysis that extended over decades. Her conclusions: Neither government regulation remote from the resource nor allowing corporations supposedly governed by the markets works. Ostrom found that allowing the commons to be managed democratically, by the local people who use them, leads most often to, not perfect, but very good management. Some resources which have global mobility like air quality and water pollution logically need state and often international regulation. In short, for most common resources, there is a better option which is neither direct state control exercised by officials nor turning resources over to absentee private owners set on maximizing profit. Co-operative control works best.

SIMPLISTIC IDEAS AND CATCH PHRASES

Former U.S. Secretary of Labour Robert Reich identifies three false neoclassical truisms and sets out in their place, real analytical conclusions based on experience: 1) big corporations do not produce new jobs and big corporate tax cuts do not lead to lower unemployment; 2) there is no crucial choice between government or the free play of market forces, but instead government defines market forces through contract law, child labour laws, patent law, bankruptcy law, etc.; and 3C) the real choice is not whether we should have big government, but in whose interest government acts.[39]

Much of the discussion of the economy is bamboozled by lines like, "open for business," "work smart," "multitask" and "career flex." These slogans are presented as if they will be our wonderful future and we need to "get with it." But what do they really mean?

- "Open for business" means that we need to lower taxes, eliminate regulations designed to protect people and the environment, and offer incentives that will compete with other jurisdictions. It means that we will go begging to the owners of capital and ask, "What is your price for investing in our state, province or country?" Since every state, province and country is supposed to be open for business, the competition is fierce. The winners are the owners of capital.
- As we move to a greater percentage of low-paying, part-time and contract work, a process that is accelerating with the robotics revolution, people have to be persuaded that this new world is great. We will do well if only we learn to "multi-task" and "work smart." What this means is that the jobs of two or three people will now be done by one, or farmed out to lower-paid contractors who, if they multi-task and work smart, will survive. Those who do not survive this brave new world are of course the ones who "just don't measure up."

- "Career flex" suggests we must not expect to have one or just a few jobs in our work lives. We should embrace workplace turmoil and accept we will have many different employers. It is really about the disappearance of long-term employment with one company. The new scheme is to earn less in unstable short-term jobs without expensive benefits and no pension at the end. For the people with capital this is far more efficient. Corporations get much cheaper work and in return make fewer commitments to the workers.

Where do all these attractive catch phases come from? Mostly it is high-priced corporate consultants with a knack for dressing up a scarecrow to look like the queen.

THERE IS NO ALTERNATIVE, OR THE END OF HISTORY

It is difficult to imagine any logical or moral grounds to defend extreme neoclassical economics or its outcomes. That is why the most popular defence for it is: "It is regrettable that capitalism and neoclassical economics have weaknesses in terms of inequality and fairness and damage to society and the natural world but, let's face it, there is really no alternative." "The poor," it is argued, "will always be with us." "Capitalism has some rough edges but it has produced immense improvements in standards of living, and has given us democracy, so we need to embrace it and try to soften the rough edges." "No other system works. Look what happened to communism!" There is no alternative, also known as TINA, was a claim that emerged into global consciousness as a slogan of Margaret Thatcher's.

A more interesting proposed justification for not questioning capitalism is Francis Fukuyama's book *The End of History and The Last Man*. Fukuyama does not dismiss most of the problems underlined in Chapter 1 but sees them as a few rough edges. The problem with his analysis is that his belief that capitalism delivers on freedom is absolutely correct only for the richest 1 percent, likely for the top 20percent and perhaps for the richest 40 percent, but for the bottom 60 percent, it is the freedom to live in debilitating or abject poverty. The problems of capitalism are not a few rough edges. "One in four of the world's *children are stunted*. In developing countries the proportion can rise to one in three.... One out of six children — roughly 100 million — in developing countries is *underweight* ... WFP calculates that *US$3.2 billion* is needed per year to reach all 66 million hungry school-age children."[40] These people are not free. How can a child deprived of the right to learn be free? For 60 to 80 percent of humanity history is not over.

"Malnutrition is the underlying cause of death for at least 3.1 million children, accounting for 45 percent of all deaths among children under the age of five and stunting growth among a further 165 million, according to a set of reports released ahead of a nutrition summit in London."[41] An economic system that regards outcomes like this as consistent with freedom, and acceptable, is ethically repugnant. Consider that 0.15 of 1 percent of the wealth that the world's 2,325 billionaires have amassed would end world hunger.[42] This unbelievably narrow idea of freedom is warped, perverse and beyond reasonable thought. It is dangerous to humanity.

The trends of Chapter 1 are neither a few rough edges, nor the fulfillment of human freedom. One can imagine a billion voices of lemmings shouting "TINA" as they pour over the cliff of environmental and social disaster. It is the ultimate curse of positive thinking and the denial of real world problems.

The problem is not just capitalism but any political economy that concentrates wealth and power in the hands of fewer and fewer people. This is what capitalism does; it is the core idea of "capitalism." The word "capital-ism" is clear. It is about capital. Naming capitalism as the problem, as the elephant in the room, is not easy. More than a decade ago I spoke at a conference and suggested that trends like I listed above could be combatted by a co-operative economy. After the session I was told by an intelligent young woman that I had attacked everything she believed in — capitalism and democracy. But capitalism incessantly undermines democracy, attacking government revenue sources, trumpeting government inefficiency while hiding its own inefficiency, calling for more government accountability while remaining almost totally unaccountable under an umbrella of "corporate confidentiality," owning the media, hiring people to post on the internet, and on and on.

The problem is not that there is a conspiracy of the super-rich and their hired managers meeting in some back room hatching plots. While their paths no doubt cross, they do not need to meet, except for PR purposes in events like the Davos conferences.[43] The reality is that their interests are the same. When they act, for example to buy the news media or endow a university or fund an extreme neoclassical think tank, they are acting in each other's interest. They do not all think the same. They do not have to. If they act in their own interest they will be generally acting in the interest of their class or group. It is not that the super-rich are all bad people or that everything they do is evil. *The problem is* that the political economy they dominate perpetuates and grows an inequality of wealth that is a disaster for humanity and the planet. Unfortunately, the most self-serving among them have come to see the problems facing humanity as irrelevant. Even someone like George Soros, who is regarded as a 'progressive' billionaire, can say: "As a market participant, I don't need to be concerned with the consequences of my actions."[44] His actions, it had been suggested, contributed to the 1997 Asian banking crisis and consequent negative impacts on millions of people.

There is another obstacle to questioning capitalism. There has been a flood of hard hitting, intelligent, data-based critiques of neoclassical economics. I have drawn on but a small selection in this book. Alas, in most, there is no alternative suggested. Books on environmental economics identify the problems but call on governments or the choices of individuals to take action to correct the problems. Some call on investor-owned businesses to change how they act. These are not viable ways forward. Consumers should act on their own whenever they can to the best of their ability, but in a complex global society this is not enough. Governments are unlikely to act against the interests of their corporate masters, who have the power to seriously disrupt economies, who fund political parties, who own the news media and who have become the "national interest."

Can investor-driven corporations become the alternative by changing who they are? I can think of some corporate leaders who have tried. Some are modestly successful, but if they push too hard they are replaced, and when viewed beside the mountain of corporate wrongdoing they are mole hills. To make a significant change they would have to abandon their overriding bottom line — maximizing the return to shareholders. But if corporations put creating strong healthy societies or ensuring a healthy natural world ahead of return to shareholders, they would no longer be investor-driven capitalist business. If you modify an elephant so it can fly, it is no longer an elephant; it is a bird. Alas, not many major corporate shareholders are likely to agree to such a shift in purpose.

The end of history is a misguided idea and TINA is absurd narcissism and hubris. We do not know how the mixed models in China and Vietnam will evolve. Neither are problem free and it is not clear if they will do better on the major negative impacts of investor-driven capitalism. Experiments in building solidarity economies are in process in Venezuela, Bolivia and Ecuador, albeit under enormous pressure from U.S. corporate interests. Cuba's drive toward democratic, co-operative social-ism is a fascinating work in progress which may provide leadership to the world. The end that is approaching is the end of capitalism, drowning in its own contradic-tions. History will go on. The planet will survive, perhaps with far fewer species, and the damage to human society may be either modest or a catastrophe. There are alternatives. The question is in what direction. This is the subject of later chapters.

THE COLLAPSE OF CAPITALISM

A core thesis of this book is that sooner or later capitalism will collapse, weighed down by its destruction of nature and human society, without which the economy cannot exist. The combination of exponential growth in a finite world with the resulting destruction of life systems and the concentration of wealth into fewer and fewer hands is simply not sustainable. Unless the nature of capitalist busi-ness (the investor-owned firm) transforms its very purpose, it will continue, like a cancer, to destroy nature and human society. If new arrangements are found that shift the focus of current capitalist business away from the concentration of wealth, it will no longer be capitalism but will have become some other "ism." The question remains as to how the collapse of capitalism will play out. It is true that capitalism has survived the predictions of Karl Marx. State redistribution of income, progressive labour laws, democratic pressure on governments to regulate capitalist misdeeds, the harnessing of some of the brightest and best, and the threat of communism all played a role. That said, triumphant capitalism has dramatically cut the ability of government to redistribute income, eroded progressive labour law, reduced government regulation, out-sourced to countries with lower taxes and increasingly bought elections. It has also proceeded as if an economy might exist without a livable natural environment.

If capitalism is to collapse how will it happen? There are multiple possible scenarios. There are peaceful and violent solutions to the problems a dying capitalism will pose. It is possible to imagine transitions that are smooth and transitions that are chaotic. Will alternatives have the time to grow slowly stronger and emerge as a new reality that can spread and endure? Will elites and governments see the need for change and adaptation, or will they resist until the implosion is a disaster? Will those with a sense of possible alternatives have the courage of their convictions and the creativity to develop the systems needed to create viable alternatives?

THERE ARE ALTERNATIVES

We need a new economics, without which the bankrupt neoclassical economic analysis will continue to dominate public policymaking. The new economics has formidable challenges. It needs to be based on a multidimensional caring, an understanding of the nature of people and a solid grasp of our relationships with each other and with nature. For example, it needs to be based on how people behave in real life, not on warped assumptions about how "economic man" might behave. (Interestingly, I have yet to run across the phrase "economic woman.") Thankfully, new directions in economics have emerged, rooted not just in narrow economic thinking and mathematical models, but drawing on the best of human thought over millennia. The new economics is based on new thinking, research and analysis. There are many threads to the new thinking: environmental economics, the economics of participation, behavioural economics, no growth economics, development economics and co-operative economics.[45] The rest of this book focuses on this last new thread.

This new economic thinking provides us with superb analysis of the problems of the dominant capitalist economy, and I drew heavily on it for the trend analysis in Chapter 1. Clearer thinking about neoclassical economic myths opens new possibilities for building a functional economy. One of the frustrations of much of the new thinking is that it often does not leave us with a hopeful set of solutions. Suggestions that corporations need to behave better or that governments need to curb corporate excess are no longer credible. Triumphant capitalism has government in retreat. Government revenues are being gutted, and trade agreements limit what corporate tribunals will allow weakened democracies to do. It is still possible for people to effect change through government, but it is limited. The trend is for governments to do less and less to curb corporate freedom, and to do more and more to curb personal and non-corporate organizational freedom. That is what government by trade agreements is about.

There are logical reasons why many of the new economists assume capitalism will continue. There is a desire to avoid sliding into pessimism. If corporations will not profoundly change and governments will not force them to change, is there room for hope? In addition, most are focused on, and are experts in, their field of economics. In arranging for Eleanor Ostrom to speak to a conference on co-operative economics in 2012, I was told at first that she was not an expert in co-operatives but rather had done most of her work on "the commons." I explained why her work on the commons was relevant to co-operatives and on reflection she agreed to contribute.[46] The new economists focus on their valuable contribution to understanding how the economy really works, but often hesitate to identify the system changes needed to accomplish change, perhaps seeing it as beyond their expertise. When I read their work, I often look in the index for the words co-operation, co-operative(s), mutual(s) or credit union(s). Those words are almost never there in spite of the fact that the performance of co-operative business, while far from perfect, has a better record in terms of worker satisfaction, social impact and environmental impact.

I make the case later in the book that co-operatives are a better fit with human nature and produce much less damage to nature and society. I also argue that the co-operative business model has the potential to make a positive contribution to correcting the negative trends outlined in Chapter 1. The case I make is that the business purpose of co-operatives, *meeting member and community need,* holds more promise for solving the problems facing humanity than does seeking efficiency by maximizing return to investors. It is important then that the definition of the economy and economics fit with this co-operative business purpose. To this point, let me suggest a new definition of the economy and a description of the purpose and work of economics.

THE ECONOMY AND ECONOMICS REDEFINED

In their introduction to *Microeconomics*, 11th edition, Christopher Lipsey and Richard Ragan define the economy as "a system in which scarce resources are allocated among competing uses," and the study of economics as "the study of the use of scarce resources to satisfy unlimited human wants."[47] These definitions allow us to rationalize unacceptable economic failures, including significant levels of unemployment that leave millions of people in despair without a role or meaning in their own society; rendering the earth less and less supportive of the existence of life; leaving millions of children and adults starving in abject poverty; and eroding families, communities and civil society. We need new directions in economic thinking and analysis to inform the development of an economy that serves humanity and respects nature.

Does this mean that co-operative economics being suggested here replaces the strands of the new economics outlined above? Clearly not! These strands of the new economics are essential to co-operative economics. They are the methodologies co-operative economics depends upon to analyze how effective the economy is at meeting human need. Environmental economics tells us how we are meeting people's needs for a healthy planet. Behavioural economics is key to understanding how to shape an economy that provides people with meaning. Co-operative economics adopts the tools and analysis of the new economics to measure how well the economy is meeting individual, family and community needs. It is not focused on a particular subset of the population, but rather on the population as a whole, including every subset. Woven together as co-operative economics, the strands of the new economics provide a profoundly better intellectual perspective to understand the role of the economy in the context of our natural world and human society in all its complexity.

The neoclassical definitions leave much to be desired. Let me suggest new definitions more in line with and relevant to human reality. Because they are linked to the purpose of co-operative business, let us call these definitions co-operative economics:

- The economy is the complex set of relationships that people use to provide themselves with the goods and services they need to lead meaningful lives in their communities.
- Economics is the study of how effective the economy is at meeting human need in a manner that allows people meaningful happy lives as an integral part of a healthy planet.

These definitions are useful and meaningful for co-operative business and humanity. It is the basis of co-operative economics. The new economy coalition's vision of the new economy, below, fits well and resonates with co-operative purpose, values and principles:

Justice: A new economy must work for all people, starting with those who have historically been marginalized and exploited by racism, imperialism, classism, patriarchy, and other systems of oppression.

Sustainability: A new economy supports regeneration of both human and natural systems. It builds community resilience by rooting wealth and power in place and in service of human needs on a finite planet.

Democracy: A new economy incorporates democratic principles into the management of economic and civic life.[48]

What do ideas about co-operation add to the new economics? As we explore in later chapters, co-operation is more fundamental than competition to human progress. The purpose, values and principles of co-operation make a valuable contribution to how we think about and structure relationships to build a new economy. The global co-operative movement has developed a business model that works.

NOTES

1   This is admittedly a contentious statement and should itself be the topic of a book. Perhaps the most convincing example would be the United States of America where corporations with their immense spending power have been accorded the status of persons, allowing them to cloak their "purchase" of elections under "freedom of speech." Many more examples could be provided of economic power used to subvert electoral processes in many democratic countries, such as the funding of "think tanks" to promote neoclassical economic viewpoints. Reflection on the crucial role of access to information in a healthy democracy, media ownership concentration and the dependence of media on advertising, raises questions as to whether voters can possibly be informed enough to vote. For a somewhat fuller reflection on democracy see Chapter 1.

2   Philanthropy is charity. It is useful to distinguish between charity and justice. Charity makes the donor feel good but often makes the recipient feel grateful but helpless, inferior or not capable. Justice is based on the concept of human dignity. That said, charity is often a necessity in a world lacking in justice.

3   Dalberg (1887).

4   Smith (1776).

5   Mill (1848: 772).

6   For a more detailed exploration of many economic myths see: Smith and Max-Neef (2011); Schweickart (2002); Chang (2010); Cato (2006), (2009); Levitt (2013); Milanovic (2011) and many more.

7   See Blythe (2013); European Trade Union Institute. (2015); Fazi (2016); Lehndorff (2015); Krugman (2015).

8   See Schweickart (2002) for a persuasive critique of Soviet socialism and an exploration of how socialist thought might fit with ideas of democracy and economic democracy.

9   Dahlberg (1887).

10 An interesting exception has been the Cuban experience. There, considerable economic and social progress has been accomplished in spite of an embargo and extreme pressure from the most powerful economy in the world. In addition, Cuba has managed a form of one party democracy that arguably is quite as responsive to its people as most multiparty systems. Cuba is currently bolstering its democratic reality by encouraging economic democracy through co-operatives. In contrast, in Canada, only 24 percent of eligible voters elected a majority government in 2011, which many saw as operating as a temporary dictatorship. For a discussion of the Cuban experience, see August (2013) and Saney (2004)

11 See Smith and Max-Neef (2011) Chapter 3 for an excellent reflection on the evolution of economics.

12 Thatcher (1987).

13 GNI — Gross National Income, GDP — Gross Domestic Product and GNP — Gross National Product are similar but equally flawed if conceived of as the key measures of progress.

14 Oxfam (2013a, 2014).

15 Greenspan (2008).

16 Stiglitz (2015b).

17 Mintzberg (2013).

18 Todaro and Smith (2003: 698).

19 To go beyond this very brief summary of the myths of the miracle of the marketplace, see Chang (2010); Todaro and Smith (2003); Cato (2009), especially "How Perfect Is the NeoClassical Market?"; Stiglitz (2003, 2009).

20 See Piketty (2011, 2014).

21 Brennan (2015: 8).

22 To understand humanity beyond the very narrow view of economics is crucial. Any understanding of the economy needs a spiritual and psychological base. To form a healthy view of the economy we should be reading several books on other aspects of our humanity for every book on economics. While there are many sources, a good start would be Frankl (1946).

23 For an interesting perspective see Ha-Joon Chang (2014).

24 Kennedy (1968).

25 Schweickart (2002: 3).

26 United States, Congress (1973).

27 GNP (gross national product), GDP (gross domestic product) and GNI (gross national income) are a set of crude measures which, while providing useful some information, are widely used but of limited usefulness.

28 Sherman (2014).

29 Wilkinson and Pickett (2011).

30 GPI Atlantic <http://www.gpiatlantic.org/gpi.htm>.

31 See GPI Atlantic <http://www.gpiatlantic.org/gpi.htm>; Genuine Progress: Moving Beyond GDP <http://genuineprogress.net/about/>; Happy Planet Index <http://www.happyplanetindex.org/>.

32 See <http://www.grossnationalhappiness.com/articles/>.

33 For a full discussion see Mander (1991).

34 An oligopoly is when a small group of large firms control a market. Size limits the entry of new small firms.

35 For a concise description, see the World Health Organization website <http://www.who.int/trade/glossary/story094/en/> and Todaro and Smith (2003: 702–705).

36 Stiglitz (2003) provides a modest list of critiques at p. 259–60, but his devastating critique of the IMF Washington Consensus policies in *Globalization and Its Discontents* has been echoed by many careful scholars.

37 In rich countries, such as Canada, there were no formal structural adjustment agreements but the government of the day simply adopted the Washington Consensus policies, perhaps driven by a fear of losing influence at bodies such as the IMF and World Bank.

38 Stan Rogers, "Make and Break Harbour."

39 Reich (2015).

40 World Food Program <http://www.wfp.org/hunger/stats> accessed 2 April 2015. Words in bold are from the source.

41 Tran (2013). This report was based on a study published in the *Lancet* in June 2013.

42 It is worth noting that the Guardian Global Development reports are supported by the Bill and Melinda Gates Foundation. For at least one billionaire family, giving something back is important. Being a billionaire does not necessarily destroy a person's human caring. The problem is an economic system that creates billionaires in the first place.

43 The Davos conferences are gala meetings organized by the global elite each year in Switzerland.

44 Clark (2003).

45 The bibliography lists the work of many of the "new economists," to whom I am most grateful. I hope I have not distorted or misunderstood their work.

46 Alas, before the conference took place Eleanor Ostrom died. The conference included a tribute to her work and its relevance to co-operative economics.

47 Lipsey and Ragan (2010).

48 New Economy Coalition (n.d.).

Chapter 3

WEALTH DRIVEN BUSINESS MODELS AND THEIR ALTERNATIVES

The previous chapter claimed: "Unless the nature of capitalist business (the investor-owned firm) changes and it transforms its very purpose for being, it will continue, like a cancer, to destroy nature and the human society, both of which depend on nature to exist." This chapter explores the basis for this controversial statement. The dominant business model globally is the investor-owned company (IOC).[1] There are other business models, including co-operatives, mutuals, and "for profit"[2] and "not for profit" social enterprises, but the investor-owned firm dominates.

INVESTOR OWNED FIRMS — A CORRUPTED IDEA

Pharmaceutical CEO Martin Shkreli's company bought the rights to an inexpensive drug, used to treat a rare and often fatal disease, and a few months later raised the price by almost 5000 percent. Asked at the Forbes Healthcare Summit,[3] "If you could rewind the clock a few months I wonder if you would do anything differently?" he responded clearly and honestly:

> I probably would have raised the price higher. It is probably what I would have done. That's my duty. I think health care prices are inelastic, I could have raised it higher and made more profits with it, which is my practice. And again, no one wants to say it, no one is proud of it, but this

is a capitalist society, capitalist system and capitalist rules and my investors expect me to maximize profits not to minimize them or go half or to seventy percent but to go to 100% of the profit curve that we are all taught in MBA class. Try to be a CEO yourself. Try to not maximize profits and not be kicked out of the company. You won't last very long. Let me know how that goes for you. Price drugs really low. It is people who make these hard choices, grow earnings for their shareholders and again try to do the right thing with those profits.[4]

In her book *This Changes Everything: Capitalism vs the Climate*, Naomi Klein weighs in on whether the capitalist system can be reformed slowly over time:

> For a quarter of a century, we have tried the approach of polite incremental change, attempting to bend the physical needs of the planet to our economic model's need for constant growth and new profit making opportunities. The results have been disastrous, leaving us all in a great deal more danger than when the experiment began.[5]

Investor-owned corporations did not always exist as they do today. Ralph Estes, a former senior manager with Arthur Anderson Inc., once one of the world's largest accounting firms, examines the roots of corporations:

> Corporations were first chartered by governments to serve the public purpose. … Sovereigns issued corporate charters to achieve a public purpose without permanently expanding the government bureaucracy — a genesis not well known today. Later democracies and states adopted this tradition to obtain needed public services — water systems, turnpikes, stage lines, colleges. For over two centuries, corporations were viewed as fairly benign servants of the public good. But they are no longer our servants, and they are often not benign.[6]

Much like a child, born in innocence and hope but raised in an increasingly immoral and brutal home, corporations have become deformed: their purpose shifted from public good to profits for investors.[7] IOCs can be publicly traded companies whose shares are traded on stock exchanges or the shares may be controlled by a partnership, small group or even single family. In either case they enjoy the protection of limited liability. The result is neither in the interests of the company — those who depend upon it for a livelihood — nor the society in which it exists. Ha-Joon Chang provides a convincing analysis of investor-owned firms, which he concludes with these words: "Running companies in the interests of floating shareholders is not only inequitable but also inefficient, not just for the national economy but also for the company itself."[8] A case is made below that small family-owned firms often operate very differently from huge family-owned conglomerates. What separates the investor-owned firm from other business models is its overriding purpose. It is the very rare IOC that consistently allows social, environmental, community or worker safety concerns to trump maximizing profit. Owners and managers of investor-owned firms talk about "the" bottom line. The idea of triple bottom lines (financial, social and environmental) is new, and for investor-owned firms the two additional "bottom lines" are clearly secondary. The share price of a firm that viewed its return to shareholders as a second or third priority would plummet. It would not likely survive, and if it did it would no longer be a firm whose purpose was return to investors.

The purpose of IOCs, regardless of what business sectors they operate in, is to provide the largest return possible to the investors who own them. The purpose of telecommunication companies is not to provide communication services, although they may do that and other things as well. Their purpose is to maximize returns to their investors. As the CEO of New Zealand Telecom told an international meeting: "Think about pricing. What has every telco in the world done in the past? It's used confusion as its chief marketing tool. And that's fine."[9] Clearly, telecommunications companies set out to confuse rather than to inform their clients. The twin of confusion is doubt. With issues like the health impact of tobacco and the threat to humanity from global warming, huge corporations and some billionaires have used their enormous wealth to create bogus science reports, obscuring scientific truth and leaving people confused and doubting real science.[10]

If a firm is publicly traded on today's markets, the pressure to maximize returns or "shareholder value" is powerful. Even a slight decline in profitability can lead to a company's share value dropping, as Apple experienced in the first months of 2013. In the words of a Forbes analyst: "Investors look to see if Apple can really produce enough profits to justify the $450 billion."[11] According to the analyst, $450 billion was the value of all Apple's shares on February 13, 2013.

The fundamentals of making maximum returns is simple. You produce a "product" for as little as you can and sell it for as much as you can, using a tool kit that includes the following:

- keeping pay and benefits to workers as low as possible;
- minimizing expenditures on improving working conditions, including health and safety;
- replacing workers with automation;
- keeping out unions;
- paying as little tax as possible;
- reducing government regulation;

- using confusion marketing or any other marketing technique that will work;
- letting society cover the costs of adverse impacts of operations, like pollution, health problems among workers or the general public, or pay levels below what is needed to provide the necessities of life, etc.;
- getting government to provide needed infrastructure such as roads, water or sewerage;
- obtaining government grants and support and low- or no -cost access to natural resources;
- ensuring a low-cost supply chain;
- contracting out[12];
- charging as much as the market will bear for goods and services produced;
- controlling markets whenever possible and reducing competition; and
- moving investments to wherever regulations allow the firm maximum use of the above tools.

Perhaps most damaging to nature and human society are the combined impacts of investor-owned firms externalizing the cost of their operational damage for governments and citizens to pay, while also demanding huge subsidies and bailouts. Naomi Klein notes of the fossil fuel industry: "Not only do fossil fuel companies receive $775 billion to $1 trillion in annual global subsidies, but they pay nothing for the privilege of treating our shared atmosphere as a free waste dump — a fact that has been described by the *Stern Review on the Economics of Climate Change* as 'the greatest market failure the world has ever seen.'"[13]

It is not an accident that many firms choose to source garments from Bangladesh.[14] Love canal, the Sydney tar ponds, the BP oil spill in the Gulf of Mexico, Union Carbide's Bhopal disaster, the millions of deaths from cigarette sales, untold more millions of deaths from food laced with addictive sugar, fat and salt, the massive environmental destruction around Canada's tar sands — these are not accidents. They are the result of profit maximization activity. This list could go on for many, many pages.[15] It could include examples of arming death squads and contracting to murder people who "got in the way."[16] Nor were the 2008 banking collapse, the 1980s "savings and loan" debacle in the U.S., WorldCom's and Arthur Anderson's demise and Enron's collapse accidents. These events, like the profit maximization tools listed above, are simply examples of the predatory activity inherent in capitalism in pursuit of profit. The investor-owned company is simply a bad technology with powerful inbuilt pressures to behave in an anti-social manner. This is a fatal design flaw. One would hope that an automobile model with as serious a design flaw would simply be banned from the roads.

Why do so many corporations commit so many corporate crimes?[17] The three main areas of corporate crime are related to safety, the environment and financial fraud. Laureen Snider argues persuasively that corporations and their owners have always fiercely resisted any limitations on what they can do with their property.[18] Since wealth brings power, they have been enormously successful in resisting regulation, promoting deregulation and ensuring that laws and regulations are not enforced. Corporations cannot be put in prison and their owners are protected by limited liability and by their ability to afford superb legal representation. The bigger the corporation and the bigger the crime, the more vigorous the defence. Unlike individual crime, corporate crime is almost never prosecuted. Snider asks us to

> consider for example the discrepancy between laws governing motorists and those protecting employees and consumers. If you kill someone accidentally in a car because you were going too fast, you will probably be charged with criminal negligence and if convicted will receive a significant prison sentence. If you kill several workers in a mine because you (as CEO or member of the board of directors) decided that safety equipment was too expensive and installing it would reduce profits (and negatively affect your bonus) you are unlikely to ever be charged with an illegal act, let alone spend a day in prison.[19]

But neoclassical economists, many business promoters and business school professors will argue: "Profit is not a dirty word." Entering that phrase into Google produces 2,390,000 hits in thirty seconds. This is a common argument. A whole chapter could be devoted to the word: to the difference between economic and accounting profit; to how it is used by different people. If by profit is meant the surplus that remains after the cost of production and operations is deducted from revenue, it is not a dirty word. If what is meant by profit is the maximization of the amount that goes to investors from the operations of a business they own, then, more often than not, in our current global economy, it is synonymous with greed. In one of the relatively rare losing court judgements addressing profit the judge said:

> Under your direction, your company has continued to allow women, tens of thousands of them, to wear this device — a deadly depth charge in their wombs, ready to explode at any time.... The only conceivable reasons that you have not recalled this product are that it would hurt your balance sheet and alert women who have already been harmed that you may be liable for their injuries.... You have taken the bottom line as your guiding beacon and the low road as your route.[20]

It is simply a fact that the richest 10 percent are using profits from investments to take for themselves more and more of the total wealth produced by humanity. The investor-owned firm is their means of accomplishing that goal.

This has profound implications for society and the economy. In an investor-owned firm, goods and services are not produced to meet human need; the purpose of production is profit. Armed with powerful marketing tools, IOCs go beyond producing what people need and create wants. This is the foundation of the consumer society. If people learn to want more and more, IOCs do well. If people can be persuaded to want things that lead to their suffering and even deaths, it is good for profit. The tobacco and food industries have clearly demonstrated this. If people can be persuaded to consume increasingly frivolous wants at levels which will destroy the ability of the planet to sustain life, it is good for profit.

Yet, increasingly, as the incomes of the poorest 60 percent of humanity decline, it is not profitable to produce for them. Food banks grow, and at the same time so do marinas with expensive yachts. Drug companies often do not research, produce or sell medicines for diseases that kill millions in poor countries because poor people cannot afford them.[21] "Every year more than US$70 billion is spent worldwide on health R&D by the public and private sectors. An estimated 10 percent of this is used for research into 90 percent of the world's health problems."[22]

The negative implications of this single overriding purpose are almost always compounded by the investors not residing in the community in which the business operates, or if some do, they are most often not identifiable in the community. The investors seldom have to live with the internal or external impacts of their business. Investors very often do not use the business, do not work in the business and have no connection with it except to be awarded the profits of its activity. Many investors do not have any notion of what companies they have invested in, much less how the companies which they partly own act or what they produce.

The claim is often made that with thousands or tens of thousands of shareholders who can vote at shareholder meetings, investor-owned firms are a form of democracy. This is absurd. Democracy is about one person one vote. Corporate shareholder voting is about one dollar one vote, where 20 percent of the population has 85 percent or more of those votes. Democracy is government "of the people, by the people and for the people."[23] Investor-owned firms are more accurately called "wealthocracies." Shareholders with a huge number of shares are usually the only ones at shareholders meetings, and they are able to outvote the few small shareholders who might attend. There is no credible way to argue that the 80 percent of the world's people who own less than 15 percent of the world's wealth have any impact on corporate decision-making.

In today's financial markets people do not even know what shares investment funds hold on their behalf. And the volume and speed of share trading is so huge and instantaneous that shareholding bears no relationship to what it meant even twenty-five years ago. Today a share is not held for years or months but days or hours. Fullerton notes: "In reality, public corporations are not 'owned' in the true sense of the word, by anyone."[24] It is much easier now for a sizable minority share-holder or management to exercise control.

Some may counter that many corporations have ethical codes of conduct and produce social responsibility reports. For the most part these standards are not accounted for in any rigorous fashion, nor are they the subject of reports by independent organizations. Rather they are PR documents. For example, British American Tobacco's award-winning social responsibility report did not deal with the health impacts of its products.[25]

But one could argue that corporations do good things as well. This is true and it brings us to a very important truth about structures and people — the core problem with the investor-owned business model is not the people in the organizations but rather the purpose and structure of the business. The investor-owned business model makes good people do bad things.[26] It exerts constant pressure, sometimes subtle and sometimes brutal.[27] Investor-owned firms as an organizational form are free of values. In the immortal words of neoclassical economist Milton Friedman commenting on corporate social responsibility: "The business of business is business." The people operating a business, the board or the management have a fiduciary responsibility to serve the shareholders.[28]

In spite of the relentless organizational pressure, board members and managers are simply people and are, for the most part, people who personally wish to "do good." Alas, far too often they succumb to the structural imperative of the organi-zation — it was created and structured to maximize the return to shareholders. Managers and board members of IOCs who do the right thing are to be greatly admired. The problem is not that all or even most business people are evil, they are just people. The problem is that the structure is based on serving greed, not need.

Finally, an argument is often made that capitalist corporations, because they are focused on maximizing the return to capital, are more efficient in using resources. It is easy to be efficient when focused on a single narrow goal. This definition of efficiency was met by Target in closing its Canadian stores. It left 17,600 workers without jobs. It left behind an estimated $5 billion in debts that will not be paid to municipalities, suppliers and landlords. It did however manage a US$61 million "golden parachute" for the CEO responsible for the mess, an amount larger than the total severance package for the 17,600 workers.[29]

But what if efficient meant meeting human need while doing as little damage as possible to nature and society and providing people with a meaningful opportunity to contribute to their communities? Judged on these standards, corporations are efficiently destructive.

What is clear is that corporations, as currently empowered by nation-states and international trade agreements, grow and merge with enormous success, and many are now clearly more powerful than individual countries. Increasingly, they dictate to nations that their economies will be run with the sole purpose of maximizing corporate profits. In his 1999 book *The Cancer Stage of Capitalism,*[30] John McMurtry makes a powerful case that just as cancer is enormously successful when examined from a narrow perspective, so is capitalism. He argues persuasively that, like cancer, the more successful it becomes, the closer the host approaches death. McMurtry's book was partly the inspiration for Joel Baken's book *The Corporation: The Pathological Pursuit of Profit and Power,* which, in turn, was the basis for the award-winning documentary film *The Corporation.* They make a compelling case that, like cancer, capitalism and its corporate expression overcome, increasingly control and destroy human society and nature. Baken also describes the corporation, as created by law, to function much like a psychopath. The logical long-term outcome of a massive growth of such organizations is the implosion of capitalism itself.[31]

The dysfunctions of corporations highlighted in these and other books include the following:

- excessive senior executive pay tied to share price performance ratchets up immoral, fraudulent and destructive behaviour;
- bribery of government officials, especially in poorer countries; support for dictatorial and corrupt regimes;
- engagement in more and more predatory behaviour using market control, technology and superior capital resources to destroy small and medium sized local business;
- forcing governments to compete with lower taxes, grants and waiving regulations;
- moving profits to tax havens for tax avoidance and evasion;
- seldom covering more than a fraction of the costs of their disasters; and
- demanding bailouts when they become "too big to fail."

This latter trait was the dominant lesson of the 2008 crisis — "socialism" for the super-rich paid for through austerity programs for the poor. The super-rich who own and control the banks were protected from losses with huge bailouts, paid for by cutting programs designed to protect the bottom 80 percent.

> It might be argued that socialism flourishes in modern Britain, but it is socialism for the rich and for corporations. The state is there to support them, to rescue them if needs be. Much of the rest of the population, on the other hand, is increasingly expected to sink or swim: their experience is capitalism red in tooth and claw.... Risk and debt have become

nationalized and carried by the population, while the profitable elements are privatized.[32]

VARIATIONS ON INVESTOR-OWNED FIRMS

There are a number of emerging variations on the investor-owned firm, including benefit corporations, low-profit limited liability companies (L3Cs) and flexible-purpose corporations (FPC). Susan Mac Cormac, a corporate lawyer from California specializing in alternative corporate forms, describes them as follows:

> All FPCs must specify at least one "special purpose" in its charter, such as promoting environmental sustainability or minimizing adverse effects on its employees. In exchange, an FPC is given a new "safe harbor" (in addition to the business judgment rule): boards and management are protected from shareholder liability when they weigh their special purpose(s) against shareholder value both in the ordinary course of business and in change of control situations. The FPC is distinguished from the L3C and Benefit Corporation in that it is primarily intended for use by for-profit companies seeking traditional capital market investment.

The FPC differs from the traditional corporate form in the following primary ways:

Qualifying Special Purpose. The FPC has one or more social and/or environmental purpose(s) agreed upon between management and shareholders, and included in the charter. The FPC is not permitted to change its purpose without a two-thirds vote of each class of voting shares.

Protection from Liability. The FPC provides protection from liability for directors and management who make decisions on the basis of the agreed special purpose(s).

Conversion of Other Forms. An existing public or private corporation (LLC, partnership, or other entity) can convert into an FPC with two-thirds vote of each class of voting shares, with dissenter's rights.

Reporting. The FPC is required to publish regular reports with objectives, goals, measurement, and reporting on the impact or "returns" of social/environmental actions.

Enforcement. As fiduciary duties include the special purpose(s), shareholders have traditional enforcement rights with respect to the special purpose(s) (removal of directors and/or legal action); other "stakeholders" will not have enforcement rights.

Benefit Corporation. The Benefit Corporation (or B Corporation or B Corp) is a new class of corporation that has passed in six states, most recently California on October 9th (2011). Often confused with the "B Corp" certification developed by B Lab and available for license after completion of a socially responsible/sustainable self-audit, the Benefit Corporation requires boards and management to consider certain public benefits in corporate decision making and issue an annual "benefit report" in accordance with B Lab's standards. Significant variation exists among the states and often the legislation was not drafted to work with the remainder of the corporate code. Benefit Corporations generally are designed for use by private companies focused on sustainability that avail themselves of socially responsible capital.

L3C — An L3C is a statutory type of LLC that has been considered in 21 states and has been adopted in eight. However, the L3C is primarily designed to assist for-profit companies with primarily a charitable purpose, hoping to obtain program-related investments from foundations.[33] end BQ

Mac Cormac goes on to make the following assessment: "As a result, organizations both in the non-profit and the for-profit worlds have been 'bending' their respective corporate forms to achieve multiple objectives. However, these approaches produce unsatisfactory results and create potential liability for managers with either shareholders (in the case of for-profits) or with the IRS (in the case of non-profits)."[34] What the long-term impact of these new corporate forms will be is too early to assess. As of April 2015 the B Corporation website claims 1,257 benefit corporations in forty-one countries. What is not known is how well benefit corporations will, in the longer term, manage the balancing act between doing good and making profits for their investors. With the unavoidable ensuing tension, it is not unreasonable to expect that for the most part the power of wealth will dominate the social purpose. If the goal of the economy is meeting human need, this is a significant drawback. There are better models than this.

THE BOTTOM LINE FOR HUMANITY

We need to shift from the unsustainable investor owned-model, which lacks intrinsic values and whose purpose is simply destructive. The IOC is an ideal business model for an economy focused on creating wealth without purpose and regardless of the consequences. It is especially successful at this single minded task when it can capture the state and enshrine corporate freedom in trade agreements that straight jacket democracy. For the good of humanity and the health of the planet it is a business model that must wither and disappear. The alternative is that, like a cancer, it will hang on until the damage to nature and human society is so severe that capitalism, like communism, simply collapses. But what shall replace it and how shall that happen? Are there business models whose single overriding purpose is not maximizing the economic return to those who already have most of the world's wealth? Fortunately there are very viable alternatives, which fall into several categories: family owned business; social enterprise and mutuals and co-operatives. The meaningful differences between them revolve around purpose, why does the business exist, and values. The best alternatives being those with the clearest values and value commitments and those whose purpose is meeting human need. The values have to include respect for the natural world and a clear understanding that we are part of nature, not above it.

FAMILY-OWNED BUSINESSES

Family-owned business is included as an alternative business model because the sole purpose of the owners is very seldom profit maximization. Financial gain is not the primary reason for the business but just one of several reasons. Another key difference is the direct involvement of the owner in the business. My father ran a small family-owned business. He would have described the purposes of his business as providing a living for his family and the workers, treating workers well, contributing to the community and providing people with the things they needed even at times when they could not afford to pay. He had no charter that spelled out his approach to business but it rested on his religious and ethical beliefs. I grew up with a positive view of the people involved in small and medium family businesses, and this has not changed.

Many family-owned businesses are run along the same lines with no formal commitment to do so. The owners are free to run the business the way they see best. They sometimes are not good employers, treating the community and workers badly or treating nature badly. They may be responding to competitive pressure or perhaps lacking competence. Their personal values may not be impressive. They may come under pressure from the banks to which they owe money but unless they have a set of "silent partners," they are free to run their business in line with their values. The people making decisions in large corporations lack that freedom. Family-owned businesses operate without the relentless pressure to serve the interests of a group of absentee investors. Family-owned businesses, unless they are very large, tend to operate in the communities in which the owner lives. They interact with the community through their family, social and business contacts. How they operate is thus influenced by community norms and values as well as their personal ones. As we see below, a large number of small- and medium-sized family businesses join together to form co-operatives.

SOCIAL ENTERPRISES

Social enterprises are businesses whose purpose is meeting identified social needs and their business activities are a means to carry out that purpose.[35] "Social enterprises, as defined by the U.K. law on Community Interest Companies in 2005, and by the Italian law on the Impresa Sociale in 2006, are public benefit organizations that pursue the satisfaction of social needs."[36] Similar definitions can be found on the websites of organizations of social enterprises. Most definitions include co-operatives, but this book deals with co-operatives as a separate group of social enterprises whose values and principles are agreed to by co-operatives around the world.

Social enterprises have a wide range of membership eligibility requirements, governance structures, purpose, values and principles. They are involved in almost any type of business that does not have an anti-social purpose. A computer service business may exist to recycle used computer equipment, charging for the service but also providing rebuilt computers to individuals or groups in need. Another may employ released prisoners to help them re-engage in society; yet another may run a hospital. They do not exist to generate a profit to a set of investor shareholders. Any surplus from operations goes to further the social purpose for which they were created.

During a study visit to the European Research Institute on Cooperative and Social Enterprises (Euricse), students explored the key differences between co-operatives and other social enterprises. "Why," they asked, "do social enterprises choose not to incorporate as co-operatives?" The answer was that the people forming the social enterprises did not always agree on the full set of co-operative values and principles. A student then asked: "Which values and principles are they not comfortable with: honesty, openness, equity, equality, democracy, education?" There are a number of possible answers. Those governing the business may or may not use it or work in it. Those working in it may or may not have any say in the operation. Those using it or benefiting from the operations may or may not have any say in governance. It may be controlled by funders. A social enterprise may be based on a group of dedicated, progressive social activists or be cleverly run for the benefit of a small clique or even as a front for other purposes. If it is involved in social services, it can identify with the needs of those it serves viewed from their perspective or seek to impose the norms of a governing group.

The social enterprise model has a great deal of flexibility, which also means that a social enterprise does not come with a set of defined expectations. While this is a weakness in the business model, it is an enormous improvement over IOC business models, whose purpose in not meeting human need beyond those of the investors. Social enterprises have a solid track record. They are very seldom dangerous. The performance of any business, regardless of its structure or built-in values, depends on the performance and values, the human weaknesses, the foibles and strengths of the people who govern it and the people who operate it.

CO-OPERATIVES

Like other forms of social enterprise, co-operatives have a straightforward purpose: meeting member and community need and aspirations. The International Co-operative Alliance Statement of Co-operative Identity clearly articulates co-operative values and principles, setting forth the difference between co-operatives and other forms of social enterprise.[37] Some will argue that they know of co-operatives that do not live up to the values and principles. Unfortunately there is no denying that. I am not aware of any human organization where every person or segment perfectly lives up to their stated ideals. The value of the declaration of co-operative values and principles is that members of the co-operative, workers and the general public have a moral right to question any aspect of operating performance that does not live up to those ideals. Such questioning does not take place as often as it should but it still is very common.

What makes the co-operative business model particularly valuable to our world today is precisely this combination of purpose, values and principles. Members are the ones who use the business and set it up to meet their needs. Almost without exception, co-operatives are created by people seeking to be treated fairly, not by people seeking to use their wealth to make a profit from the needs of others. The process of choosing the co-operative model forces founding members to ask "why these values and principles?" Members who join later may do so without much reflection on values and principles, but research shows they at least have a vague sense that co-operatives have a different purpose and are value-based and more trustworthy.

Co-operatives emerged in response to the excesses of the Industrial Revolution. Co-operative pioneers developed a set of values and principles designed to shape and guide the structures and processes of co-operative businesses and to ensure that co-operative business provided a distinct alternative to investor-owned corporations. The values and principles have played a strong role in various jurisdictions in shaping the legislative requirements under which co-operatives are incorporated. These values and principles form the touchstones for co-operative practice, including democratic functioning.

These values and principles have evolved over the years since they were first developed as an alternative to the frequent excesses during the Industrial Revolution. All co-operatives and co-operators around the globe are united by their acceptance of the International Co-operative Alliance statement of values and principles:

Co-operative Organizational Values

- Equality — Every person is worthwhile in his or her own right and has the right to have his or her life, dignity and abilities respected and valued equally.
- Equity — Each person should be treated fairly and have access to all that is necessary to live a meaningful and productive life.
- Mutual Self-help — People are interdependent and benefit from joining their individual efforts with others to achieve their aspirations and improve their lives.
- Self-responsibility — Each of us is responsible for our own actions and the impact of those actions upon others and ourselves. Groups are also responsible for the impact of their actions on individuals, other groups and society in general.
- Democracy — The human spirit is liberated by democratic processes and structures, through which control is shared, and each person shares in the ability to influence decisions. Every person has the right to have a say and influence all decisions that affect their lives. Democracy is not limited to the actions of the state but extends to all decisions that have an impact on the lives of people.
- Solidarity — Shared, coordinated action between individuals and groups is the best way to create a society and economy characterized by equity, equality and mutual self-help. After participating in an open democratic process to determine a position or course of action, members support it. Solidarity limits our individual freedom only to the extent required by a real respect for the dignity of others being equal to our own.

Personal Ethical Values for Co-operators

These are values that are logical extensions of the co-operative values. Without seeking to live by these values, co-operators are not able to nurture strong co-operatives.

- Honesty — Reliable honest dealings with members, customers, suppliers and the community rest on an appreciation for the dignity of people and are a key foundation of trust.
- Openness — Honesty reaches full meaning only with the open disclosure of information about products and services, the way they are organized and presented and the operations and governance of the business. Openness is also the foundation of equitable access to participation.
- Social Responsibility — The interdependence of people and recognition of their dignity leads to a realization that individual and group action has

profound effects on individuals, groups and their relationships.
- Caring for Others — Caring implies not just charity but active concern about how to act and create structures so as to enable others to realize their potential and live full and satisfying lives.

ICA Co-operative Principles

The following seven co-operative principles are operational guidelines as to how the co-operative values can be put into practice. They exist to help us organize how the co-operative operates and set standards by which we can assess our achievements and make decisions.

- Voluntary and Open Membership — Co-operatives are voluntary organizations, open to all persons able to use their services and willing to accept the responsibilities of membership, without gender, social, racial, political or religious discrimination.
- Democratic Member Control — Co-operatives are democratic organizations controlled by their members, who actively participate in setting their policies and making decisions. Men and women serving as elected representatives are accountable to the membership. In primary co-operatives, members have equal voting rights (one member, one vote) and co-operatives at other levels are organized in a democratic manner.
- Member Economic Participation — Members contribute equitably to, and democratically control, the capital of their co-operative. Each person should have the same access to ownership. At least part of that capital is usually the common property of the co-operative. They usually receive limited compensation, if any, on capital subscribed as a condition of membership. Members allocate surpluses for any or all of the following purposes: developing the co-operative, possibly by setting up reserves, part of which at least would be indivisible; benefiting members in proportion to their transactions with the co-operative; and supporting other activities approved by the membership.
- Autonomy and Independence — Co-operatives are autonomous, self-help organizations controlled by their members. If they enter into agreements with other organizations, including governments, or raise capital from external sources, they do so on terms that ensure democratic control by their members and maintain their co-operative autonomy.
- Education, Training and Information — Co-operatives provide education and training for their members, elected representatives, managers and employees so they can contribute effectively to the development of their co-operatives. They inform the general public — particularly young

people and opinion leaders — about the nature and benefits of co-operation.
- Co-operation among Co-operatives — Co-operatives serve their
  members most effectively and strengthen the co-operative movement
  by working together through local, national, regional and international
  structures.
- Concern for Community — While focusing on member needs, co-operatives work for the sustainable development of their communities through
  policies accepted by their members.

Mondragon Co-operative Principles

In addition to the seven ICA principles, there is a second set of principles developed by what many would argue is the most successful network of co-operatives
in the world, the Mondragon Co-operative Corporation (MCC).[38] Mondragon is a
network of primarily worker-owned co-operatives in the Basque Country of Spain,
concentrated in three valleys in the Pyrenees.[39] The Mondragon co-operatives
follow ten basic principles, not seven, and they reflect the thinking of Arizmendi
and his colleagues on the importance of worker co-operation. Of the ten, five are
significantly different or add to the ICA principles.

- Open Admission — Similar to ICA Voluntary and Open Membership
- Democratic Organization — Similar to ICA Democratic Member Control
- Sovereignty of Labour — Mondragon co-operators believe that labour is
  the primary factor in productive activity and that workers have primacy
  in the governance of co-operatives. The operational expression of this is
  that the Mondragon group is built on a base of worker co-operatives.
- Instrumental and Subordinate Character of Capital — Similar to ICA
  Member Economic Participation
- Participatory Management — The Mondragon co-operatives strive to
  engage workers in self-management with an emphasis on channels of
  participation, access to information and business education.
- Payment Solidarity — The wage gap between the lowest and highest
  paid is agreed to within each co-operative and for the system as a whole.
  Wages are to be in line with those in the community unless those wage
  levels are not a living wage. In current practice the gap between highest
  and lowest in individual co-operatives cannot exceed 6:1 and for the
  whole system 9:1.
- Interco-operation — Similar to ICA Co-operation among Co-operatives.
- Social Transformation — A commitment to building a freer, more just
  society characterized by solidarity. This includes the continuous devel-

opment of co-operatives; community development; social programs; a commitment to the promotion of the Basque language and culture; co-operation with other institutions and organizations in the Basque Country.

- Universality — Solidarity with all those working for economic democracy, peace, justice and development around the world.
- Education — Similar to ICA Education, Training and Information

Given the success of the Mondragon group and the value of the additional principles, these are highly recommended to all co-operatives and especially to worker co-operatives. The additional Mondragon values enhance the ICA principles and deepen their meaning.

ECOLOGICAL PERSPECTIVE

The co-operative values and principles continue to evolve and there is much pressure to respond to the enormous and growing threat to our environment. Some are pushing to add a strong specific statement regarding the environment to the principle of concern for the community. Others see the assault on nature and our interdependence with it as demanding a new and separate principle. It has taken many years to get recognition of the ICA Co-operative Identity by states from around the world and from international organizations like the United Nations and the International Labour Organization. The bolder path would be a decisive eighth principle, which seems likely to have more potential both as an educational tool and in attracting public support. Whichever path is chosen, the content needs to be along the following lines:

> Co-operatives recognize that the human species is but one part of an interconnected and interdependent universe and that respecting nature and life in all its expressions is not separable from respect for the dignity and value of each person.

The co-operative values and principles are of tremendously practical. They have been chosen and modified over time because they make co-operation among a group of people work. If an organization wants to foster co-operation as a way of working together, putting these values and principles "up on the wall" is a powerful influence. When people treat each other in line with these values and principles, groups function well. This is a strength that other forms of social enterprise lack. The co-operative purpose sets co-operatives apart from investor-owned firms, and the values and principles deepen that difference and also set the bar higher than in other forms of social enterprise.

With that in mind, the Co-operative Management Education program at Saint Mary's University, in Halifax, partnered with Polish scholar Ryzard Stocki and worker co-operative organizations in Canada and the U.S. to develop the Co-op Index, a management tool based on a total participation approach. The Index helps co-operatives to diagnose and develop their participatory character and align their daily operations with their co-operative values. An integral part of the Index is its linkage to the co-operative values and principles, based on the belief that, when followed, they are a powerful source of business strength that can drive financial and membership health.[40]

In those relatively rare instances when a social enterprise (SE) or co-operative performs badly, it is usually a result of a moral or competence failure of individuals or of the social enterprise model being abused. Of the millions of social enterprises around the world, none have produced cases of criminal, immoral or irresponsible actions on the scale of infant formula marketing, the Bophal disaster, the blood diamonds trade, the Sydney tar ponds, Goldman Sachs profiting from selling junk securities or the rupture of Enbridge's ill maintained pipelines.[41] The difference between IOCs on the one hand and social enterprises and co-operatives on the other is that IOCs are bad structures pressuring good people do bad things and the co-operatives and social enterprise are good structures influencing good people to the right thing. Co-ops and social enterprises cannot make people perfect but they nurture the best in people. These are business models that offer hope.

A FLEXIBLE MODEL

The co-operative business model is very flexible. There are several different types of co-operatives, hybrids and variations within types. Following the values and principles above, each member of the co-operative is a user. Not all users are members but membership is open to all users.[42] The different types of co-operatives based on different types of membership are as follows:

- Worker/Employee Co-operatives — Members are those who work in the business, which could be in any industry, such as food, agriculture, retail sales of goods or services, social services, financial services, etc. This model varies, from "collectives" which operate without a management structure, through to forms with hierarchical management structures. The co-operative's general assemblies have final authority over the structure and operating policies.
- Consumer Co-operatives: Members are consumers of commodities, such as food, insurance, funerals, financial services, including credit unions, housing, utilities, such as electricity or gas, farm and garden supplies, travel services, etc. This model includes mutuals, which are almost always

co-operative-type insurance businesses where the policy holders own the business and have an equal say in its governance and direction.

- Small Business Co-operatives: Members are producers of goods and services, such as dairy farmers, fishers, motel/hotel owners, hardware or other retail stores, electricians, plumbers, family grocers, etc. They provide themselves with shared services, such as procurement, marketing, business expertise, government relations, etc. These are generally small- and medium-sized family-owned businesses. The co-operative form makes sense to them because it allows them to protect themselves from predatory competition, to achieve greater buying power and to share certain functions, like marketing, while keeping control of their own business in their own community. It also makes sense because family-owned firms often have multiple purposes which can override profit, like making a contribution to the community, treating workers well or just supporting the family rather than maximizing return.

- Solidarity Co-operatives: These involve members who have an interdependent relationship with each other (dairy workers and farmers, parents and daycare workers, social workers and clients, consumers and workers, etc.) and form a co-operative with different classes of membership to work toward a shared goal — e.g., providing quality daycare for children — which is the basis of their solidarity. Solidarity co-operatives might have differences in conditions of membership and member benefits. Solidarity co-operatives have different classes of members, for example consumers and workers, with different conditions of membership and benefits of membership. For example workers get an income and consumer members may get special discounts but both get to vote for members of the board.

- Community Co-operatives: People from a community seeking to accomplish ad hoc projects or broad based community improvement join together to achieve shared goals, for example, building a community hall or developing a plan for community renewal.

- Second and Third Tier Co-operatives: Members are co-operatives rather than individuals, and there is often a variation of the "one member–one vote" practice to reflect varying co-operative membership levels. For example, a local co-operative with ten thousand members might be represented at a second tier co-operative meeting by five voting delegates, while a co-operative with a couple of hundred might have just one delegate. The International Co-operative Alliance is a clear example of a third tier co-operative. The ICA members are for the most part second tier co-operatives. It is also worth noting that there also "sector organizations," like international associations of agricultural or consumer food co-operatives, depending on the number and size of active co-operatives sharing a particular focus. The ICA has a number of such organizations

A VIABLE BUSINESS MODEL

It is difficult to obtain accurate statistics about the extent of social enterprises worldwide because of the large variety of forms and because statistics between countries are not comparable. Co-operatives on the other hand are much more uniform, have an agreed-upon international co-operative identity and while statistics are not perfect they are reliable and comparable.

Co-operatives exist in almost every country in the world, having an appeal to every culture and language group. They have appeared under every form of government, although almost every fascist regime has restricted them, and dictatorships are often an uncomfortable fit as a result of the commitment to democracy, openness, caring and education.[43] Excessive state control has blunted their effectiveness and brought discredit to the model from time to time. But co-operatives have a tremendous resilience and bounce back from excessive state control as happened in most of the countries of the former Eastern Bloc. Co-operative values resonate with every major religion, although extremist religious cults and fanatical sects are likely to be exceptions, again because of an uncomfortable fit with values like democracy, openness and education.

The global reach of co-operatives is impressive The International Co-operative Alliance website lists the following facts:

- The United Nations estimated in 1994 that the livelihoods of more than three billion people around the globe were made more secure by co-operatives.
- Co-operatives provide full-time or part-time employment to more than 250 million people worldwide.
- In France, 21,000 co-operatives provide over 1 million jobs, representing 3.5 percent of the active working population.
- In Kenya, 63 percent of the population derive their livelihoods from co-operatives. Approximately 250,000 Kenyans are employed or gain most of their income from co-operatives.
- In Colombia, the co-operative movement provides 137,888 jobs through direct employment and an additional 559,118 jobs as worker-owners in workers co-operatives — providing 3.65 percent of all jobs in the country.
- In Indonesia, co-operatives provide jobs to 288,589 individuals.

- In the United States, 30,000 co-operatives provide more than 2 million jobs.
- From 2009 to 2012 the turnover of the largest 300 co-operatives grew by 11.6 percent to reach 2.2 trillion USD in 2012, equivalent to the GDP of Brazil, the world's 7th largest economy.
- The overall turnover of the nearly 2,000 co-operatives in the 65 countries surveyed by the World Co-operative Monitor totals 2.6 trillion USD.

Clearly this is a business model that works. This is not to claim that co-operatives do not fail or that the model is flawless. The co-operative model's strengths are explored in Chapter 5 and some of its short-comings in Chapter 7.

NOTES

1   A more recent form of business, "B" Corporations, are a variation on investor-owned companies. See below.
2   A "for profit" social enterprise is one where any surplus of revenue, once expenses have been paid, is not paid out as a private gain but rather used to further the objectives of the social enterprise. Social enterprises are discussed more fully later in the book.
3   <forbes.com/healthcare-summit/>.
4   Diamond (2015).
5   Klein (2014: 26). For anyone unsure of the reality of climate change, or the impact of capitalism on it, this is a must read.
6   Estes (1996). The level of corporate crime is a mystery. The Center for Corporate Policy points out that while statistics are kept on individual crime, even though corporate crime is far more costly, law enforcement agencies do not keep corporate crime statistics. They also suggest there is less investigation and even less prosecution. <corporatepolicy.org/issues/crimedata.htm>.
7   For an early reflection on corporations losing their way, see Heilbroner (1972).
8   Chang (2010: 22).
9   Nowak (2006).
10 Oreskes and Conway (2010); Goldenberg (2015).
11 Viswanathan (2013). Hundreds of other stories could be cited but on this occasion Apple shares fell even with strong profits that were just a bit less than speculators wanted.
12 Loomis (2015). This is a superb reference book on corporate outsourcing.
13 Klein (2014: 70).
14 For specific impacts see Social Europe Report (2015) and Sommer (2014).
15 This is not a transient problem. For example see Estes (1996); Madeley (1999); Hawken (1993).
16 For an understanding of how corporations act in the developing world, see Perkins (2006)
17 See Mokhiber (1988).
18 Snider (2015).
19 Snider (2015: 15),

20 Judge Miles W. Lord, Chief U.S. District Judge for Minnesota, on February 29, 1984, cited in Mintz (1985: 267).

21 Boseley (2015); Ridley, Grabowski and Moe (2006).

22 Jamison et al. (2015: 4).

23 Lincoln (1863).

24 Fullerton (2014).

25 See the BAT social responsibility website <http://www.bat.com/ar/2011/corporate-governance/corporate-social-responsibility/>.

26 Estes (1996).

27 Bayerl (2014). For a fuller version see Perkins (2006).

28 It is widely thought that corporate CEOs and boards must maximize profits or be legally vulnerable (Page and Katz 2012). I have not found a study that explores the veracity or lack thereof of this claim on a global but there is evidence that in the U.S. this is not true. That said, the organization is structured to pursue a single bottom line and market and corporate culture pressures are relentless.

29 Press Progress (2015b). See also Hodgson (2014).

30 There is now a 2013 edition published by Fernwood Publishing.

31 Information about the movie, including review comments, can be found at <thecorporation.com/>.

32 Jones (2015: 179).

33 Mac Cormac(2011).

34 Mac Cormac (2011).

35 For definitions of social enterprise, see European Research Institute on Co-operative and Social Enterprise <euricse.eu/sites/euricse.eu/files/db_uploads/documents/1269529638_n360.pdf>; The Centre for Social Enterprise <centreforsocialenterprise.com/what.html>; or The Social Enterprise Alliance <se-alliance.org/what-is-social-enterprise>; Social Enterprise Canada <socialenterprisecanada.ca/en/learn/nav/whatisasocialenterprise.html>.

36 Borzaga, Depedri and Tortia (2009).

37 See International Co-operative Alliance website at <ica.coop/en/whats-co-op/co-operative-identity-values-principles>.

38 This description of the Mondragon principles draws heavily on Ormaechea (1993).

39 Chapter 5 will provide more information about the MCC Co-operatives.

40 Novković and Brown (2012).

41 See: Infant formula <multinationalmonitor.org/hyper/issues/1987/04/formula.html>; Bophal <theatlantic.com/photo/2014/12/bhopal-the-worlds-worst-industrial-disaster-30-years-later/100864/>; Tar Ponds <tarpondscleanup.ca/>; Goldman Sachs <sec.gov/news/press/2010/2010-59.htm> and Fullerton (2015); Enbridge <desmog.ca/2013/08/26/official-price-enbridge-kalamazoo-spill-whopping-1-039-000-000>.

42 There are practical exceptions to open membership. For example, in a housing co-operative, because the number of users is limited by the number of houses, membership is not open to everyone in the society. In worker owned co-operatives there is usually a trial period during which new "users" are employees and in some cases, such as in construction companies, it may make no sense to have temporary workers become members.

43 For example, during the military-led government in Guatemala there were massacres of co-operative members in several co-operatives over a decade. Co-operatives in Latin America have been attacked by various military and extremist right wing governments. See for example Human Rights Watch (1992); Williams (1986); Also OAS-IACHR (1992).

Chapter 4

A SOURCE
OF HOPE

For a business model that provides work to 250 million people, whose output is equal the seventh largest economy in the world and which has more than a billion members, co-operatives have been the focus of surprisingly little research.[1] Co-operatives and credit unions have been largely ignored in courses on economics and business, not just in North America but around the world.[2] For every research paper on co-operatives there are hundreds on investor-owned firms, although there has been increasing interest in studying co-operatives, especially since the 2012 International Year of Co-operatives. Nevertheless, the co-operative movement is growing and as we explore in this chapter, they are less destructive and more stable than investor-owned business.

IS CO-OPERATION A VIABLE ALTERNATIVE?[3]

Since the earliest human settlements — and even before that — human beings have worked together to overcome difficult circumstances, such as challenges posed by nature and providing the basic necessities of human life — food, shelter, and company. Without co-operation, individuals would have had greatly reduced chances for survival — indeed, it is questionable whether the human species would have survived at all without elaborate and steadily more complex forms of mutual support and reciprocal relationships.[4]

The previous chapter identified the basics of the co-operative business organization and its flexibility of form. It explored the purpose and the values and principles that make co-operatives unique. But why should we think that co-operating, people working together in groups, will work better than the dynamism of the rugged individual, vigorous competition and the triumph of the strongest and most fit to survive? Is co-operation a better strategy for humanity? Neoclassical economics and right wing philosophy would tell us that the most powerful driver in human nature IS individual self-interest in the rational pursuit of maximum wealth for minimal effort. Wouldn't that mean that co-operatives were just utopian dreams out of touch with what drives "economic man" and destined to remain on the fringe of the economy? Are people social and co-operative by nature, or competitive and self centred? These are questions that need to be responded to by both heart and head because they go to the very core of what it means to be human.

In considering scientific answers to these questions we begin with a reflection on the emergence of life on our planet. In his 2012 book *The Super Cooperators*, Martin Nowak, one of the world's leading theorists on evolution, points out that for life to move beyond single-cell organisms cells needed to co-operate. As life became more and more complex, it was an explosion of co-operation that made it possible. If the cells in your eyes did not co-operate you would not see this line of words. If the cells in your brain did not work together you would not understand anything. All complex life is based on cell co-operation, without which there is no intelligence and no emotion.[5] When cells cease to co-operate and begin to multiply, simply reproducing themselves, it is called cancer. The absence of co-operation in cells leads to death.

Not all individuals co-operate, and, as game theory demonstrates, some will most certainly undermine and/or exploit those who do co-operate. Again, the cancer metaphor is useful. Cells whose ability to co-operate with other cells is diminished or absent operate in a selfish fashion and grow out of control, forming tumours. Later they invade the immediate surrounding tissue, and still later they spread into the whole organism, eventually destroying it. In a system in balance, antibodies and natural defences stop cancer at an early stage.

The danger to society is not a result of creative individual effort but rather, as with cancer, when self-interest becomes the overriding driving force of that effort. We can, for example, visualize many millions of small businesses, with a variety of motivations, seeking good for themselves, their families and their communities. Normal human temptations would be countered by the "antibodies" of family, community and societal pressure. It is also easy to imagine a small percentage of family businesses, like cancer cells, losing their balance and becoming predatory, seeking individual gain above all other goals. As the businesses amass more and more wealth, they spread beyond their communities and eventually metastasize to the whole society and globally.

As small- and medium-sized family businesses that have become predatory grow, they become more and more dependent upon and controlled by an over-developed, one might say carcinogenic, system of financial market forces and players. The overriding value becomes efficiency in maximizing the return to capital. If any remnant of the balanced mix of goals they had as small firms remains, the pressure to abandon them mounts. This describes capitalism today. So, we have accepted the argument that our best way forward, as a species, is to build our economy on a business model prone to become predatory[6] and to reward and celebrate predatory growth. Small family business is not capitalism until it becomes focused on maximizing the return to the holders of capital. The "I am a tycoon like the big guys" shift can be seductive and is one that can corrupt managers of social enterprises and co-operatives as well.

The crucial role of co-operation in evolution is not limited to the level of cells. Throughout nature there are numerous examples of the co-operation between members of a species that enhances their survival. "There are other ways of understanding nature that, while not ignoring its obvious competition, give primacy to cooperation, symbiosis, and the merging of organisms into larger wholes. This new understanding is actually quite ancient, echoing the indigenous understanding of nature as a web of gifts."[7] Many living creatures survive by living in groups. Biological research, Nowak tells us, shows a large number of small and medium-sized groups of organisms tends to be more successful than a small number of very large groups — another reality of life on the planet that should add to our discomfort about corporate concentration. Solitary creatures, unless they are asexual, co-operate at some point in their lives or they disappear. After more than twenty years of studying orcas, Tiu Simila of Norway observed: "When you have spent so much of your life around beings that live in co-operative societies, remember their past and care for their weakest you learn to be open to what else they may be capable of."[8] Had she spent twenty years studying capitalist society, with its constant messages that we cannot look after our most vulnerable and that co-operation is inefficient, it is doubtful she would have highlighted the same traits. Perhaps it is time to rethink human society. This does not deny the survival of the fittest or perhaps more aptly stated the demise of individuals whose genetic inheritance reduces the chance of survival. Nor does it deny the contribution of individual effort. Most individual contributions make a contribution to the wellbeing of a group. Life is complex. People are a mix of competition and co-operation, individual and social. Perhaps the best way to understand the "survival of the fittest" is to see it as those who can best use their individual talents and attributes to benefit their group. High levels of altruistic behaviour make a group or species more fit to survive.

Nowak discusses the linking of genes on chromosomes, noting: "The relative advantage of having all genes linked on a chromosome dramatically increases with their number, so the more genes that co-operate this way the better." Genes linked on a chromosome are more effective in passing on their message to the life form of which they are an essential part. This is a kind of interdependent relationship where the self-realization of individuals is enhanced by a co-operative relationship. The genes are more effective co-operating than competing. This pattern of individual fulfillment through interdependent co-operation is repeated over and over in the natural world, creating magnificent ecosystems. It is the glue that holds life on the planet and human society together. Co-operation between groups is always more productive in meeting human need than conflict, especially armed conflict. Only in our economy have we chosen to celebrate destructive competition and parasitic relationships, where the few use relationships based on raw power to exploit the many.

Co-operation is a celebration of the balanced human being. It celebrates both healthy individualism and social relations. Justice is the description of humanity in balance — of the social, economic and political in harmony. If we wish to maximize justice, health and happiness, we will co-operate. The co-operative business model, when followed, provides the best opportunity for humanity to prosper. It is not perfect. It needs to be improved, as I suggest later. It is the best chance for our species to live in harmony with life on this planet, and live satisfying lives, because it springs from the best of natural life and the best of our humanity.

Co-operation was the dominant force with the cells from which all life evolved and with the species from which we evolved. Throughout human history co-operation has played a major role, whether in hunting parties, tilling the land, digging wells, building barns and a thousand other endeavours. The co-operation practised by early humans in gathering, farming, fishing and providing shelter dramatically enhanced their chances of survival. Even within investor-owned corporations, while lacking in co-operative purpose, daily examples of co-operation make them more endurable. Over millennia examples of co-operation can be found in every culture on every continent. It is consistent with the best in religious belief around the world.

These informal forms of co-operation made the emergence of formal co-operatives a natural evolution as people moved from the land into cities during the Industrial Revolution. The survival techniques of the rural society emerged in the more intense life and exploitation of the cities.

In the past other forms of tyranny have seemed equally as normal as capitalism seems today. There was a time when to question shaping the society and economy entirely for the benefit of the king was treason. There was a time when feudalism was regarded as clearly the only sensible way to run an economy and society. There was a time when slavery was seen as acceptable. Five hundred years ago political democracy would have seemed an unworkable idea. Today it is seen as reasonable and normal that we should base our economy and society on capitalism — control of the economy and society for the benefit of those who own great amounts of capital. Some government leaders regard limiting corporate freedom for the sake of protecting the natural world as treasonous. The investor-owned corporation, and its economic theory, neoclassical economics, are a relatively new phenomena in the broad sweep of human history. The damage they are inflicting on the natural world and human society will have our great grandchildren shaking their heads wondering why anyone would have found this to be acceptable. "Why," they will ask, "were our grandparents so foolish?"

Today we live in partial and eroding political democracies. Our economy is at war with political democracy. Neoclassical economics and the neoliberal political policies based on it insists that when "one dollar–one vote" comes into conflict with "one person–one vote," the dollars acting in the marketplace should prevail. What is missing is economic democracy. In his superb book *A Preface to Economic Democracy*, Robert Dahl raises a key question: If the rationale for democracy makes sense for our political lives, why does the same rationale not apply to our economic lives? If it is good for humanity and the dignity of people to apply democratic ideas to political and social decision-making, why do the same ideas not apply to economic decision-making? If we have an inalienable right to democratic institutions and process in organizations related to political decision-making, why do the same rights not apply to the economic organizations in which we participate and upon which we depend for the goods and services we need?

It is not just that we are being inconsistent in applying ideas about human dignity and the most desirable values upon which to base our human relationships, but our failure to do so will eventually undermine and destroy political democracy. Dahl makes the following argument: "Ownership and control contribute to the creation of great differences among citizens in wealth, income, status, skills, information, control over information and propaganda, access to political leaders, and, on the average, predictable life chances, not only for mature adults but also for the unborn, infants and children."[9] As Thomas Piketty's extensive research conclusively demonstrates, the enormous income inequality is increasing and is the natural product of capitalism.

Would a dominant economics based co-operatives, whose public policy was informed by co-operative economics, be any different? As Sidney Pobihushchy, one of Canada's foremost co-operative scholars, noted, economic arrangements and arguments are based on values: "What is very critically important to know is that underlying those arrangements there is a set of Values. So the Co-operative Economy is based on a very different set of Values than is a Capitalist and global Corporate market economy. Therefore those two economies are very different and the Co-operative Economy exists to serve the people, all the people, in respect of nature."[10] Capitalism is based on the value of individual liberty, and its guiding principle is the right to property. These trump all other considerations. The values and principles underlying co-operation are varied and require balancing many factors in reaching decisions.

Co-operatives grew out of the cruelty, suffering and turmoil of the Industrial Revolution. The so-called advanced countries were dominated by inhuman working conditions, abysmal poverty for most people and the use of child labour. These are the conditions capitalism has now exported to countries with weak laws against them, like Bangladesh.

> Co-operators at that time were looking for an alternative to the Industrial Revolution and the growth of capitalism. They had a strong appreciation for the wisdom that had been generated over the ages, that community is by far the optimal condition within which to achieve human fulfillment. They borrowed the values from community life and incorporated them into the Values of Co-operation and the Co-operative Economy. The Co-operative Values and Principles were drawn from the experience of community life because the people who initiated the Co-operative Movement had respect for other people and for the importance of community.... The Co-operative Values and Principles convey a very important central message: Respect for the dignity of life, all life, not only human life but the life of nature as well.[11]

Community, Pobihushchy argues, is essential to human dignity because it is in relation to others that we develop our sense of personal meaning. Nature is essential to human dignity because we developed out of it through the process of evolution. Our minds, senses and emotional lives are rooted in the life that surrounds us, and our continued wellbeing depends upon the thin layer of life that covers the planet. If we respect human dignity, we will not degrade community or nature. Capitalism, without opposition stemming from values or principles, degrades both. The values and principles of Co-operation, if adhered to, generate tension when confronted with the degradation of human dignity, community or nature.

INTERDEPENDENT RELATIONSHIPS

A key question for society, in seeking an alternative to an investor-driven economy, is how to deal with interdependence. Farmers depend on those working in retail and wholesale, and both depend on consumers. Up and down supply chains, and among supply chains, there are interdependent relationships. In capitalism they are dealt with through competition and exploitation. Power is in the hands of those with capital. At each step, those above and below try to take as much and give as little as they are allowed to get away with. The holders of wealth are always in the position where they can wait out the other players, who depend upon their own labour for short-term survival. That is why farmers, fishers, workers and small business owners often struggle just to survive; why the workers in Rana Plaza, in Bangladesh, were so vulnerable; why lobster fishers in Nova Scotia saw their incomes collapse in 2010–2014; and why in 2009, the super-rich saw their incomes rise in the midst of economic collapse.

In co-operatives, the multiple interdependent relationships among people are approached not from the perspective of how to exploit them for profit but how to use reciprocity to meet each other's needs. Reciprocity is based on a belief that all human beings deserve to be valued equally and that their dignity should be respected. Truly followed reciprocity is co-operation. It is violated when a couple or several people co-operate with each other to exploit others. The best route to practise reciprocity to its full potential is to use and follow the co-operative principles and values. We know from our experiences that when we exploit others or treat them unfairly, they are much more likely to treat us the same way. Mean behaviour produces mean responses, and kind behaviour produces kind responses. Violence breeds more violence. Revenge produces more revenge. Forgiveness produces more forgiveness. Competition almost always produces more losers than winners. Win-win solutions come from co-operation and reciprocity.

Co-operatives are formed in response to exploitation but, as bears repeating, are not perfect. While some types of co-operatives leave room for exploitation (for example, consumers or producers exploiting workers or workers exploiting consumers) the more closely a co-operative follows the values and principles, the less likely it is to exploit.[12] For example, it would be possible to imagine a set of circumstances where consumers in pursuit of lower prices or fishers seeking a larger share of the revenue from the sale of their fish might be tempted to offer less than fair wages to workers or allow unsatisfactory working conditions. It is possible to imagine circumstances in a worker-owned co-operative where decisions regarding product or service quality or safety might impact negatively on the health or safety of consumers. Clearly, unfair wages, unsafe working conditions or shoddy or dangerous products violate the co-operative values and principles. Integrity demands the values of co-operation being applied to everyone impacted by the co-operative. Even though these possibilities exist, there is the "solidarity co-operative" option, where workers, consumers, suppliers — anyone with a significant interdependency — can be members and work through co-operative relationships. Thousands of such co-operatives exist in Italy, in the province of Quebec in Canada, and in many other countries.

CO-OPERATIVES AND ALTRUISM

Nowak relates examples of individual altruistic behaviour and the praise they elicit from society — from governments and organization as well as other individuals. As Canadian observers will note the acceptance of 25,000 Syrian refugees and the thousands of acts of kindness it has entailed have made millions of people feel good about themselves and their country. "Why do groups react this way? Why do the group's social norms value this extraordinary co-operative behaviour? Most likely the social norms of indirect reciprocity require another mechanism of co-operation. Groups with meaningful social norms outcompete other groups. In this way indirect reciprocity can co-operate with group election to shape humanity."[13] He notes Darwin's belief: "There can be no doubt that a tribe including many members who... were always ready to give aid to each other and to sacrifice themselves for the common good, would be victorious over most other tribes, and this would be natural selection."[14]

> The competition ethics of the economic liberal, which glorify predatory behaviour, are diametrically opposed to this view of justice. Civilization is based on working together, on co-operation to reach common goals, competing to see who can contribute the most towards achieving this. Community is the key word of civilization.... We must be clear about this though. It goes without saying that competition is a normal part of human behaviour and, when counterbalanced with co-operation, is a necessary stimulus for improving humanity's lot.[15]

HEALTHY DECISION-MAKING

Economic and social decisions are inseparable. Given the depressing trends outlined in Chapter 1, humanity is at present not making sensible or constructive decisions. Decision-making based on profit maximization, or even narrowly defined economic efficiency, is dangerous to society and the planet. The co-operative business model not only allows, but its very purpose is to achieve, a balance of social, economic and political goals — meeting member and community need. The model also creates a democratic structure that is open to social and community pressure and to input from those who are impacted by the co-operative's activity.

The natural structure of a co-operative is to be community-based. This means decisions are aligned with the idea of subsidiarity, that decisions are made as close as possible to the people who will be affected by them. It is true that there are more and more very large co-operatives, very often a result of the corporate concentration implications of capitalist business. To survive in a world where cancerous oligopolies compete in a predatory fashion means that a co-operative must grow through mergers or become another predatory victim. Competing with capital-driven firms distorts co-operatives and diminishes their benefits. Yet, it is something they must do daily. Often, but not often enough, co-operatives compete with much larger scale capital-driven business by networking — as when a number of small- and medium-sized co-operatives form a consortium to take on a very large project they could not accomplish on their own.[16] Other times they survive and thrive by focusing on their co-operative difference and advantage; people would rather deal with a business they can trust. To the extent that they mimic their competition, they diminish the benefits of the co-operative business model to their members, communities and society. To the extent they become more like investor-owned business, they reduce our grandchildren's hope for a better world.

CHANGING THE NATURE OF POWER

There are two conceptions of power — "power over" and "power to." "Power over" is top down and about control, dominance and coercion. It uses manipulation, threats and violence, legitimized by a sense of entitlement. The more of this type of power one has, the more power one can get, and the more power is concentrated in fewer and fewer people the larger the portion of society that is powerless. Power over is comfortable with capitalism, investor ownership and the erosion of democracy. Power over relationships are destructive.

In contrast, "power to" is about equalizing and spreading the ability to control one's life. It is horizontal, based on relationships among equals. It does not manipulate or use violence or threats. It is about enabling and empowering people. It is used and shared rather than exercised. Co-operatives are about "power to." A world dominated by "power to" businesses will be far different. "Power to" relationships are constructive and build community and a better world.

NOTES

1   International Co-operative Alliance (2015).
2   Lynch, Urban and Sommer (1989); Hill (2000) and Chamard (2003).
3   For a short succinct look at co-operatives as an alternative see Joyce (2013).
4   MacPherson and Emmanuel (2007).
5   Ridley (2001).
6   For example when a firm like Walmart uses its enormous resources to wipe out competition in a community.
7   Eisenstein (2011) *Sacred Economics* suggests a profound rethinking of the role of money in the economy and society.
8   Morell (2015).
9   Dahl (1985: 54–55).
10 Pobihushchy (2003).
11 Pobihushchy (2003: 4).

12　For example in the late 1980s, Co-op Atlantic consumer and producer members passed a resolution authorizing the Board and Management to make as many as possible work positions full-time, provide benefits to part-time workers and to lobby governments to make retail companies maintain a higher level of full-time workers.

13　Nowak (2012: 83). Direct reciprocity is when we agree to help each other. Indirect reciprocity is when we help another person with no understood expectation they will help us.

14　Nowak quotes from Darwin's 1871 *The Descent of Man.*

15　Smith and Max-Neef (2011: 41).

16　See Menzani and Zamagni (2010).

Chapter 5

ENVISIONING A CO-OPERATIVE ECONOMY

The trends sketched out in Chapter 1 are horrifying and daunting. That said, the co-operative business model offers a healthier alternative. It does not drive the worst trends. Its different purpose, values and principles, lack of need for a growth economy, bottom-up nature and ability to put people and nature before profits, are an enormous opportunity. People in co-operatives can choose to do bad things, but they are in a business model that not only allows them but encourages them to do the right thing. An investor-owned business management or board that consistently does the right thing is to be admired. A co-operative business, board or management that does the wrong thing has to answer to its membership for going against its purpose, values and principles.

ECONOMIC STABILITY

During the 2008 Great Recession, my retirement savings, along with those of millions of others, shrank as a result of criminal and immoral corporate activity. In the casino world of corporate finance and on the stock and bond markets, chaos erupted. But one part of my investments remained stable — my small investments in co-operatives. But why were my investments in co-operatives so small compared to my "capitalist" investments? The answer is that Canadian taxation policies and regulation of financial instruments makes investment in co-operatives difficult, as does the failure of co-operative financial institutions to create co-operative capital funds. My casino economy investments fell by 24 percent. But, the market specula-tors, out making windfall profits for the already exceedingly rich, could not get at my co-operative investments. Although the co-operatives in which I had invest-ments were impacted by the economic chaos around them, they remained stable while many capitalist firms lost a third of their value in a month, week or even days. Dividends on those investments in co-operatives dropped and recovered later, but the value of those co-operative shares remained the same.

This experience was the same for co-operatives around the globe. The following traits of co-operatives are worth noting in terms of economic stability:

- They do not cause instability. They did not pump out bad mortgages to inflate short-term profit, nor did they pump out the derivatives based on the bad mortgages.
- They continue to invest and make loans based on meeting member need in spite of recessions and without the massive subsidies of taxpayer funds to banks and tax breaks that failed to stop the capitalist investment strike after 2008.[1]
- Their share value does not collapse or fluctuate wildly based on irrational or predatory speculation. Co-operatives are more difficult to start but have lower failure rates than private capital start-ups. There needs to be more research on this, but the studies that have been done all confirm the lower failure rate, as does the remarkable record of the Mondragon group of co-operatives in Spain and the co-operatives of Emilia Romagna region in Italy.[2] Studies in Canada[3] consistently show that the failure rates for co-operatives are lower than for investor-owned firms.
- When co-operatives, especially worker-owned co-operatives, do fail they are less likely to treat their workers with callous disregard. The process involved in the closure of Fagor, an appliance manufacturer in the Mon-dragon group, stands as a contrast to investor-owned business closures.[4]
- They are almost always focused on long-term, basic needs — food, cloth-ing, shelter, credit, productive work — rather than fads.
- In both the Emilia Romagna and Mondragon regions unemployment increases were substantially less after 2008 than in regions dominated by capitalist firms. In Spain unemployment reached 27 percent, in the Basque Country 14 percent, and in the three valleys dominated by the Mondragon Cooperative Corporation it did not exceed 5 percent. Co-operatives perform well even though they are profoundly limited by hav-ing to operate within the destructive dominant capitalist economy. They have to compete with firms that pass on huge environmental and social costs to society and with predatory companies with deep pockets.

Casino capitalism is seductive with its open-ended possibilities for return on investment. The messages are clear: "You can become fabulously rich beyond your wildest dreams! All you need do is invest in a winner. It is all legal. Profit is not a dirty word, it is what happens if you are smart." I remember my worry and anger in October 2008 as the extent of my retirement savings losses — a 24 percent decline — became clear. If instead, my retirement investments had increased in a few months by 24 percent, I might have been reluctant to ask: "Whose money is this that I did not earn?" The stability of an economy dominated by co-operatives will not offer huge windfall profits to those who did little to earn them, but it will provide a stable base for people to provide themselves, and each other, with the goods and services they need to live fulfilling lives.

INCREASED TRUST AND LESS ALIENATION

For years, surveys in the English-speaking world of people's attitudes toward co-operatives have been positive, with slight improvements in times of corporate crisis. People trust co-operatives more than they trust investor-owned business, even though their understanding of the co-operative business model is relatively shallow. A project undertaken by the Extension Department of St. Francis Xavier. University in Nova Scotia, the Co-operative Development Institute of Greenfield Massachusetts and the National Co-operative Bank looked at multi-year opinion research in Canada, the U.S. and the U.K. The results were consistent.[5] For example, in a 2012 survey in the U.S., respondents rated co-ops higher than for-profit businesses in each of the following value indicators, often by margins of 15–20 percentage points: have the best interests of the consumer in mind; run business in a trustworthy manner; committed to/involved in their communities; committed to the highest quality of service; offer fair, competitive prices; can be counted on to meet customers' needs; and provide products/services of high value. For-profit businesses scored higher only in the "offer customers more choices" category, and only by 5 percentage points.

COLLABORATION AND NETWORKING

Drive any distance and you'll witness an excessive number of cell phone towers, owned by different companies, and you'll understand the waste of resources resulting from destructive competition. Not only is the countryside disfigured but the cost is passed on to customers in user fees, much like a tax without representation. The principle of co-operation among co-operatives nurtures efficiency, as can be seen, for example, in the consortia in the highly developed co-operative economy of Northern Italy.[6] After exploring the impressive growth of co-operatives in Italy over the last forty years, Manzini and Zamagni conclude that, while privately owned firms do sometimes network (often in a competitive context), it is the normal way of business for co-operatives.

The co-operatives of the Mondragon group are also practised in networking and forming consortia, for instance, to take on more complex or larger projects than any one co-operative might be able to accomplish on its own. For investor-owned firms, a "strategic alliance" carries with it a risk of being a dance to the death, with the largest, strongest firm reaping the profit and benefits by swallowing its partners. Collaborative networking makes more sense for co-operatives because of their values. Additionally, their bottom-up structures and multiple goals make preda-tory behaviour much less likely. This ability to network in a non-predatory fashion allows co-operative businesses to achieve economies of scale, greater adaptability, multiple portals for innovation, complex operations and sharing of research and development. In our current investor-owned dominated economy, co-operatives are often forced to merge in the face of enormous predatory competitors. In a co-operative economy, if there is a merger, it will happen because it is in the interests of the member users of the co-operative businesses, not because some financier has added a company to his portfolio to strip it of its assets. The merged co-operative's purpose will remain to meet member and community needs.

ENVIRONMENTAL RESPONSIBILITY

Pobihushchy's theoretical base for the respect of nature inherent in co-operation has been noted above. But there are powerful practical aspects of the co-operative model that influence environmental behaviour of co-operatives. Because they are bottom-up, community-based businesses (even the big ones started that way) and because it is clear who owns them, they are more easily influenced by people in the communities where they operate. They are also more vulnerable to commu-nity pressure because they have openly adopted a set of values and principles to which people in communities can point. Being chastised for values you claim to hold is more uncomfortable than a critique based on the values of those making the critique. While it is true that a deep understanding of co-operative values and principles is not widely held, it is a rare community that does not have someone who understands them and is prepared to hold an offending co-operative account-able. These two influences explain in part why co-operatives do not often make the news for environmental irresponsibility and to be more often than numbers would suggest named on lists of environmentally responsible firms.

This does not mean they are perfect environmental performers, always making the best choices. As noted earlier, co-operatives must remain roughly cost competi-tive and so face some limitations on their freedom of action in a world where their competition faces minimal environmental regulation and enforcement. Those of us who believe that co-operatives are strongest from a business perspective when they are clearly living their values are from time to time disappointed that more co-operatives do not play a leadership role on environmental issues. The point about co-operatives is that the business model, with its values, principles and a democratic structure, pushes them to more responsible performance. There is no other way to explain why the giant outdoor equipment co-operative REI decided to close on the Black Friday shopping binge in the U.S. and suggested its workers and customers that going hiking would be better for the world than a day of super consumption.[7]

LIMITED-GROWTH ECONOMICS

Reflecting seriously on the causes of environmental problems points to capitalism as the elephant in the room. We live in a finite world and infinite growth is simply not a possibility. The super-rich are clearly not willing or able to reduce their share of the world's resources. The top 20 percent of income earners with 87 percent of the world's wealth remain committed to levels of consumption that wildly exceed their needs, yet three billion people struggle to obtain basic food, clothing, shelter, health care and education. The world must move to a more sharing economic system, where 1) the richest 20 percent significantly reduce their footprint on the natural world; 2) the bottom 60 percent of humanity's share of the world's wealth allows them the basics of a comfortable life; and 3) the good life is measured not by quantity but by quality. This will mean a decline in excessive consumption and the provision of economic basics far more widely. The rich will have to let go of their search for meaning by accumulation of material goods and turn to a greater appreciation of relationships and community. Capitalism and its children — neoclassical economics, neoliberal governments, a consumer society and investor-driven business — have demonstrated they cannot deliver on any of these three necessities. They are in fact driving the world in the opposite direction.

Co-operatives do not need constant growth to remain financially healthy. They do not need spiralling consumption. They do not have shareholders demanding maximum returns, nor do they have the same pressure from money markets that plagues publicly traded companies. They do have to be efficient at meeting member need. For co-operatives, growth should be limited to meeting additional or new basic needs and increasing market share by meeting the needs of new additional members. Co-operatives can grow capacity by networking with other co-operatives. These forms of growth do not add to the impact of humanity on the planet, a major additional environmental plus.

Co-operatives do not need to constantly drive new consumption by creating new wants. They are not likely to create a "motorized disco skate board" and then hire a psychologically savvy advertising company to create a need for it. They do not need to "invent" pet rocks. They do need to respond to member and community need, constantly assessing it and developing innovative solutions. They are more likely to respond to the need of a community for a clean water supply, a school, health care, decent housing, affordable healthy clothing or food. For three-fifths of the world's population, these basic needs are not now met by the capitalist economy. They are not met because that part of the population does not have the income. They do not have the income because it is increasingly concentrated in the hands of those who already have far more than they need.

The "growth at any cost" imperative of capitalism is foreign to co-operative purpose, values and principles. Co-operatives do not exist to maximize profits by maximizing human consumption, but to meet member and community need. Co-operatives can grow by offering many more people a way to meet important human needs without destroying nature. The principle of education urges co-operatives to help members understand environmental issues, and meeting member need suggests that co-operatives offer alternatives that protect the environment. Co-operative education can also help people understand that after wealth reaches the level needed to meet basic needs, additional wealth does not provide significant increases to happiness and satisfaction but rather increases stress and is usually associated with less time with family, friends and social life. The richest 20 percent of humanity can shed a significant amount of their 87 percent share of the world's wealth and still lead happy, satisfying lives with less stress and a richer family and community life.

EQUALITY AND JUSTICE

As part of co-operative values and principles, the idea that one person's work is worth 300, 200 or even 100 times as much as another person's work is repugnant and an assault on human dignity. It is therefore not surprising that the gap between highest and lowest paid people in co-operatives is smaller than in investor-owned firms. In some large financial co-operatives, the ratio approaches 100:1 but far more common is 10:1 or perhaps 20:1. In what is arguably the most successful co-operative system in the world, centred in Mondragon, Spain, "pay solidarity" is a key additional principle. In the individual co-operatives that make up the network, the ratio of highest to lowest paid is 6:1. For the whole network the highest to lowest pay ratio is 9:1.[8] I am privileged to take a group of master's students to study the Mondragon co-operatives every second year. They are always doubtful about how these co-operatives can attract the necessary management competence to manage a co-operative system that provides more than 100,000 mostly industrial jobs and has its own university, financial institutions and robust research and development without paying twenty times more to chief executives. Mondragon spokespersons have a two pronged response: a) tell us if you see signs of weak management as you visit our co-operatives, and b) we believe that if a person believes they deserve one hundred times the income to be a leader, they do not have the skills and attitudes to run a co-operative.[9] Fairness is a fundamental principle for not just Mondragon co-operatives but for co-operatives around the world.

Co-operatives are formed almost always out of a sense of injustice as a result of market failure. Farmers and fishers form co-operatives when the marketplace fails to provide a fair price for their product or charges unfair prices for their inputs. Workers form co-operatives when wages or working conditions are unfair or exploitive. Consumers form co-operatives to get quality goods at fair prices. In each of these cases, the impact is to raise the value of the income of the co-operative's members, either by lowering costs or improving salaries and benefits. Often the emergence of a co-operative in a marketplace will have a ripple effect, improving fairness beyond the members of the co-operative by lowering prices, improving quality or improving pay and working conditions in competing firms. The co-operative business model gives the bottom 80 percent of people in the world a powerful tool to create a more fair society. The logic of co-operation creates win/win dynamics where many people win by working together, while economic competition creates a small group of winners and many losers.

MEANINGFUL WORK

In a capitalist society, there is enormous pressure to consume. Powerful advertising efforts worth trillions of dollars per year shape our minds to judge ourselves and others by the quality and quantity we consume. This is a denial of our humanity. This is not who you are or who I am. It is a pervasive warping of humanity to meet the needs of capitalism.

For the vast majority of people, our contribution to our families and communities is the main source of meaning in our lives. The work we do for a living should provide a major source of meaning in our lives by contributing to our families and communities and making this a better world. Whether it is growing food or providing people with goods and services they need, it should leave people with a good feeling about their contribution. Most people work in groups, and the way groups function and the work process should also be a source of meaning in people's lives. The structure of the investor corporation is an obstacle. Workers in poorly functioning consumer or other co-operatives might be exploited for the benefit of consumers or farmers or small business owners, but this violates co-operative values and purpose and usually is the result of the predatory nature of the dominant capitalist economy. Far more often co-operatives reduce exploitation.

The co-operative model that provides the best structure for meaningful work is of course the worker-owned co-operative. One of the earliest economists to study the higher productivity of worker-owned firms was Keith Bradley, who was interviewed in the 1980 BBC Horizons documentary *The Mondragon Experiment*.[10] He noted that Mondragon's worker-owned firms showed about 15 percent higher productivity than comparable investor-owned companies. Higher productivity is a logical outcome in a firm where the workers own the business, choose the general manager and make decisions about productivity, salaries, benefits, workplace safety and who sits on the board. I used to have a sign on my filing cabinet that said, "Let the people who do the work tell you how the work is done." During a recent visit to Cuba to work with agricultural co-operatives, I had occasion to visit several worker co-operatives recently created from former state-owned companies. One of their products was school uniforms. They were proud that they had been able to cut the prices to families by 20 percent. They were also very pleased that they had been able to increase their wages from 350 to 1,050 pesos a month. How, we asked, was it possible to cut prices and increase their incomes at the same time? "Because we work better now" they said. "We can help each other work better and we don't need supervisors." This is a business model that out performs state ownership and capitalism.

Neoclassical economic ideology would have us believe that financial gain is the best motivator. However, research by behavioural economists shows a much wider and more complicated basis for motivation. Daniel Pink's top three motivators are 1) workplace autonomy, 2) the desire to be the best we can be at what we do and 3) the desire to make the world a better place. Aside from pressuring workers to produce more for less, which is not at all the same as being the best they can be, the investor-owned business model is destructive of all three prime motivators, although some managers or owners may make efforts to tap into these motivation streams. The worker co-operative model, based on meeting member and community need, is structured to focus comfortably on all three. A worker co-operative may not achieve perfection but workers expect the following:

- to be more satisfied with job quality and their employment environment;
- to feel that work is a key source of self-fulfillment;
- to feel that they work in an environment of shared values;
- to have a say in the decision-making and delivery of services; and
- to have access to professional training and career advancement.

Most countries' regulations governing public financial institutions forbid workers in credit unions and co-operative financial institutions from sitting on their boards. However, the Mondragon co-operative group's Laboral Kutxa, with workers sitting on the board, is one of the most stable financial institutions in the world. Credit unions in the rest of the world are inappropriately regulated as if they were investor-owned businesses. Solidarity co-operatives allow people who share a common purpose but play different roles to participate in governance in a way that recognizes their interdependence. As John Restakis and others have noted, there is an abundance of such co-operatives in Italy,[11] and on my numerous visits to them, workers uniformly spoke positively about a workplace that gives them a strong say but also creates a sense of solidarity with those they serve.

DEMOCRACY AND FREEDOM

Co-operatives extend democracy past institutions of political governance and into the very heart of economic relationships. They carry the possibility of a much deeper democracy, especially in their worker co-operative and solidarity co-operative forms. In a 2003 speech to New England co-operators, the respected co-operative scholar and theorist Sidney Pobihushchy noted:

> The two Co-operative principles of Democratic Member Control and Member Economic Participation really underlie the meaning of Co-operative Democracy which is so very different from what we know as Liberal Representative Democracy. In Co-operative democracy the authority resides in the members/people. In a Liberal Representative democracy the authority resides in the few Representatives that are somehow selected and then they have the authority to control the people. Co-operative democracy is fundamentally different from Liberal Representative Democracy.

Pobihushchy also talked at length about education and learning without which democracy is hollow.

Owen Jones suggests: "Public ownership that involves service users and workers would help democratize the economy, posing a genuine alternative to both the market and rigid "statism." The whole approach of endlessly moving towards a society run on the basis of profit for a small elite would be dealt a sizable blow."[12] Solidarity co-operatives can include workers, service users and representatives of the community in ownership and governance. Democracy is at its fullest expression when all those who share interdependence based on an economic activity have a say in how it is done.

But it is not just these co-operative principles that shape and deepen the democratic possibilities of co-operatives. The following co-operative values deepen democracy and make it more meaningful, possible and workable:

- Equality — Every person has the right to have their life, dignity and abilities respected and valued equally.
- Equity — Each person should be treated fairly.
- Mutual Self-help — People are interdependent and benefit from joining their individual efforts.
- Self-responsibility — Each of us is responsible for our own actions.
- Democracy — Democracy is not limited to the actions of the state but extends to all decisions that have an impact on the lives of people.

The personal ethical values of co-operators add another dimension. Is democracy possible without honesty and openness? Is democracy enriched by social responsibility and caring for others?

The main obstacle to a democratic political economy is the cynicism created in large measure by investor-driven business. Because its foundation rests on the baser traits of human nature, its best defence is cynicism. I have been told: "Believing people will act on co-operative values and principles is naive!" Co-operative values and principles are not naive, they are aspirational. Creating an economy on the excuse that people are not perfect, so we should forget about values and principles, is to aim for the bottom. A business system which promotes the pursuit of self-interest and whose aim is maximum return to those who own capital is socially destructive. It is simply madness to create our economy with structures and thinking based on the worst of human nature. It is little wonder that the biggest obstacle co-operators face is being immersed in a business culture founded on humanity's less altruistic characteristics.

Nurturing a functioning democratic society in the face of economic thought and structures that undermine and disparage it is an uphill struggle. It is why we are seeing the massive assault by much of the business community against democracy and any role for government other than to protect the interests of big business. Imagine a society dominated by co-operatives in which the values and principles of co-operation were promoted in the workplaces of society and championed as reflecting the best values to which people can aspire. Imagine if the economic system and the political system worked to reinforce each other's values. The result would be a democratic political economy. Economics scholar Stefano Zamagni states: "When people spend their working lives in a democratic workplace they become accustomed to thinking and acting in line with democratic values and expecting the same of others. When they work in an autocratic workplace they absorb dictatorial ethics as natural and carry autocratic ways of behaving into their lives outside of work and lower expectations of how others will act."[13] Economic democracy and political democracy strengthen each other.

Liberty, as defined by neoclassical economics, is the freedom of an individual to do whatever they want with their property without interference from government or society. This liberty is to be achieved by letting the markets regulate. In practice this has meant, for example, the "freedom" to pollute beyond any realistic possibility of a market response. When pollution fuels climate change, makes water a thousand miles away undrinkable, causes dead areas in the ocean or punches a hole in the ozone layer, markets have failed to produce an automatic correcting response. It is the "freedom" to distribute an overabundance of food in a manner that ensures millions starve to death and hundreds of millions suffer from crippling malnutrition and/or from obesity. It is the "freedom" to use your property and the power it confers to undermine markets! This is not liberty but abuse of liberty. Real liberty is bounded by our interdependence. Real liberty accepts limitation on our personal ability to injure others. Real liberty and true freedom rest on the ability of all persons to be able to reasonably influence the decisions that impact their lives, their families, their communities and their society. When a person, individual or corporation can make decisions that affect others without any restraint, liberty is truly crushed.

Co-operatives offer a powerful tool to achieve real liberty. Co-operatives and other forms of economic democracy offer the only hope that democracy can survive the pervasive attack it is now under from the super-rich and their corporations. In the words of pioneering researcher into international co-operative economies John Restakis: "What we need is a generative democracy — a democracy that is recreated constantly through the everyday mechanisms and decisions that go into the design, production, monitoring and evaluation of the goods and services that people need to construct and live a truly civic life."[14] Decisions are not either social, economic or political but all three at once. Co-operatives allow people a democratic option they can use that is comfortable with all the aspects of every decision.

SOCIAL COHESION AND PROGRESSIVE SOCIETY

If we had a co-operative economy would it create a better world? Logic and theory say yes, but is there any evidence? Dr. David Erdal, who sold his family's paper mill to its workers, studied three towns in the Emilia Romagna region of Northern Italy for his PhD thesis. Emilia Romagna is noted for the high co-operative production as a percentage GDP. Erdal picked three towns with differing percentages of co-operative production and compared a set of social indicators in each community to determine whether a higher presence of co-operatives would have any impact on the social indicators. The correlation was very strong. Almost without exception, the greater the presence of co-operatives as a percentage of GDP, the higher the score on social indicators.[15] This is a study that needs repetition in more countries and with different types of co-operatives, but such strong relationships between a greater presence of co-operatives and better performance on indicators like crime rates, health, income inequality and social cohesion are too important to ignore.[16]

In a lecture to Saint Mary's University masters students Flavio Delbono[17] reviewed the impact of Emilia Romagna's strong co-operative presence on social cohesion and noted the following significant impacts:

- Opportunities for women to work are higher in areas with a strong co-operative presence. He noted that this did not always mean equal opportunity or equal pay but that co-operative performance was better.
- Co-op jobs are more stable and pay relatively well. Again not perfection but a better performance.
- The Coopfond for co-operative development has been successful in helping workers take over failed investor-owned companies. In forty-seven "rescues," 1242 jobs were saved with a Coopfond investment of €7.1 million.
- The work environments in co-operatives are generally better.
- Consumer co-operatives have kept prices fair.
- Communities with more co-operatives have more citizens active in civil society.
- Income gaps are less in co-operatives, with much less sense of division between managers and workers.

The more people are surrounded by co-operation and co-operative values the greater the impact on a society's culture. Our customs, attitudes, beliefs and ways of doing things will become more co-operative — people centred, caring, sharing, respectful, fair, honest and open. This is vastly preferable to a culture that is predatory, acquisitive, competitive and abusive, valuing things over people.

In 2014 Dave Grace and Associates did a study for the U.N. Secretariat, Department Economic and Social Affairs, which again strongly suggested the positive impact of co-operatives on social progress. "In compiling our results on the most co-operative economies in the world we were amazed that two-thirds of the countries listed in the top ten most co-operative economies also make up eight of the top twelve spots on the Social Progress Index (SPI)."[18] In large measure co-operatives generate social cohesion through allowing people a say in decisions that affect their lives and through their much smaller gap between highest and lowest paid workers.

PEACE AND SECURITY

Co-operatives are an expression of the best in human nature. They reflect our social essence and yet provide scope for the individualism that reflects our whole selves. But it is that social interdependent part of us that seeks peace. In reflecting on the relatively peaceful transition after decades of repressive violent apartheid, Desmond Tutu spoke of *ubuntu* and reconciliation, which made the transition as peaceful as it was:

> *Ubuntu* speaks about how we need each other. God, quite deliberately, has made us beings that are incomplete without the other. No one is self-sufficient. People who had been ill-treated, subjugated, instead of seeking revenge, were ready to speak about reconciliation, forgiveness. Of course, they were given a wonderful example by the magnanimity of a Nelson Mandela, who came out of prison not spitting blood and fire, but saying we need to understand the other person and we need to forgive. And our country was saved from devastation by this willingness to understand and to forgive.[19]

I have often described co-operation as being in the radical centre. Co-operators do not spit "blood and fire" like the extreme right or the extreme left. They reject the rhetoric of fear and hatred, and reject violence and revenge as solutions.

Co-operatives are virtually absent from the arms industry. Nor do any but the largest co-operatives have a presence in foreign countries. The major exceptions are large co-operatives which have found it necessary to locate plants abroad in order to compete with investor-driven competitors. The massive growth of investor-driven firms is more about resource and market control than about efficiency. The Mondragon group and some of the larger co-operatives in Italy and other European countries are the main examples of "multinational co-operatives." As long as they are forced to compete with investor-driven firms that have no limits on their growth, this will continue to happen. Such growth is not the natural path for co-operatives. Their tendency is to grow in their countries of origin and to remain rooted in communities. In Mondragon there is an ongoing debate about how they might "co-operativize" their holdings abroad.

Most war is now carried out in the name of protecting national interests. Those national interests are not the wellbeing of citizens, but almost invariably the interests of investor-driven corporations. These are the same investors and corporations that are shaping trade agreements that attack the ability of democratic governments to act and that drive down tax revenues around the world by threatening to move their investments. Much of the huge global arms industry is directed at producing weapons to protect the interests of these investors and companies.

Co-operatives, in contrast, are very often found working for peace rather than driving the engines of war. There is every indication that an economy dominated by co-operative firms would greatly reduce the pressures for war that exist in our current capitalist economy.

The landmark book *Co-operatives and the Pursuit of Peace*, edited by Canadian co-operative scholars Ian Macpherson and Joy Emanuel (2007), pulls together papers from a 2007 conference focused on the topic, using examples from South America, Africa and Asia. It explores the historical record; the roles played by co-operatives in addressing the causes of violence, such as gender inequality and poverty; and co-operatives' involvement in reconstruction and conflict resolution. As an example, the chapter by Rafi Goldman relates the case of an agricultural co-operative (Produce for Peace) that brings together Israelis and Palestinians.

PROMOTING AND SHARING INNOVATION

The claim is sometimes made that investor-driven firms are innovation leaders, as if no other source of innovation ever existed. But the reality is clearly different. Canada's first debit card was introduced by a credit union. The Mondragon co-operative group has been an innovation leader in robotics, solar electric, plastics, forged metal and machine tool design, among other areas. Its R&D business park includes sixteen facilities and it has others in different locations. Many more examples exist but the most important thing about co-operative innovation is their tendency to share knowledge and innovation with sister co-operatives. North American credit unions, for example, have not hesitated to share new ideas with savings and loan co-operatives in Africa. Why? Because they do not have aspirations to launch competing branches in Africa. The credit union idea in North America was born in Quebec. Its founder, Alphonse Desjardin, did not hesitate to share the idea with department store magnate Edward Filene, who saw the idea as being good for his employees. Filene in turn shared it with the Extension Department of Saint Francis Xavier University, which in turn shared it with black co-operative developers in the Southern United States. This approach to sharing innovation with people who need it is in stark contrast with the intellectual property ideas of investor-driven firms, the price gouging by major pharmaceutical companies related to AIDS drugs in Africa and efforts by some companies to patent the genes, some even stolen, from human tissue samples.

It is also true that perhaps the most prolific source of innovation in our times has been governments. Government research in space, health and communications has produced a flood of new products and services, including miracle drugs and the internet. This plethora of innovation flowed from the very institution most ridiculed by corporations and neoclassical economists. There is also significant government support for university-based research. It is crucial for society and for co-operatives that the principle driver of research not be commercial return. Investor-driven research will not explore the impact of pesticides, plastics and other chemicals. It will not explore the impact of humanity on nature nor drugs for the diseases that plague the poorest 50 percent of humanity. Indeed, history shows that corporations will fund "cigarette company science" to confuse the public on crucial issues like climate change. Non-commercial science is crucial to co-operatives. Without it they cannot serve and protect their members and meet their needs. Co-operatives offer an alternative to scientists which public policymakers should consider and nurture. They offer the possibility to carry out research in the public interest without a commercial driving focus and with a layer of insulation from the government but still subject to public audit.

FAIR TRADE

We know that not every country in the world produces everything and there has been trade almost as long as people began living in cities. During the colonial era terms of trade were set by force of arms and much trade has remained unfair. Colonized lands and peoples received low prices for the goods they produced and paid high prices for the goods they bought. Resources were extracted from the colonies and manufactured goods sold back to them. Much of the wealth of the super-rich had its roots in colonial exploitation and slavery and is now possessed by descendants. Now, rich country corporations place their manufacturing plants in poor counties with the weakest regulatory environment and lowest wages, and bring the product back to rich countries, often selling them at high prices and reaping a very large profit. Control is still very much with rich countries' business interests.

Poor countries still produce cheap commodities — oil, minerals, coffee, tea, cocoa and other food crops — for low prices, enforced by large companies who largely control the supply chains and by the home country governments, for whom "national interest" is the welfare of their mega corporations. The result is stifling poverty in poor countries, increasingly exacerbated by so-called "free trade agreements," designed to prevent governments from acting to protect their citizens.

One response has been the fair trade movement. Fair trade organizations in rich countries work with co-operatives in poor countries to develop a fair supply chain. Rich world co-operatives, like Equal Exchange in the U.S., the Co-operative Group in the U.K. and JustUs and LaSiembra in Canada, are key partners with co-operatives in poor countries rather than exploiting them. The result has been openness about pricing and significant increases of the prices paid to producers in poorer countries. In addition, profits from rich world sales are used for projects in the poor country co-operative's community, such as efforts to provide clean water and education. Fair trade is not charity but justice. The participating rich world co-operatives make a reasonable but modest surplus, which makes fair trade businesses stable even in weak market conditions and recessions. Producer/consumer exchanges are also promoted, allowing people on both sides of the trading relationship to learn about each other. The improvements have been dramatic. Farmers producing cocoa in Ghana can now afford to send their five-year-old children to school instead of to the fields. Villages have schools and clean water. Another development has been "domestic fair trade," based on the idea that if farmers in the Global South deserve fair prices, rich world farmers deserve the same.

Unfortunately, large corporate players have eroded fair trade progress. Fair trade organizations largely welcomed companies like StarBucks, Cadburys, Nestle and Walmart as an opportunity to expand the benefit of fair trade. Even when the fair trade purchases of the mega corporations represented less than 1 percent of their volumes, they dwarfed other purchasers and led to significant increases in organizational resources and staff of fair trade organizations. It was seductive, but it has also left fair trade organizations vulnerable to pressure to lower prices and accept products from large plantations, where workers are not protected. The result has been to create divisions in the fair trade movement and render it less successful in the long run. It is necessary to remember that investor-driven firms exist to maximize returns to shareholders — not to promote fair trade.

Fair trade fits with co-operative business purpose, values and principles, but it does not fit with the purpose and principles of investor-driven business. The pressures that drive investor-owned business will undermine fair trade as inevitably as they undermine democracy. In an economy dominated by co-operatives, co-operative-to-co-operative trade systems stress mutual self-help, equity and equality, openness, honesty — all the values and principles of co-operation. It is time to begin building a "co-operative trade" system that will not be undermined and destroyed and will also underline, for the public, the co-operative difference.

FOOD SECURITY AND SOVEREIGNTY

The co-operative business model has had a long and close association with food. It has stabilized family farms and local food production for generations and played a key role in ensuring that consumers have access to quality, healthy food at fair prices. Consumer co-operatives emerged in the United Kingdom in response to rock in the coal, chalk in the flour and weighted scales in investor-driven stores that made fourteen ounces into a pound. Farm co-operatives grew because farmers were at the mercy of merchants and food processors who forced prices for the food farmers produced down and over-charged for farm supplies. Fishers faced the same problems, high cost inputs and rock bottom prices for fish. The following are just a few examples of the relationship of co-operatives to food security and sovereignty:

- In the U.S., one of the world's finest networks of retail food co-operatives emerged passionate about the ideas of co-operation, providing healthy food, providing local food, fair trade and sourcing food that was grown with respect for the environment.
- In India, the price of fertilizer led farmers to create their own successful fertilizer co-operative.
- In Kenya, where 40 percent of GDP is produced by co-operatives, the foundation of the co-operative network is agricultural co-operatives, allowing many rural people the option of not migrating to Nairobi's slums.
- In Italy, concern over the deteriorating quality of food led Coop Italia to refuse to buy beef from cattle that had been fed animal parts like chicken feathers. Consulting closely with thousands of consumer members, Coop Italia established strict quality guidelines for food. As a result, when people were faced with the risk of mad cow disease, consumers flocked to Coop Italia for meat they could trust.
- In Cuba, the massive collective farms have been replaced by co-operatives, with 85 percent or more food now being produced by them. They are among the world's leaders in high efficiency organic food production.

Food co-operatives are the result by the repeated market failures of investor-driven business. The net result is safer, healthier food, local food security, fair prices for farmers at home and around the world, and for consumers, and a healthier environment. Co-operatives allow farmers to stay on the land and produce food for the communities around them, thus slowing urbanization with its vast degrading urban slums. A healthy network of farm co-operatives producing for local communities means less malnutrition. Food produced in poor countries for export often means local people cannot compete with the prices rich people in other countries can pay. In turn, subsidized food from rich country farmers is often "dumped," destroying local agriculture.

DECENTRALIZATION

Investor-driven firms tend by nature to concentrate power in ever larger businesses. Co-operatives by nature are local. They are created by the people who use them. "Co-operative businesses require a different kind of 'ecosystem' than what fuels today's online monopolies."[20] Co-operatives grow reluctantly to achieve economies of scale, to make most efficient use of scarce capital and to match patterns of development set by competitors.[21] They also grow in response to the need to defend themselves from hostile multinational competitors and predatory anti-market behaviour. More often they "spread" rather than grow with new co-operatives emerging to serve additional people and to increase the percentage of the population they serve. This pattern of reluctant growth fits with the principle of subsidiarity, first articulated by the Roman Catholic Church's first Vatican Council in 1870 and since been adopted as an article of the European Union.[22] In essence, it calls for decisions to be made as close as possible to those who are impacted by them. It is a natural fit for co-operatives. It fits with the research findings of Elinor Ostrom, which show that decisions made closest to and by the people they impact, are the most reliably sound. Common resources are used most efficiently, not by the marketplace nor distant government, but by those on the ground who depend on the resources and those impacted by their use.[23]

SENSIBLE TECHNOLOGICAL ADOPTION

When co-operatives operate in line with their purpose, values and principles, their membership and governance include those who are significantly impacted by their co-operative's performance; they educate them about technology choices; they are open and honest with information; and they benefit from information sharing with other co-operatives around technology choices. In this co-operative framework, technological choices are made with meeting human need in mind rather than maximizing return to investors regardless of "externalities." In an investor-driven economy, unintended costs of technology choices are passed on to citizens, who have no say, or to increasingly tax-starved governments hemmed in by so-called free trade agreements. For a co-operative business, their purpose, values and principles dictate that they should not pass on the costs of their business decisions to their members or to society. But the competitive atmosphere of the investor-dominated economy in which co-operatives operate does not allow them the latitude to make fully responsible decisions on behalf of their members. In addition, government regulatory frameworks are increasingly constructed by bureaucrats who move back and forth between large corporations and government or even worse are abandoned for corporate "self regulation." Investor-owned firms are resistant to regulation but at the same time they compete in a race to the bottom that demands they use a technology if it is used by their competitors. This corporate culture, abetted by government, drags co-operatives in its destructive wake.

Large IOCs and their experts capture the attention of governments in shaping regulations. The regulatory frameworks they devise are seldom beneficial to small- and medium-sized business or co-operatives. In an economy dominated by co-operatives, this is less likely to be the case than in one dominated by investor-driven firms.

PRUDENT USE OF RESOURCES

In a well-functioning co-operative, especially where the workers are members, there is a consciousness of how resources are used and how waste is minimized.[24] Concern for community includes a concern for the natural environment. Many co-operatives have strong environmental programs. An exemplary example is the consumer food co-operatives in the U.S. where a passion for healthy food is combined with a passion for environmental protection and renewal. The logic of the co-operative business model is tempered by the dominant investor-driven corporate culture — its concepts, ways of thinking and analysis are so pervasive they are often accepted without critical thought. That said, co-operatives are freed from the financial quarterly performance treadmill and expected by members to take a long-term perspective. They are also expected to balance financial performance with a wider range of goals. The markets, especially financial markets, are relentless, impersonal and focused on short-term gain, whereas co-operative shareholders exercise control through member meetings. While investor-owners may not even know what corporations they hold shares in, co-operative members are keenly aware and much more able to reach elected and management leaders. The co-operative business model offers more hope for environmental responsibility and sustainability simply because of its long-term focus and "multiple bottom line" flexibility.[25]

MEANINGFUL PARTICIPATION

One of the frustrations of consumerism is the lack of consumer choice and the poverty of consumer information. The shirt you bought last year that you liked so much is no longer available. The information you want about products is not available from a resource you can trust. Companies "tax" you as part of the purchase price to fund advertising to mislead you about what you bought. Corporate advertising is paid for by the people who buy the product but they have absolutely no say in whether it is honest, informative or confusing. The internet has limitless information and disinformation. The investor-driven firm offers no solution. It is simply not possible to determine if the information they provide is accurate without considerable research. In providing information they have conflict of interest. Often corporations and the super-rich fund dishonest and biased research.[26] The tool serves the owner. Consumers, lacking time to do research themselves and unable to trust available information, slide into apathy.

Consumer co-operatives and solidarity co-operatives provide a solution. Owned by consumers or a combination of consumers and workers, a co-operative provides a business model that, if working reasonably well, can be relied upon. The firm you own is much less likely to lie to you. In a complex world, the co-operative allows consumers to pool their resources to not just provide themselves with the goods and services they want, but with the reliable information they want and need if they are to behave in a responsible and informed manner. In today's world it is not possible to have real "consumer power" without consumer co-operation. It would take many years to research where the things you buy in the run of a year came from, who made them, under what working conditions and with what impact on nature and society. By the time you finished the answers would have changed. Co-operation is the only way to solve these problems. Consumer co-operatives constitute a huge opportunity to provide members and the community with the information they need to meet their needs.

TREATMENT OF PEOPLE AND NATURE

In Chapter 1, stimulated by the thinking of Stefano Zamagni and others, we looked at the labour market trends emerging as a result of robotics. For much of humanity a capitalist global economy is foreboding and dismal. According to Frey and Osbourne, 47 percent of jobs in the U.S. will be at risk due to computerization.[27] Existing inequality which has grown steadily over the past thirty years will accelerate. The vast majority of humanity will experience downward income pressure and part-time and short-term work.

Even more appalling is the possibility of "super intelligent" machines, which can design and produce themselves, being developed for commercial purposes as opposed to for the benefit of humanity. Decisions about the future of humanity and the planet will be made with profit maximization as the driving goal, and increasingly weak "democratic" governments will play a marginal role, mostly confined by trade deals to ensuring that their right to make a commercial profit is not impeded. A co-operative economy focused on the needs of people, with firm democratic government regulation, is far more promising and far more likely to confine the development of artificial intelligence to meeting human need and to rule out antisocial and apocalyptic developments.

In contrast, a global co-operative economy will be very attractive for the vast majority of humanity. A democratic workplace guided by co-operative values, principles and purpose will stress making jobs meaningful. There will also be a diminishment of the gap between lowest and highest paid and an increase in worker requested practices such as time sharing and job rotation. Incomes will be more evenly distributed between lower skilled, lower responsibility work and higher skilled, higher responsibility work and technology's financial benefits used to shorten work weeks and encouraging more job sharing. In the 1960s, universities led discussions about the coming "leisure society." Technology did deliver enormous productivity gains but investor-owned firms delivered the benefits to the super rich. In a democratic co-operative economy, improvements in technology will benefit the vast majority of people rather than just making the super-rich much richer.

Sceptics argue that they know of co-operatives where wage gaps are high or where jobs are not enriching or where working conditions are less than one should expect from a co-operative adhering to co-operative values, principles and purpose. They are of course correct; such examples exist. However, I defy them to compare randomly chosen co-operatives to investor-driven businesses. I am confident the co-operatives will on average significantly out-perform in terms of the treatment of people. In addition, co-operatives will on average out-perform IOCs in terms of environmental and social issues and worker satisfaction. If investor-owned firms were forced to cover the costs of their externalized social and environmental impacts, many and perhaps most would flounder. That is why they lobby so hard to be self-regulating or not regulated at all. The co-operative logic is compelling — workers are controlling capital and with it working conditions, wages and the distribution of surplus. Bottom-up ownership and control make co-operatives more responsive to community pressure on social and environmental impacts. The more co-operatives dominate the economy, the better it will perform in meeting human need.

Because of their democratic nature, co-operatives are more accountable. Investor-driven firms are accountable to shareholders and hide vital information behind a screen of commercial confidentiality. In co-operatives, those who make decisions are accountable at democratic meetings where members have the power to remove management. In an economy dominated by co-operatives people accustomed to democratic accountability would increasingly demand more accountability from investor-driven firms. Co-operatives make people accustomed to democracy while investor-driven firms accustom people to autocracy.[28]

THE NEED FOR A CO-OPERATIVE ECONOMICS

Neoclassical economics, the economics of capitalism, is bankrupt. It is like the fabled story of the emperor who has no clothes.[29] The emperor's tailor has fashioned him a new set of clothes to be worn in a grand parade. He has told the emperor that the clothes can only be seen by honest and just people. The emperor cannot see the clothes but does not want to admit he is dishonest and unjust. The crowd gathers along the street to watch the parade and everyone marvels at his new suit. In the fable only an innocent child has the freedom to say, "He is naked." Almost all political and business leaders know deep down that our social economy is in trouble. They know it is unstable and is destroying the natural world. Even the staunchest defenders of the status quo talk about the very fragile world economy, using it as an excuse to accelerate the destruction of the environment. They care only about short-term narrow economic gain and are blind to long-term, profound and widespread economic and social pain.

The environmental challenges, the inequality challenges, the challenge to democracy, the erosion of civil society are beyond being solved by a capitalist market economy. It will only make them worse. But many people want to be optimists and "think positively," and many refuse to think deeply about the contradictions they know are there in front of them. They fear the scorn that will erupt if they say "The emperor has no clothes — capitalism must cease to dominate the political economy." Some want the approval of the rich and powerful. Some adopt the "curse of positive thinking" and lack the courage to acknowledge reality. Some fear that thinking about the real issues that face us will be too depressing. The tough truth is that there is no hope without facing reality. Burying one's head in the sand provides a false sense of security. Hope comes from developing solutions, not denying reality. Hope is only possible when people face reality. The dominance of neoclassical economics and increasingly destructive capitalism is but a passing nightmare. It fogs our thought while we are in the midst of it and seems inescapable. To go on with a meaningful life we must slough off the nightmare and return to the real world thoughts and feelings that preceded it and the productive thoughts and feelings that will replace it. There are pre–neoclassical ideas from great thinkers[30] we will wish to retain as we move forward and many recent ideas from what I loosely call the "new economists."

The new economists and alternative economic thinkers fill me with hope when they accurately and honestly document problems. People focused on reducing environmental damage fill me with hope. People striving to lessen human suffering fill me with hope. The peacemakers fill me with hope.

There are more and more of these people. They outnumber those committed to protecting the status quo at all costs. They are well documented by Paul Hawken in his hope-filled book *Blessed Unrest.*[31] They do not have the resources of the corporations and the super-rich and are as a result less visible, but they are growing in number. There are also new breeds of economists — behavioural economists, environmental economists, no-growth economists and genuine progress measuring economists to name just a few — producing brilliant analyses as if people and the planet mattered more than protecting the super wealthy. But often, as I read these analyses, they are not able to offer a convincing alternative.[32] They suggest more regulation or strong action by governments that are nominally democratic but as we have seen are controlled by the wealthiest 20 percent of humanity. Some, like Paul Mason, see hope in new information technologies forcing change: "Without us noticing, we are entering the post capitalist era. At the heart of further change to come is information technology, new ways of working and the sharing economy.

The old ways will take a long while to disappear, but it's time to be utopian."[33] An alternative will not emerge in this fashion.

Bruni and Zamagni, in their book about the need for a "civil economy," note:

> It expresses the difference in our approach from those authors who think in terms of ideally dividing society into three separated spheres. Although the spheres are adjoining, these authors believe that they must separately realize only one of these three principles. There would be the market sphere, the state sphere and the civil society sphere. This divisional logic of separation could only bring about truly paradoxical results.... But how does a person living in all three of these spheres behave in accordance with antagonistic symbolic codes and canons without becoming schizophrenic?[34]

If the investor-driven corporation remains the core and dominant institution of economic activity, change is not possible. Those who own and control the current destructive economy are perfectly capable of employing the new technologies using the business model they have perfected to serve themselves. How we go about providing ourselves with the goods and services we need to live meaningful lives must happen through a shift to a different business model. We need a model that will use technologies for the good of humanity rather than in the service of greed. As Bruni and Zamagni observe, it is not possible to solve the problems created by three theoretical spheres of society, each operating on different values. "Instead, it is necessary to intervene also at the moment production takes place. Under the present circumstances, acting only upon redistribution is too late. The firm is required to become 'social' in its normal economic activity."[35]

The New Economics Foundation describes the challenge this way: "Our purpose is to bring about a Great Transition — to transform the economy so that it works for people and the planet. The U.K. and most of the world's economies are increasingly unsustainable, unfair and unstable. It is not even making us any happier — many of the richest countries in the world do not have the highest wellbeing. From climate change to the financial crisis it is clear the current economic system is not "fit for purpose." We need a Great Transition to a new economics that can deliver for people and the planet.[36] If and how this might happen are explored in Chapter 7.

As I read the new economic thinkers I am always struck by how their work fits together like pieces of a jigsaw puzzle. In the words of the New Economics Foundation in the U.K., it is "economics as if people and the planet mattered." In 2012, we celebrated the International Year of Co-operatives by bringing together the ideas of a small group of the new economy thinkers — Stefano Zamagni and Vera Negri from the University of Bologna; Manfred Max-Neef from Chile; Elinor

Ostrom, Neva Goodwin, John Fullerton and Stephen Smith from the U.S.; David Erdal, Richard Wilkinson and Kate Pickett form the U.K.; Claudia Sanchez-Bajo from Belgium; and Ron Colman, Bill Rees, Thomas Homer-Dixon and Peter Victor from Canada. The synergy was powerful. The conference was called Imagine 2012: An International Conference on Co-operative Economics.[37]

Why do we need co-operative economics? First, neoclassical economics has failed to provide a convincing explanation of the real world, how we got here and how we might solve our mounting problems. A second compelling reason is clearly stated by Mike Nickerson in his book *Life, Money and Illusion*:

> While economic exchange is the foundation of human communities, we are stuck in a model that is on a collision course with planetary limits. To adopt another model, we have to overcome the perception that the present model is the only form possible. The human family has come to what is probably the most critical choice we will ever make. It is now necessary to question what we are trying to accomplish.[38]

Neoclassical economics is based on a desire to explain why capitalism based on the investor-driven business model is the only alternative. Neoliberal policies are then set out as the only way to make capitalism work. If we reject capitalism and the investor-driven business model because they are creating an exploding mix of interconnected problems, then we need to replace capitalist economics and neoliberalism with viable alternatives that rest on an alternative business model. The most viable alternative that is reasonably consistent around the world is the co-operative business model. It is a form of economic democracy. In *Making Another World Possible — Social Economy, Cooperatives and Sustainable Development*, Jean-Francois Draperi suggests there is a strong base upon which to build an alternative. "That alternative is expressed as an original school of thought, which is structured around the idea that the alternative to the inequality produced by the capitalist economy can be constructed in a peaceful fashion through collective action that transcends class conflict."[39] He argues that the main legal forms upon which to base this alternative are associations, co-operatives and mutual societies. Other forms of social enterprise, it may be argued, are also viable. That is true, but the social enterprise model is reinvented every time it is created. It does not have a consistent purpose, values and principles. It is not a consistent business model, and as a result, while not as destructive as IOCs, it is much more difficult to use as a foundation to build an economic theory and analysis.

Over time an economy based on co-operation will evolve and improve, especially as the co-operative business model becomes dominant and less distorted by capitalism and as co-operative economics analyses results in terms of how human need is met. Public policy promoting more co-operation will also have a powerful influence. In some future time we will develop even better co-operative business models. In the meantime, let us build on the best foundation available.

NOTES

1 European Parliament (2012); Ketilson and Birchall (2009); Ferri (2012).

2 Gasaway (2012). For a clear analysis of the destructiveness and futility of tax giveaways see O'Heagan and Shaxon (2013).

3 Murray (2011; Ministry of Economic Development (2008; Stringham and Lee (2011; Gasaway (2012).

4 During a visit to the Mondragon co-operatives in June 2014 with a group of students, several of our meetings shed light how the Mondragon co-operative group had handled the failure of their flagship co-operative, Spain's largest appliance maker. With 27 percent unemployment in Spain and a deep recession in the rest of Europe, appliance sales collapsed for five years running and showed little likelihood of recovery in the foreseeable future. The decision to close Fagor was painful but it was accomplished with not one worker being simply thrown out on the street. They lost the value of their co-operative shares but not pensions. All were absorbed by other co-operatives, took early retirement on full pensions or went for training for different jobs in new or existing co-operatives. It was a remarkable contrast to the behaviour of capitalist firms.

5 Webb et al. (2005).

6 Menzani and Zamagni (2010).

7 Khandhar (2015).

8 Ormaecchea (1993: 164–68).

9 Based on study visits to Mondragon in 2014, 2012, 2010, 2008, 2006, 2005, 2004.

10 BBC Horizons (1980).

11 Restakis (2013).

12 Jones (2015).

13 Presentation by Stefano Zamagni to Saint Mary's Master of Management students, University of Bologna, 3 June 2015.

14 Restakis (2015).

15 Erdal (2012). The social indicators included: Crime: victimization, policing, confidence, feeling of security, domestic violence; Education: level attained, age leaving school, truancy, expected truancy, post-school training, perceived importance of education; Health: physical health, emotional health, mortality; Social Environment: perceived gap between rich and poor, helpfulness of authorities, supportiveness of social networks; and Social Participation: membership of clubs, voting, blood donation.

16 For a broader discussion of social cohesion, its importance and the relevance of regions in Italy, see Helliwell and Putman 2004.

17 Flavio Delbono, 8 June 2015, lecture to Saint Mary's University masters students in the Co-operative Management Education program.

18 Grace and Associates (2014).

19 Davis and van Gelder (2015).

20 Schneider and Scholz 2015.

21 For example, Mondragon auto parts manufacturers located plants close to auto assembly plants when required.

22 Eur-Lex, Access to European Union Law 2015.

23 Ostrom (2012, 1990).

24 International Co-operative Alliance (2013).

25 Bibby (2014); SustainAbility (2014).

26 Oreskes and Conway (2010).

27 Frey and Osbourne (2013).

28 For the general thrust of this section, I am grateful to presentations by Dr. Stefano Zamagni and Dr. Flavio Delbono to masters students in the Saint Mary's University Co-operative Management Education program on June 8, 2015, Economics Department, University of Bologna, Bologna, Italy.

29 Nadeau (2008).

30 Kagawa (1937).

31 Hawken (2007).

32 See, for example, the Carey Center for Democratic Capitalism <www.democratic-capitalism.com/> and the recent books by former Clinton Secretary of Labor Robert Reich (2015) or eminent Oxford University and London Business School scholar John Kay (2015).

33 Mason (2015).

34 Bruni and Zamagni (2007: 22).

35 Bruni and Zamagni (2007: 18).

36 <neweconomy.net/organizations/new-economics-foundation>. See also The New Democracy Collaborative, <democracycollaborative.org/> and The Next System Project <democracycollaborative.org/content/next-system-project> and other websites listed in the Bibliography.

37 See Novković and Webb (2014). A DVD video set of the conference presentations is also available from Global Co-operation, 232 Main St., RR3, Mahone Bay, NS, Canada, B0J 2E0 or via <tom.webb@smu.ca>.

38 Nickerson (2009)·

39 Draperi (2005: 70).

Chapter 6

CO-OPERATIVE RENEWAL AND REFORM

The core idea of this book is that our grandchildren need a co-operative economy focused on meeting the needs of people, families and communities. But can co-operatives really deliver? Will they be as good as I am suggesting, or will a co-operative economy look far too much like the deteriorating capitalist economy we need to leave behind? The answer is: it depends and perhaps. I have repeatedly suggested that co-operatives are not perfect and their performance is not perfect. No one should believe for a moment that there is some manifest destiny that will see co-operatives become the dominant business model. Major co-operatives can fail. Their overall failure rate is lower than IOCs, but as I write, some large Italian co-operative banks are likely being forced by the government of Italy to privatize because they have ceased to function as co-operatives. In this they follow the path of a number of large mutual insurance co-operatives over the past twenty years. Co-operatives in Atlantic Canada had to sell their wholesale food and petroleum business to a competitor because of a series of business errors and erosion of their co-operative identity over the years. The Co-operative Group in the U.K. ceased co-operative governance following a number of years of disastrous management leadership and weak governance. Each of these disappointments share a common thread — they all failed to maintain their co-operative identity, and in each it played a key role in the reverses they suffered.

If co-operatives are to meet their potential, they need to improve performance in the following key areas:

- deepening co-operative identity;
- increasing co-operative education;
- stewarding the environment;
- developing new co-operatives;
- forming co-operative capital;
- using co-operative accounting and reporting;
- developing more robust governance;
- reducing large salary gaps;
- enhancing international values and principles; and
- developing courageous vision and leadership flowing from their purpose, values and principles.

Each of these performance areas are challenged by internal failings and external threats. The internal failings come from the imperfection of humanity. The external threats have two points of genesis. The first is predatory activity from investor-owned firms, and the second comes from the dominant capital culture. Co-operatives require leaders and members to think differently. A co-operative culture is a set of beliefs, customs and ways of doing things that is in line with co-operative purpose, values and principles. Because co-operative leaders and members live surrounded by a capitalist culture, their actions often are automatically conditioned by that culture. For example, in a corporate retail culture, strong marketing includes placing high margin items at the end of the aisle and at eye level, candy near the checkout, inducements to buy things we do not need with "buy one, get one free" and other offers, psychological manipulation of packaging, adding chemicals to mimic nutrient tastes in nutrient deficient foods, researching taste "bliss points" achieved by adding fat, salt and sugar, and many other sophisticated marketing techniques. These actions fit the capitalist corporate culture.

A co-operative culture rejects these actions because they are not directed to meeting member and community need, and they violate co-operative values and principles. The most common reason co-operatives use the above "capitalist" marketing techniques is that it is done without thinking — done because that is what people do all the time. The second major reason is that they believe this is the only way to compete and have the co-operative be financially healthy or, still thinking within the capitalist culture, to make the co-operative more profitable. The irony is that when co-operatives act from a corporate culture mindset, they put themselves at risk. Why should members and communities be loyal when there is no difference? When they act based on their co-operative culture, they provide people with an alternative rooted in member and community need and in line with widely admired values.

Co-operative performance needs to improve significantly if co-operatives are to rise to the challenge posed by the collapse of capitalism. The worst outcome would be the eventual collapse of capitalism without a better, progressive alternative.

DEEPENING CO-OPERATIVE IDENTITY

A co-operative's most valuable asset is its co-operative identity, and the value of that identity increases as the need for an alternative to the investor-driven economy becomes more and more urgent. The threats to co-operative identity are complex and reinforce each other. It is true that co-operatives tend to copy many of the not very co-operative practices of their competitors. For example, a grocery co-operative may use grocery flyers with two items for the price of one and other marketing tricks in order to boost sales volume. They may place high margin items in impulse-buy locations to increase margins, for example, placing candy at checkouts so children will pester parents while they are waiting in line. Clearly getting children to pester their parent is not meeting the parent's needs, nor is it meeting a member's needs to be pressed to buy more than they need. Or a credit union will offer such similar services as a bank that if you simply changed the signs people would be hard pressed to tell the difference. If there is no difference, if co-operatives and credit unions look and operate just like investor-owned firms, then they are useless.

Co-operatives do these things for many reasons but it is primarily because they have not nurtured their co-operative culture (see Figure 6-1). Many members have come to expect such behaviour from business. Managers may copy the competition because it is easier than answering the question: "Reflecting on our purpose, values and principles, how would we do things differently?" But lazy or weak management is only one explanation for loss of co-operative identity.

Figure 6-1 Pressures on Co-operative Identity

Sound Co-operative Identity

Absence of education programs

Absence from education programs

Low levels of research

Competitive pressures

Standard accounting

The search for skills

Business culture pressures

As co-ops and CU's grow and succeed, key pressures lure them away from their co-operative identity.

Faltering Co-operative Identity

Co-operatives are islands in a sea of capitalist economics, politics and culture. People have to work at learning about co-operatives and co-operation. We are surrounded by news media, books, clever consulting companies and education institutions that all either push the ideas of investor-owned business or accept them uncritically. For example, CBC news reported that the government of Greece was refusing to implement the "reform" package being demanded by the IMF, the European Central Bank and some Eurozone leaders. The so-called reforms were a ramping up of the austerity measures that had shrunk the Greek economy by 25 percent; raised unemployment to 25 percent of the labour force and to 50 percent among youth; greatly reduced government revenues and sharply drove up Greek debt. This is the same "reform" package that was not working in Italy, Spain, Portugal and Ireland. This is the same bankrupt neoclassical "reform" package that leading new economists are denouncing.[1] But CBC News portrayed Greece as being irresponsible for protesting failed economic policies. Why? Because, even as a state-owned business, they have uncritically accepted capitalist culture as the only possible way of thinking.

There are many ways for co-operatives to build their identity. Figure 6-2 illustrates how co-operatives can build the co-operative difference into every aspect of their business operations, from the development of products and services to every interaction between members, boards, workers, the community and society. They need to be driven by the question: "How would we do it differently from investor-owned business if we reflected co-operative purpose, values and principles?"

Figure 6-2 Creating the Co-operative Difference

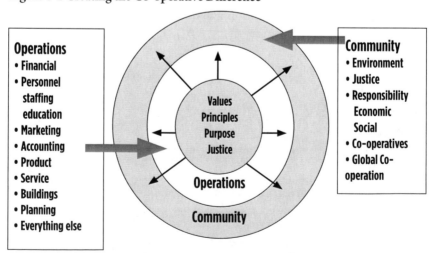

INCREASING CO-OPERATIVE EDUCATION

The key to maintaining co-operative identity is the often-ignored principle of co-operative education. Founders of co-operatives deliberately chose the co-operative business model, but as time goes on, they retire, new managers are hired and new members are recruited, sometimes resulting in the decline of the understanding of co-operative purpose, values and principles. New people are not educated and older members become focused on day-to-day "hows" rather than long-term "whys." If the co-operative hires "capitalistic hardnosed managers" to bring in new skills, they tend to regard the expense of education as a frill to be cut at the first sign of a downturn. But maintaining and renewing the organization's co-operative identity demands intelligent and consistent education of management, board, members and the public.

Resisting capitalist ideas and thinking about how to run a co-operative business requires critical thinking. But, how can managers, boards, workers and members adhere to the values and principles if they do not know about, understand or believe in them? In developing the Saint Mary's University Master of Co-operative Management Program, I made presentations to hundreds of co-operative managers, many of whom were long-term co-operative workers. I often heard the following two statements:

- "Managing a co-operative is not different from managing any other business."
- "We don't need to spend time on the co-operative values and principles — we know them."

I usually responded by asking: "What is the difference between equity and equality?"[2] Almost always the answer was either silence or confusion. If the management, board and workers do not understand the purpose, values and principles, making them a daily reality of operations is simply impossible. The co-operative's image will be confused at best, and at worst, a source of contempt. Members who do not know the purpose, values and principles may be demanding, but they are often demanding the wrong thing. The purpose, values and principles need to be on the walls in every meeting room where decisions are made about the operations of the co-operative. New board members, managers and workers all need sessions on their meaning, particularly how they might apply to their co-operative. The most powerful educational tool a co-operative can have is what it does, how that is different and how it explains the difference. Following the purpose, values and principles requires constant innovation. It is how a co-operative meets member and community need, which is how it maintains member loyalty and attracts new members.

Pamphlets and courses alone will not convince members there is a difference. The most effective co-operative education is producing or providing products and services that embody the values and principles. If a co-operative does not treat people well and has disregard for social and environmental wellbeing, a pamphlet will not make anyone feel there is a co-operative difference. If the people who work for the co-operative "just don't get it," a co-operative's identity will certainly suffer. This is true from the shelf stockers in a grocery, to the tellers in a credit union and receptionists in a worker-owned firm. They likely have more member and public contact in a day than board members and most managers do in a year. They are the face of the co-operative. They answer questions and reflect the co-operative culture or lack of it.

The larger the co-operative, the greater the need for potential board members to participate in education programs before they are permitted to serve on the board. Co-operatives cannot afford board members who do not understand co-operation and the nature of the business.

A core requirement of the hiring process for managers and workers should be exploring their comfort with co-operative purpose, values and principles. It is unfair to them, and to the organization, to have them earn their living in an organization whose values cause them discomfort. Newly hired managers and workers, even for the most senior positions, who express comfort with co-operation but know little about it, should agree as part of their new responsibilities to take an appropriate level co-operative education program. Senior managers, hired from the outside for their technical skill, are among the greatest threats to co-operatives' single most important asset — their co-operative identity. They are a major risk for business failure or demutualization. As part of their hiring process, they should agree to a strong co-operative education program, at least as strong as the Saint Mary's University master's program.

Education of members and the general public should be a major source of business strength. In a world where information was never more available and is often unreliable, information from a co-operative business you own and can trust carries immense possibilities for success. Using social media to provide trustworthy information is a great opportunity for co-operatives, but only if they adhere to the purpose, values and principles.

Public education systems are infused with courses and programs for business but few courses are designed for the co-operative business model. But co-operative members pay taxes and so do co-operatives. Why do we accept an education system that uses our tax dollars to educate people to, at best, know nothing about co-operation, and at worst see it as a second-rate business model? It is rare that co-operators demand equal educational coverage, and often they themselves pay for the development of curriculum, while governments heavily subsidize or provide

IOC supportive curriculum for free. In many business texts and courses, the co-operative model is ignored or even mocked. From elementary school to university, curriculums and research are heavily biased. The media, another key source of "education," are almost entirely owned by huge-investor driven firms, usually presenting biased information. For example, the failure of a co-operative is most often presented as another example of why co-operatives do not work while the failure of investor-driven business is presented as the miracle of the marketplace weeding out a weak player. Co-operatives far too often see internal education programs as a financial burden and seldom adapt their accounting systems to measure how well they use their resources to achieve educational goals.

When co-operatives simply copy the competition, they *become just like* the competition. When the resemblance is complete they have destroyed their co-operative. Their members still need an alternative that meets their needs better than a capitalist business but they have just lost that alternative. The less co-operatives reflect their purpose, values and principles, the less useful they are to society as a remedy to capitalism.

STEWARDING THE ENVIRONMENT

Humanity is on a multifaceted course of destruction of the natural world. We depend on plankton in the oceans and the trees for the oxygen we need to live. We are destroying both. Climate change is the greatest single threat to public health facing humanity. The negative economic implications of climate change are obvious to all but the wilfully or ideologically blind. The implications of plastics in the oceans are established, with more consequences becoming apparent each year. Environmental irresponsibility is a direct threat to our members, our communities and our societies. If our purpose is meeting member and community need, our co-operatives need to act in harmony with nature. If we believe in the values and principles we need to act.

Many co-operative leaders and co-operatives have stepped up to meet the challenges facing our planet,[3] but not enough of them and not with enough conviction and depth of action. Co-operatives may be disproportionately represented in lists of environmentally responsible businesses, but too many have weak programs. Not enough co-operatives have reacted to the growing environmental disasters facing their members by:

- developing serious internal environmental programs rigorously based on measuring their own negative environmental impact and reducing those impacts;
- educating members, boards, managers, workers and the public;
- seeing threats to the environment as threats to their members;

- working to spawn new co-operatives to meet member and community environmental needs;[4] and
- developing advocacy programs to spur government action.

Co-operatives belong not just to their current members but to their parents and grandparents and even more importantly to their children and grandchildren and to the communities of which they are part. It is difficult for co-operatives to be fully environmentally responsible and internalize costs in a competitive system where investor-owned rivals are focused on externalizing costs. Governments bear a significant responsibility for not setting the bar high enough on environmental issues and not enforcing the laws and regulations that do exist. If co-operatives are living up to their purpose, values and principles, they will set their internal bar as high as possible while maintaining financial health, and they will push governments to protect their members and their children and grandchildren.

DEVELOPING NEW CO-OPERATIVES

If co-operatives are to position themselves as an alternative, they have to significantly increase the share of global goods and services they provide. This is not a simple task. All new business ventures need a range of business development skills and expertise to survive. They need expertise in planning, the law, management, marketing, financial matters, accounting, government relations, technology and organization. They also need capital, especially if they are to be able to move into increasingly capital intensive businesses. (Capital needs are dealt with separately below.) The fewer areas of expertise they have, the less likely they are to succeed past the first few years. They need to be able to access this expertise in a timely fashion. But co-operatives also need expertise that is co-operative friendly. Specialists in Taylorist[5] management techniques would destroy a worker co-operative. Financial expertise that does not grasp fully the difference between people hiring capital, and capital hiring people, will be destructive. Marketers who specialize in manipulation will give inappropriate advice. Accountants need to be able to modify the accounting to measure other goals as well as financial health. Sources of expertise must clearly grasp that the fundamentally different purpose of the business.

The ability to deliver the full range of co-operative friendly business development expertise in a timely basis formed the foundation for success for the Mondragon Co-operative group, which was also able to provide "co-operative capital" to the co-operatives it developed. The Empresarial Division of the Caja Laborale Popular, established in 1959, not only facilitated start-ups of new co-operatives but tracked the performance of existing co-operatives in the group, identifying business problems and advising boards of directors on solutions. The Caja appointed a "godfather" to work with groups wanting to start a new co-operative until it was up and running. When the performance of a co-operative faltered, the Caja's team of experts assisted with the management change, modernization or whatever was needed to restore it to healthy functioning. Another role played by the Caja was opportunity identification. The result was many years with no business failures in the creation and continuing operation of 110 co-operatives.

Unfortunately, the Empresarial division was disbanded as a result of horribly inappropriate regulation by the Bank of Spain under pressure from the European Central Bank. The regulators felt the Caja's activity, both financing and developing businesses, was far too risky. Had it been a capitalist bank they would have been dead on. Instead, forced to shift its investments to the private marketplace to lower risk, the Caja held a large investment in the AAA "low risk" Lehman's Bank when it went under. While Mondragon has created alternative mechanisms to develop new co-operatives, the rate and quality of new co-operative development has deteriorated. No other co-operative system in the world has matched the Caja's Empresarial Division for the rate, quality and success it achieved.

Co-operative failure rates are directly related to the level of timely, co-operative friendly expertise and access to capital. The co-operative development agencies in the U.K. in the 1980s were low on expertise and high on failures. The contemporary Société Cooperative des Ouvrières Productif (SCOP) in France had greater expertise but was not resourced to the level of the Caja. It had significantly a higher success rate than in the U.K. but not as spectacular as that of the Caja. And capitalist business development efforts and success rates fall far, far short of those of the Caja. What the International Cooperative Alliance's co-operative decade needs is dozens of Caja-like development centres around the world co-operating with each other and sharing risks, technology and capital. It is possible. It could be built over a decade or two, but whether the vision or determination exists among the leadership of the co-operative movement remains to be seen. The other vision vying for their attention is the desire to be seen by their capitalist counterparts as acceptable partners and players in the larger capitalist business world.

FORMING CO-OPERATIVE CAPITAL

Co-operatives have always had difficulty raising capital in markets dominated by investor-owned firms. People are accustomed to thinking of capital only from a capitalist perspective, in which the purpose of the economy is to serve capital. In this paradigm, capital is meant to receive the maximum possible return. In a co-operative paradigm, capital is meant to serve people — it is a tool to be used to provide us with the goods and services we need to live fulfilling lives. Capitalist capital is not attracted to co-operatives, one of whose principles is to pay a limited return on investment. There is no fit. Capitalist capital does not have the behaviour and characteristics needed by co-operatives.

Co-operators have allowed themselves to be boxed in by the capitalist concept of capital. Instead, I suggest that we think about capital as we would think about dogs. When we see the word dog, an image comes into our mind. If we see words "sheep dog" the image changes. If we see the words "pit bull," the image changes again. We would not consider putting our young prize lambs into a pen with a pit bull, nor would you expect a chihuahua to pull a sled. We would look for different behaviour and characteristics. Co-operatives need capital with suitable behaviour and characteristics. Co-operatives need to develop their own "breed" of capital: co-operative capital.

The following conceptual framework for co-operative capital was presented to the 2010 Euricse Conference in Trento, Italy:

> Co-operative capital must behave in such a way as to not erode the co-operative business model comprised of its purpose, values and principles. None of these considerations are essential to other business models. In contrast, in the investor-owned business model any considerations such as these are essentially secondary and must be reconciled with and be subservient to maximizing the return to capital. The purpose of capital in a co-operative and the purpose of the members or others providing the capital has as its primary focus meeting member and community need. Members and others who invest in co-operatives expect, as long as the co-operative is successful, that they will be able to get their money back and that they will get a limited return of the investment. They also expect that member and community needs will be met in a fair and equitable manner consistent with co-operative purpose, values and principles.

The framework goes on to describe the behaviour and characteristics one could expect with co-operative capital:

- makes possible meeting a human need in a fair and equitable manner;
- conducts its operations in a manner that respects the co-operative values and principles, specifically equality, equity, mutual self-help, self-responsibility, democracy and solidarity;
- conducts its operations in a manner that respects the personal co-operative values of openness, honesty, social responsibility and caring for others;
- operates in a manner that reflects the following co-operative principles: open and voluntary membership; democratic member control; member economic participation; autonomy and independence; education, train-

ing and information; co-operation among co-operatives; and concern for community;

- returns equity upon request unless it puts the co-operative in financial jeopardy;
- pays a limited return or fair return and does not expect a windfall at the expense of others;
- allows the creation of a pool of capital that is owned collectively by the members and is the indivisible common property of the membership;
- respects the values and principles and does not act in such a way that it would inflict suffering on others through pollution or damaging the environment or community; and
- respects the values and principles and acts in a manner that will respect the dignity of its workers and give them a meaningful way to contribute to society.[6]

It is possible to find such capital. Millions of people have sought ethical investment funds, slow capital funds, social impact funds and socially responsible funds in which to invest. Such funds have attracted trillions of dollars. Investments in tobacco, high pollution industries, fossil fuels and arms manufacturers are high on the list of those to avoid. People want their savings to do good in the world. Close inspection of the so-called "ethical funds," including some created by co-operative financial institutions, shows investments in dirty oil and banks, with the claim that they are doing their best to influence oil companies and banks. But the arms industries, tobacco and fossil fuels are still being financed by those banks. My personal savings are invested in Co-operators Ethical Funds, but I would move them tomorrow — every cent — if there was a co-operative capital fund focused on fueling co-operative development and other activities such as "green energy."[7]

There are more than a billion co-operative members around the world, whose co-operatives were almost all started to correct the injustice of market failures. Assuming only half of them share co-operative values (a pessimistic assumption) that would be 500 million. If the average savings of each were just $1,000 (and many in the rich world have savings in the hundreds of thousands), that would indicate a potential co-operative capital fund of $500 billion. Alternatively, one might assume that co-operative members are more likely than the general population to wish to make truly ethical investments. Since the general population had invested $21.4 trillion by the start of 2014,[8] perhaps co-operative members could achieve one-twentieth of that amount, a modest $1 trillion. Around the world, co-operative financial institutions have assets in excess of $2.5 trillion. If they invested just 5 percent of those assets in co-operative capital funds, that would add another $125 billion. In short, the funds are there, the people are ready, but what is missing is the co-operative capital funds for them to put the money in.

But what about risk? As the Mondragon example showed, the real risk is capitalist financial institutions. Using prudent lending and management practices, without the aim of making a windfall profit at someone else's expense, in an organization without excessively paid management on a bonus system and seeking to improve their communities, the Caja Empresarial Division never lost money in any appreciable amount. This is not a surprise to co-operators. Co-operative financial institutions are less risky, and the risks they do pose are different from capital-based firms. In addition, the more co-operative capital funds exist, the more they can share risk. Finally, given the different nature of co-operatives, we are not likely to see co-operatives producing the toxic assets that capitalist banks produced in the years before 2008 (not to mention the savings and loan mess less than thirty years earlier), nor will we likely ever see a bailout of co-operative financial institutions in the billions, much less the trillions. Even if such a bailout did occur it would be ordinary people bailing out ordinary people rather than ordinary people bailing out the super rich. To contain risk in capitalist financial institutions requires tougher legislation and regulation than emerged after 2008, and one might consider a savings plan funded by the banks to cover the next bailout. Co-operative financial institutions pose much lower and different risks and should be regulated well but differently.

If the ICA plan for the co-operative decade and beyond is to have any real impact, co-operative capital development is crucial. Over the next twenty years, as a wide swath of the economy shifts to become more capital intensive and driven by robotics, the co-operative world will face being shut out of more and more of the economy unless it solves its capital development failure. Fewer and fewer people will be needed to produce more and more, and a smaller and smaller portion of the jobs will be well paid. Millions of white-collar jobs will be replaced by robots. Capitalist business has been a disaster at sharing the wealth of increased productivity. If robotics are left to capitalist firms, the following negative results will emerge:

- The economy will become increasingly unstable as fewer and fewer people on declining incomes will be able to afford anything beyond very basic goods and services.
- Income inequality will accelerate.
- Government revenues will continue to fall as corporations and the super-rich insist on lower and lower taxes, enforcing their demands with capital mobility and the use of tax havens.
- Government-supported social services and income redistribution will wither.

- Co-operatives will become truly marginal and the support to social co-operatives will be dependent on the generosity of the investor-driven economy — in other words, they will be marginal and likely wither and die.

Never has there been a time when an alternative to the investor-driven business model was needed more, but unless co-operatives solve their capital development failure, their role in a robot-dominated economy and society will be marginal. The capitalists will own all the capital intensive robots.

USING CO-OPERATIVE ACCOUNTING AND REPORTING

The job of an accountant is to make it possible for an organization to account for how efficiently it uses its resources to achieve its purpose. For investor-owned firms this is a much simpler task than for co-operatives. Standard accounting systems are focused on the efficient use of resources to maximize the return to invested capital. But for co-operatives, whose purpose is to meet member and community need, that is inadequate, with both measurement gaps and distorting existing measures that need to be modified. During the development process for the Saint Mary's Master of Co-operative Management Program, an accountant with Co-op Atlantic, Brian Murray, suggested that the standard accounting system actually subtly erodes co-operative identity. He suggested that you can only manage what you measure, and if you primarily use a measuring system that focuses on return on investment, your measurement system will distort your co-operative purpose. More and more, he suggested, co-operatives will make decisions to meet investor-owned firm goals and purposes. "What we needed," he advised, "was an accounting system to measure the efficiency of resource use to achieve co-operative purpose and goals."[9] We also knew that we needed a new approach to issues such as how are co-operative members to know if their "par value shares"[10] could be redeemed at full value.

In the late 1990s, the idea that co-operatives might require a rethinking of how they did their accounting and reporting was not a point of discussion. Investor-owned accounting and reporting standards were simply accepted without question. Following Murray's advice, we added a second accounting course, and to develop curriculum for it, organized the International Symposium on Co-operative Accounting with participants from five countries. We also needed to get an understanding of how accounting professionals and standards bodies would react to the idea of developing a new approach for accounting and reporting for co-operatives. The answer from the Canadian Institute of Chartered Accountants was a resounding vote of confidence. They responded to a grant request for $5,000 by offering core funding for the Centre of Excellence in Accounting and Reporting for Co-operatives (CEARC). CEARC is still running and publishes a journal.

Of course co-operatives still have to report on their financial soundness. Clearly, bankrupt co-operatives do not meet either member or community need. But the rate of return on investment (ROI) is not their sole or even their key measure of success. Co-operatives have to determine the indicators of financial health, which is different from return on investment (ROI), and may well differ from co-operative to co-operative and industry to industry. They also need to develop measures for how well they use resources to meet member and community need. What is their impact, positive or negative, on the community? A unique co-operative index has been developed by the Saint Mary's program to measure member engagement linked to co-operative purpose, values and principles. Initially developed for worker-owned co-operatives, it has been translated into Spanish and is being used in North America and several countries in Europe. It has been adapted for agricultural co-operatives in Cuba, and there are plans to adapt it for other types of co-operatives. The importance of measuring member engagement goes to the very heart of the co-operative difference. The index measures the health of relationships in the co-operative and, because of its link to purpose, values and principles, measures the overall co-operative health as well.

The development of a comprehensive approach to co-operative accounting is a gradual process, which we hope will be speeded up by growth of the co-operative share of the global economy. Ideally it should never become static but be subject to continual improvement. It also needs to have graduated levels that allow small co-operatives to develop more and more sophisticated accounting systems as they grow. Finally, it needs rigorous standards. If co-operatives are to honestly claim to live by their values, their openness and transparency need to be above reproach. Investor-owned firms have to be accountable only to their shareholders, and marginally to government. Co-operatives have to be accountable to members, the community they impact, their workers and government. They need an accounting system that is robust and up to the task.

DEVELOPING MORE ROBUST GOVERNANCE

It is clear from the turmoil in The Co-operative in the U.K., the proposed demutualization of the biggest co-operative banks in Italy and the collapse of Co-op Atlantic in Canada that there are too many governance failures. Co-operatives cannot stake out a moral high ground and brush failures of such large co-operatives aside as anomalies. It is also clear that too often membership growth and successive mergers of co-operatives take place with virtually no changes in governance. The following are clear signs of governance problems:

- when a consumer co-operative grows from 500 members to 10,000 members with no appreciable change in governance to engage them;
- when a worker co-operative begins to exclude most full-time workers from membership;
- when boards come up with lists of "recommended" and "not recommended" candidates for board elections based on the decisions of a board committee; and
- when co-operatives fail to admit to and solve serious problems over a period of years.

Consumer co-operatives, such as food co-operatives and credit unions, seldom have more than 5 percent of their members involved in any way other than use of the co-operative. A co-operative with even 10,000 members would face a real challenge if they all wanted to volunteer or attend the annual meeting. In an age that allows online voting, the number of members voting can and should be a significantly greater percentage, but democratic functioning in a co-operative goes beyond voting and attending meetings. The internet allows members to engage with their co-operatives in diverse ways and permits their views to be expressed and followed. It allows them to rate products and services. Few boards have committees that encourage and track member engagement and ideas. As a co-operative grows bigger, if it does not deepen its member engagement, members will increasingly see the co-operative as "they," and member loyalty will decline. A co-operative with limited member engagement, run by a tiny fragment of the membership, more and more resembles an IOC and is increasingly at risk.

A common problem co-operatives face as they grow is the diminished ability of a volunteer board of directors to give policy direction to more and more sophisticated management. Too often, board members' sophistication, learning and ability to understand the growing complexity of the business stagnates. Too often too many board members of large co-operatives are people you would trust with your children but not with your co-operative. They have lots of integrity but not enough expertise at their disposal. Managers with high levels of expertise can become tempted to manipulate their boards or find themselves growing frustrated at being directed by boards not up to the job. Senior managers hired from the outside, with no understanding of co-operative purpose, values and principles, often become frustrated with the co-operative business model. For example, Peter Marks, former chief executive at The Co-operative in the U.K., regarded the co-operative business model with something close to contempt. Boards can become split with more competent and less competent members resenting each other. They can also become unreasonably suspicious or even afraid of a chief executive. Over the past thirty years, I have too often witnessed this board-management turmoil, both close up and at a distance. It is complex, and even the best boards and CEOs can drift into misunderstanding that breeds distrust. These problems are common in capital-driven firms as well, with the glorification of competition making them even worse.

The key issues related to the expertise gap in boards are board eligibility criteria, education appropriate to the size of the co-operative and access to expertise. When a co-operative is small, board education can be left until after a board candidate is elected, as long as they agree to post-election learning. As the co-operative grows, it needs to expand its board education offerings and requirements, and begin making some board education a qualification for candidates. When co-operatives become truly large they should have evolved sophisticated education programs for board members, linked to eligibility criteria and to a set of volunteer positions below the board level with their own eligibility and educational requirements. The Co-operative in the U.K. was developing such a board education system, but earlier weak practice and poor CEO selection caught up with the process. Far too often education policies are non-existent or weak. A co-operative without a board education policy is a time bomb. The bigger the co-operative, the higher the risk. What was once the largest co-operative in the world, The Co-operative in the U.K. still supplies co-operatives but can only be described as a quasi-co-operative.

Access to expertise is a touchier issue. Significant board education should relate to the basic expertise needed to understand the business, but board members should not be expected to become as expert as their managers but they should be able to ask the right questions. How are boards to know whether their CEO's expert advice is sound or manipulative? How do they know when the CEO is in over their head? The board and senior management should trust each other, but the desire to trust cannot replace due diligence and fiduciary responsibility. The board must control their access to expertise and must be able to access expertise independently of management. There is a good argument to be made for having the corporate secretary position in a large co-operative be a board "direct hire," who answers to the board but sits in on all meetings of senior management. The corporate secretary role can become a bridge that provides the board a window into operations, and a person who can head off distrust. They also become the person who can find the expertise the board needs to ensure they are comfortable with management directions and explanations and able to remain focused on member and community need.

I can understand the discomfort of CEOs and senior managers with this idea. They will argue that if the board does not trust them, they should be replaced. Trust is seldom blind trust or total distrust. The reality is always in the middle. A board that accepts all advice from the CEO, on the basis that the CEO is the expert whose direction they should accept, is simply not functioning. A CEO should know that the board can ask for other opinions. It will improve communication efforts. There is, as with all positions that interact, a risk of personality disputes between the CEO and the corporate secretary. The corporate secretary, like a board chair or any senior manager, requires careful selection. Although many co-operatives have corporate secretaries, most are hired by management and report to the CEO. Their responsibilities are often "care and feeding" of the board to keep them happy. This is not sufficient. Good governance requires a strong board chair, a strong CEO and a strong, wise corporate secretary.

REDUCING LARGE SALARY GAPS

Generally speaking, the gap between the lowest and highest paid workers in co-operatives is much smaller than in IOCs. The ideas of equality, equity, solidarity, mutual self-help and caring for others lead to the conclusion that one human being's abilities do not merit an income 100 or 200 or 300 times that of another. Nor does any level of responsibility justify such gaps. Government leaders with far more responsibility earn a fraction of what the top corporate CEOs are paid. In small- and medium-sized co-operatives, salary gaps are almost invariably less than 1:10.

While it is hard to reconcile large gaps in pay in co-operatives, in many of our largest financial, agricultural and consumer co-operatives, pay ratios can be as high as 1:100. In a presentation to students in the Saint Mary's University program, Bob Burlton, a well-regarded former CEO of a large U.K. consumer co-operative, suggested one source of the problem: "When co-operative committees set executive compensation they compare the scope of the positions with other co-operatives but also with investor-owned firms. The latter comparison pulls the pay packages up. Often absent in the comparisons are references to salaries in social enterprises or government."[11] Another source of upward salary pressure is a sense of entitlement held by those in positions of power. That this sense of entitlement is shared by some leaders in co-operative world is disappointing. It is hard to imagine leaders being paid 100 times what their lowest paid worker receives and squaring this with co-operative purpose, values and principles.

Large pay gaps in co-operatives stand in sharp contrast with the attitudes of leaders in the Mondragon co-operative group, who have refused to become part of this sense of IOC entitlement. Earlier, I quoted a Mondragon spokesperson expressing the opinion that if a leader needs to have an income many times the level of the lowest paid, they are not capable of leading a co-operative business. Far too often, profound damage is done to co-operatives by leadership the corporate world would admire, but which is enormously destructive in co-operatives. A move by any or all of our largest co-operatives to lower pay ratios to 1:20 or even lower would send a clear signal to the general public, workers, members and boards. It would be easiest to announce as a policy going forward for newly hired CEOs. If large co-operatives are truly serious about building "the Co-operative Decade," this would be a credible, powerful and popular message.

ENHANCING INTERNATIONAL VALUES AND PRINCIPLES

We live in a world that is changing more rapidly each decade. It is now twenty years since Ian MacPherson and a group of international scholars led the revision of the co-operative principles. The rate of growth of income inequality has accelerated. Environmental issues are escalating. The interrelated trends outlined in Chapter 1 present new challenges to humanity and the planet. There are two admirable sets of co-operative principles, one adopted by the ICA, based largely on the consumer co-operative traditions of the U.K., and the other focused on the enormously successful worker co-operative tradition of the Mondragon co-operatives. All seven ICA co-operative principles and the ten Mondragon principles remain valid, but changes need to be seriously considered in light of current realities, taking into consideration especially the mounting destruction of the natural world and exploding income inequality.

Neither the Mondragon nor the ICA principles adequately address the business-driven environmental destruction of today's world. The seventh principle was not, at the time of its formulation, nor is it now, up to challenging the profound environmental destruction driving climate change or destroying life in the oceans. Co-operatives need a principle that clearly rejects the notion that we can create a healthy economy by destroying nature. All damage we do to nature is directly or indirectly damage to the network of life upon which we depend. Our present dominant business model is one that implacably resists knowing about or paying for its damage to nature. Instead, IOCs pass the costs along to society, while insisting on destroying the ability of society to deal with the costs by demanding less government and lower taxes. It is crucial, if co-operatives are to offer a credible alternative, that they have a strong statement of principle addressing our interdependence with nature. The following might serve as the basis of discussion: "Co-operatives recognize that the human species is but one part of an interconnected and interdependent universe and that respecting nature and life in all its expressions is not separable from respect for the dignity and value of each person."[12]

The second major change is the need to merge the two sets of principles. Worker co-operatives are demonstrating a deep strength to make more profound changes in global society. Solidarity co-operatives, with more than one class of member, offer the opportunity to weld together the various strands of the co-operative movement and focus on our interdependence — consumer, producer and worker solidarity — as opposed to our differences. Key innovative Mondragon principle ideas, such as pay solidarity, universality and participatory management, are much needed additions to the ICA principles. It is hard to argue that these ideas did not play a vital role in the emergence of the Mondragon Co-operative group, perhaps the single most powerful expression of co-operative success around the world. There is much merit to exploring merging the ICA and Mondragon values.

It has been argued that the current ICA principles have finally been accepted by many governments and international bodies, and that changing them would be a step backwards. But giving up our ability to renew and develop the co-operative values and principles is an enormously larger step backwards. The process of looking at changes should be the purview of an ICA permanent committee, mandated to suggest modifications every ten years. If we are worried about the recognition by international bodies, we should grant them observer status on the committee so that they can keep our "recognition" up to date. If we are not able to adapt the values and principles that serve as the foundation of our co-operative identity, decade by decade in a rapidly changing world, we will become more and more irrelevant.

DEVELOPING COURAGEOUS VISION AND LEADERSHIP

Co-operative renewal and reform requires a courageous vision shared by a growing leadership group, including management as well as board members. Most, but not all, co-operative leaders do believe that the co-operative business model is superior but shy away from developing a vision of global co-operation. In 1999, Bob Burlton, then president of the U.K. Co-operative Congress and chief executive of a major co-operative, asked the audience how many chief executives had been removed in the past year. Someone suggested one and another said two. Both wrong, Burlton replied, the answer was "too few." The relatively few CEOs who do not believe co-operatives are a better business model should be reviewed by their boards and given the opportunity to work somewhere else. They will be happier in the long run and so will the co-operative movement. Co-operatives need leaders who understand and can utilize the benefits of the co-operative difference.

Co-operatives need leaders who can address the big issues as well as operational ones. As Dave Gutknecht, editor of *Co-operative Grocer* in the U.S., pointed out while addressing the issue of infinite economic growth: "The subject of global growth leads to a larger discussion that is usually deferred in favour of things seemingly closer at hand. Yet it is a topic that will not go away in our lifetimes — quite the contrary"[13] Leaders need to be able to deal with the day to day issues and deal with the big issues just as vigorously.

Canadian co-operative thinker Sidney Pobihushchy was fond of saying: "If you do not know where you are going, any road will do." Co-operatives need a clear dynamic vision. The vision should be a variation of the general idea of global co-operation. It should be a vision of what the world would look like if co-operatives were the dominant business form. Would co-operatives compete with each other, each trying to gain advantage at the expense of each other? Would rich world co-operatives set up branches or subsidiaries in foreign countries to compete with local co-operatives? Would co-operatives, grown too large and remote from their members, decentralize, forming service co-operatives to ensure economies of scale? Would co-operatives come together and review everything they buy, identifying opportunities to create worker co-operatives to supply them? What kinds of structures and processes would they need to remain efficient if they eliminated competition? Every area of business structure and practice would need to be challenged with the question: "If we implemented the co-operative values and principles, how would we do it differently in a co-operative?" This and many other questions need to be answered to develop a conceptual framework for global co-operation. With a billion members around the globe and trillions in assets, a lesser vision than global co-operation will leave us in the position of "any road will do."

NOTES

1　The austerity approach has been sharply criticized by, among others, Nobel Prize winners Joseph Stiglitz and Paul Krugman.

2　See Chapter 3, section on Co-operative Organizational Values.

3　As a group, the food co-operatives in the U.S. are exemplary in terms of environmental stewardship, with a combined focus on healthy food and environmental issues.

4　For examples of how proactive co-operatives can be, explore the following links: Midcounties Co-operative, U.K. <cooperativeenergy.coop/>; The Co-operators, Canada <cooperators.ca/en/About-Us/about-sustainability.aspx>; VanCity Credit Union, Canada <vancity.com/AboutVancity/VisionAndValues/ValuesBasedBanking/EnvironmentalSustainability/>; The Co-operative Group, U.K. <co-operative.coop/our-ethics/sustainability-report/protecting-the-environment/> or almost any of the hundreds of food co-operatives in the U.S.

5　Frederic W. Taylor developed the concept of "scientific" management. The tasks of workers were studied, every motion timed, jobs broken down into small segments of the task.

6　Robb, Smith and Webb (2010).

7　As it now stands there is a solar energy co-operative in Ontario, Canada, that issues "preferred shares" but the Co-operators Ethical funds cannot invest in them. The problems are largely regulatory and require a concerted effort to change, but at present there appears to be no movement to try and make change possible.

8　Global Sustainable Investment Alliance (2015).

9　Conversations between Brian Murray of Co-op Atlantic and the author, October 1996.

10　Par value shares are not traded in the marketplace and can only be redeemed by the co-operative for the same value as the purchase price.

11 Presentation by Robert H. Burlton to Saint Mary's University Master of Co-operative Management Program, Bologna, Italy, June 2015. Mr. Burlton was the CEO of Oxford Swindon and Gloucester Co-operative and led its merger with West Midlands Co-operative to form Midcounties Co-operative. He was also chair of the boards of directors of Co-operatives U.K., the Co-operative Group and Co-operative Financial Services.

12 Imagine 2012 Conference on Co-operative Economics contribution to the ICA International Year of Co-operatives Declaration. The Imagine 2012 Declaration was submitted to the ICA but the recommended suggestion, that the statement on the environment be added to the Seventh Principle was not immediately adopted.

13 Gutknecht (2015).

Chapter 7

CO-OPERATIVE-FRIENDLY PUBLIC POLICY

Public policy is not neutral. At present it is very heavily biased toward investor-owned, private-profit business development. According to a 2015 IMF study, world governments are providing a $5.3 trillion "post tax" subsidy to the fossil fuel industry alone by failing to account for its harmful effects on the environment and human health.[1] "Pre-tax" direct subsidies were $480 billion in 2011, with Canada a leader, having given the industry subsidies of $34 billion in that year alone.[2] Some, like neoclassical economist Milton Friedman, claim that investor-owned business is and should be "value free." But that is impossible. No human creation or action is value free. The question that must always be asked is: "What are the underlying values?" Henry Mintzberg, former dean of the McGill University business school, is a leader in the exploration of the values of economic actors. His comment on the economic crisis in the United States is revealing:

> Corporate correctness dictates that publicly-traded enterprises maximize "Shareholder Value." Don't confuse this with anything of real value, let alone any human values. Shareholder Value is a fancy label for pumping up the price of a company's stock as quickly as possible, so that those in the know can cash in and run before the stock sinks.[3]

Governments, if they were acting on behalf of all their citizens, would ask: "What are the human values public policy ought to promote?"

PUBLIC POLICY BENEFITS

Where do co-operatives fit in public policy between the extremes of complete government control the right-wing ideal of total individual freedom? The intellectual founder of the Mondragon co-operative group, Don Jose Maria Arizmendiarrieta, expressed it eloquently: "It is the third way, distinct from egoist capitalism and of the mastodon of depersonalizing socialism."[4]

> Cooperativist philosophy rejects both the collectivist and the liberal conceptions of human nature. It recognizes instead the unique value of the human person, but insists that this person cannot be totally him or herself until entering into creative as well as spiritually and materially productive relationships with the world he or she is part of.[5]

It might also be described as the "radical centre." It is radical in that it is rooted in the dual social and individual nature of humanity. It espouses socialist goals of equality, equity, solidarity and respect for human dignity and celebrates individual contributions. Co-operatives are different. They do not have an institutional pressure to externalize costs. Externalized costs from business and tax avoidance produce enormous demands on public revenues and expenditures. As a business form, co-operatives have several public policy benefits:

- Co-operatives, especially worker co-operatives, are rooted in their communities and do not threaten governments that they will leave the community unless they get tax concessions, grants and relaxed health, safety and environmental regulations. Co-operatives cause very little economic dislocation and wasted social and economic infrastructure and make communities more stable.
- With their local bases, co-operative management and boards can more easily be reached by people in communities when their business has a negative environmental or social impact. When a community experiences a rise in environmental activism and concern, local co-operatives are faster to respond than remotely owned firms.
- The wage gaps between lowest and highest paid workers in co-operatives are smaller. This has a positive impact on tax revenues and economic stability, as middle-income people spend a higher portion of their income on day to day living and pay taxes rather than tax lawyers.
- When worker co-operatives face economic downturns, they are less likely to dispose of workers, and if they do have to reduce numbers, they do not just throw their workers on the streets. Worker owned co-operatives are harder to start but have lower failure rates.

- Owned by their savers and borrowers, co-operative financial institutions do not make bad loans to fatten short-term profits. They did not produce the toxic paper that crippled economies around the world. Co-operatives, with their focus on meeting member and community need, are not contributing to the excessive, unproductive and destructive growth of the financial industry.
- Co-operative financial institutions keep making loans during economic downturns without trillion dollar bailouts.
- Co-operatives model democracy as a way of living and as a culture. They promote the best in human nature.
- Healthy families and communities are a vital foundation to a healthy society. Co-operatives, as a group of businesses, are far more community friendly than investor owned firms. Research evidence has shown that the higher the percentage of co-operatives in a community's economy, the better the community scores on a set of social indicators related to health, education, crime, social integration and social environment. This leads to less need for pubic expenditures.

This is an impressive list of public policy benefits. The major problem for co-operatives is the transition that has been underway since the mid-1980s to regard corporate interest, as opposed to the interests of citizens, as the public interest. Citizens have been demoted to being clients and government increasingly run as if it were a business. People would benefit more if it were run in line with co-operative purpose, values and principles.

PUBLIC POLICY NEEDS

The good news is that public agencies, including all levels of government, can increase social capital and social development through providing the means and opportunities for citizens to interact, cooperate, and engage in their communities.[6]

The operational dynamics of a co-operative are different from investor-driven business because:

- the people who use the business (workers or farmers or consumers) are at the heart of the business and borrow most of the capital they need, rather than the owners of capital being the heart of the business and hiring the people they need;
- the business focus is on meeting member and community need rather than maximizing the rate of return on capital;

- in co-operatives the return to borrowed and member share capital is limited, as opposed to being unlimited; and
- the business is democratic and operates with a declared set of values and principles that create expectations among workers, management, boards and the general public.

Legislation, regulations and programs designed for investor-owned business are not appropriate for co-operatives and seldom work well. The dynamics of raising capital for a co-operative are simply different. The autocratic decision-making processes of investor ownership are easier to organize. Co-operatives need significant upfront investment in member education and organizational development. Co-operatives need their own tailored statute for incorporation that takes into account their public policy benefits and their unique business dynamics.

The purpose of the state and public policy is to benefit the public. When members of the public wish to co-operate in order to provide themselves with the goods and/or services they need there is every reason for public policy to be supportive. Given the many public policy benefits of co-operatives, public policy should create a climate for co-operatives that is stronger than the powerful pro-business policies that are now ubiquitous from the local to the international levels. Positive public policy toward co-operatives would include the following:

- The right to form a co-operative should be embedded in a bill of rights and freedoms, or in the constitution. This exists, to my knowledge, only in the Italian constitution. The sad truth remains that, in a number of countries around the world, for example some in Central America, forming a co-operative can only be undertaken under the threat of violence. It is a global problem wherever extreme right-wing groups come to power and death squads appear. It was included in the Italian constitution after the excesses of the fascist era.
- Public policy should nurture and encourage the development of co-operatives based on their economic, social and democratic process benefits.
- An incorporation statute should facilitate the formation of co-operatives and protect the "internationally accepted co-operative identity" by setting a standard for operating in a co-operative manner. It should recognize the different forms of co-operatives — consumer, worker, solidarity, community and small business co-operatives. It should also recognize logical exemptions for housing co-operatives from legislation respecting landlords and tenants and worker co-operatives from labour management relations while ensuring member protection.
- Appropriate regulation should be drafted specifically with co-operative

public policy benefits in mind. Regulations should also aggressively recognize and promote "co-operative good governance" as opposed to "investor-owned corporate good governance." Regulations designed to curb the worst abuses of investor-owned firms should not be automatically applied to co-operatives in the name of equal treatment. Equal is not equitable. Co-operative purpose, values and principles are more in line with the public good than is investor-owned business purpose. While there has been some improvement in requirements, in general, co-operatives raising capital have to meet the same prospectus demands as large, more predatory investor-owned firms and speculative market players. Because co-operative shares are not traded they do not attract the same "quick buck artists." The regulators of co-operatives should be required to take extensive education about the co-operative business model.

What co-operatives need is appropriate, not equal, regulation. For example, regulators often tell co-operative boards that they need "expert members," chosen from outside the membership. They believe that because this is the way big corporations build their boards, it must be right for co-operatives. There are two problems with this approach. The track record of big corporations at doing anything but making profits and passing on their costs is very poor. They are the real drivers behind the issues painfully documented in Chapter 1. In terms of fiscal responsibility, one has to only ask: "How much did taxpayers around the world have to pay to bailout IOCs repeatedly over the past three decades?" Answer — trillions. How much was spent bailing out co-operatives, which did not cause the 2008 crisis or the savings and loan debacle? Answer — globally less than $250 million. Why is copying IOCs' corporate governance model good advice? The co-operative governance model needs improvement, but copying Lehman's, Worldcom, Arthur Anderson and Goldman Sachs is going backward. Co-operative governance needs reform, not deform.

This is not a call for weak, ineffective regulation. Co-operatives need a regulatory framework that is effective. People are not saints because they sit on a co-operative board or belong to one or work for one. The bigger co-operatives become, the further they are geographically from their members and the more their concentrated power encourages entitlement.

- Public policy should facilitate the development of co-operative capital, which is different from investor capital. Co-operative capital has characteristics and behaviour consistent with co-operative purpose, values and principles. Public policies to stimulate private investment (which often do not achieve their goal) will not work for co-operatives. Tax policy, legislation and regulation to stimulate co-operative capital development do work.

The tax treatment of co-operatives should encourage the development of co-operative capital, especially indivisible reserves,[7] whose purpose is not individual gain but community gain. Indivisible capital reserves in a co-operative are almost always generated over more than one generation and will be there for our grand-children and their communities. Indivisible co-operative capital is a community resource to be encouraged and protected. Public policy should prevent the current members of a co-operative from appropriating indivisible capital, because it was not solely created by them, does not belong to them and was created for community benefit.

The Italian approach to encouraging the development of co-operative capital works fairly well. Legislation in Italy recognizes member loans as a valuable form of financing and provides financial incentives for them; allows co-operatives to put profits into indivisible reserves without paying taxes on them[8]; permits co-operatives to have members (within the one member, one vote limitation) who do not use the services of the co-operative but only invest in it[9]; and requires co-operatives to contribute 3 percent of their profits to two funds controlled by the national co-operative federations for the purpose of co-operative development.[10] One of the funds has more than €450 million and an enviable track record in financing new and existing co-operatives. In addition, Italy allows workers to put their unemployment benefits into an emerging co-operative. The strength of co-operatives in Northern Italy flows from these measures and other supports, such as those to social co-operatives.

Personal tax provisions and financial regulation often reward investments in investor-owned firms, but investment in co-operatives or in co-operative capital funds is seldom encouraged. The regulatory pressure is to imitate the investment patterns of private-sector financial corporations. Regulators believe co-operatives should use the same risk reduction concepts that make sense for private companies. They believe a wide range of investments in investor-owned firms minimizes risk, even if those firms include companies like Lehman's, Worldcom and Arthur Anderson. They believe those investments will reduce risk in spite of the volatility of markets and the contrasting stability of co-operatives.

Co-operative members who wish to place their retirement investment savings in co-operative development have only very limited opportunities but are able, in fact one might say are encouraged, to invest in private-sector financial instruments. Taxation policies that encourage co-operative financial institutions to facilitate member investment in co-operatives should be part of the public policy mix. It makes sense for public policy to reward those who invest for a limited return and play a role in building up community capital, more than those who invest solely to maximize their own personal wealth. Community economic development investment funds, providing tax credits, work well in a couple Canadian provinces and if adapted to co-operative capital would attract ethical investors.

For European co-operatives, capital issues may become even more urgent if debt capital becomes much more difficult to obtain under Basel II, which includes a risk assessment based on the performance of for-profit, capitalist companies with a business purpose different from co-operatives.[11]

- Programs to promote co-operatives should also include support for early development. Co-operatives, while having lower failure rates and more stability, are more complex to start. Canada's co-operative housing program, which for years provided funding for Co-operative Housing Resource Groups, achieved excellent results.[12] It provided groups wishing to form a housing co-operative with vital expertise regarding the soundness of the proposal, real estate, land suitability, construction, legal issues, maintenance, financial issues and management. During its lifetime the program produced more than 2,200 housing co-operatives across Canada, providing secure non-market housing for almost 100,000 families. Those housing co-operatives continue many years later to provide affordable non-market housing across Canada. The public policy aim should be for the creation of co-operative development mechanisms as effective as the Mondragon Co-operative's Empresarial Division of the Caja Laborale Populaire. This was a model that worked.
- Pubic policy should promote the positive use of existing programs and policies to encourage co-operative formation. For example, the unemployment insurance system could allow workers in closed plants to use their benefits to facilitate shifting the company to worker ownership or tax policy could reduce the capital gains on proceeds generated by the sale of a company to its workers.
- Tendering policies could favour worker co-operatives. For example, in Italy the process gave a small advantage in rating bids to worker co-operatives and allowed a consortium of worker co-operatives to bid as a single entity.
- If governments have a pressing reason to outsource internally produced goods or service, like electrical services, rather than create a private monopoly to replace the public monopoly, they should create a co-operative service owned by users. It could be set up as a consumer co-operative, a worker-owned co-operative or a solidarity co-operative. Co-operative utilities work very well in supplying electricity to millions of people in

the U.S. and natural gas to three quarter of a million people in Alberta.

- Policies should be developed to engage with workers when a business closing is announced, such that if the workers are interested in taking over the business, government will work with them to assess the operation's viability and develop a plan, as well as seeking other potential purchasers.

- Incentives should be created to encourage the owners of small- and medium-sized family businesses, one of the main sources of new job creation, to sell the business to their workers when no family member is interested in taking it over when the owner exits. Costs to governments will be reduced if these firms continue and if they are sold to owners with community commitments.

- Research and development needs to be taken back as a domain of public policy and the emphasis shifted from seeking commercially viable technologies to research for the benefit of humanity. Public policy has to define the purpose of education as learning to live a full and meaningful life, not solely preparation for jobs. Co-operatives need information and analysis that is rounded and balanced.

- While co-operatives and IOCs should not be regulated in the same manner nor subject to the same legislation, there does need to be a level playing field. IOCs pass on to society trillions in externalized costs. This makes it much harder for co-operatives to compete with them because co-operatives resist externalizing costs due to values, principles and openness to member and community pressure. Governments must get serious about requiring IOCs to either pay for externalized costs or stop these practices.

- Funding to education institutions should require that curricula have significant content about co-operatives. With more than a billion members worldwide and economic output sufficient to be part of G7, it is incredible that secondary and post-secondary curricula, business schools and economics texts almost completely ignore the co-operative business model.

- Public policy must allow for co-operatives to remain autonomous. This does not mean they would be free from the rule of law, but that in their day to day operations, members not governments make the decisions. Government decision-making has occurred in extreme right and totalitarian states like fascist Italy and the U.S.S.R. Wherever states, including some less extreme examples, have forced co-operatives to be tools of government policy, they have fallen into disrepute. Co-operative socialism can legitimately ensure that neither co-operatives nor investor-owned corporations pass on costs to society or exploit people or communities.

Democratic governments must have faith that their citizens, empowered by economic democracy, will do the right thing and require far less regulation and control than autocratic organizations whose purpose is to make the super-rich richer. In this respect, how co-operative socialism evolves in Cuba over the next twenty years will be of great interest.

- Public policy should promote social co-operatives. Governments find it increasingly difficult to provide high quality social services, for two reasons. First, the rich and corporations both pressure governments to lower taxes and avoid taxes using tax havens, resulting in shrinking government revenues around the globe. Second is the difficulty for government to provide services through large, unwieldy bureaucracies; any large bureaucracy, public or private, is inefficient. Workers in social co-operatives in Italy have repeatedly told visiting students in the Saint Mary's Co-operative Management Education Program that they were willing to accept modest pay reductions to work in a co-operative, where they have much more control over their workplace, than in a large bureaucracy. They feel strongly that the service they provide is better and that they are helping to make a better world. A good case can be made for using the social co-operative model to provide better service at the same cost. No good case can be made for making those who provide public services live in increasing poverty while service quality declines. Austerity programs lower levels of service and reduce the tax base. Nor can a convincing case be made for turning social services over to for-profit firms.

- Public policies should promote "green" economic democracy. Governments should give preference to promoting economic democracy, especially in new and emerging green industries. Utilities owned by local users are less likely to pass costs along to the local community. Community acceptance of siting is far easier when it is the community that is doing the siting. Utilities owned by local communities retain surpluses in the community rather than act as a vacuum sucking wealth out. They build community stability and contribute to the local economic base. Moreover, they are efficient and successful, as is evident in Danish wind co-operatives, Midcounties Co-operative Energy in the U.K. and TREC Renewable Energy Co-operative in Toronto, Canada.[13] Green energy co-operatives need the right to connect to the electrical grid, the legal requirement that utilities purchase their electricity and a guaranteed fair price. Governments concerned about the erosion of rural communities and small towns can use energy co-operatives as a valuable tool.

FAIRNESS MEANS APPROPRIATE BUT NOT EQUAL

The role of government is to protect all of its citizens and ensure them, as far as is possible, the opportunity to have meaningful lives in reasonable comfort. Rather than being "open for business," and under that slogan, dismantling useful regulation to protect people and the environment, governments should be "open for co-operatives and economic democracy." Government policies would not be anti-IOCs but they should demand that IOCs stop or pay for the enormous damage they do to human society and nature. Co-operatives provide citizens with "power to" meet their needs through collective action, and they foster an economic democracy to complement and reinforce political democracy. Nurturing co-operatives should be part of every state's public policy.

NOTES

1   Coady, Parry, Sears and Shang (2015).
2   IMF (2013).
3   Mintzberg (2013).
4   Whyte and Whyte (1991).
5   Azurmendi (2004).
6   Elgar (2014: 57).
7   An indivisible reserve is capital that belongs permanently to the co-operative as a whole and to which individual members have no personal claim. It is a recognition that the value of the co-operative was created by past members and is wealth to be used by future members. It is a pool of wealth owned by all members for the benefit of the group rather than being individually owned.
8   Zamagni, Battilani and Casali (2004).
9   This individual investor member provision has not had any positive impact on funding and Italian co-operative scholars Vera and Stefano Zamagni are critical of the concept, arguing that it did not work in large measure because it is "indefensible" Zamagni and Zamagni (2010).
10   Menzani and Zamagni (2010: 7).
11   The G10 committee which develops recommendations for international banking regulation is called the Basel Committee on Banking Supervision, meets in Basel Switzerland. Basel II is the second in a series of recommended regulations developed as a result of the irresponsible activity of banks that triggered the 2008 Great Recession. Credit unions and co-operative banks were not involved in those irresponsible activities but are subject to the regulations as if they had been involved. See Zamagni and Zamagni (2010: 86).
12   See "Co-operative Housing Facts" <chfcanada.coop/eng/pages2007/about_2_1.asp>.
13   For a brief review of the Danish wind co-operatives, see <chelseagreen.com/blogs/a-case-study-in-community-wind-denmark/:> for Midcounties, see <cooperativeenergy.coop> for TREC, see <solarbonds.ca/ http://trec.on.ca/>.

Chapter 8

DREAMING OF A BETTER WORLD

There are those who look at things the way they are and ask why. I dream
of things that never were and ask why not. — Robert F Kennedy

I hope that this book lifts people's spirits following its initial sobering wake-up
call to face the daunting issues engulfing our world. Chapter 1 reviewed a series,
but not all, of the interconnected destructive trends challenging the globe. The
purpose was not to depress and dishearten, but to establish the need for action and
stimulate the belief that we can do better. Our current reality is a bit like roaring
down the highway in a car with faulty steering, suspension and brakes. It is essential
for the survival of the driver and passenger, and bystanders as well, that we know
what needs to be fixed. To say, "Don't tell me about the problems. I don't want to
be depressed," would be a foolish reaction offering no hope.

It is crucial that we know the enormous risks facing humanity and the natural
world. It is essential in fashioning a solution to our problems that we understand
the key drivers of the problems. If the brakes came from a supplier who cut cor-
ners, then we should know so we do not buy the same brakes again. If the steering
problems came from driving too fast over a pot-holed road, we need to know that
as well. Critical analysis that tells us our current economic arrangements have
negative impacts, but mainstream economics says that there is no alternative to
capitalism and its principle tool, the investor-owned corporation. Fortunately,
there are indeed alternatives.

Corporations have a history dating back 400 years or more. For most of that .

history, corporations were chartered by governments to serve a public purpose. Estes aptly notes: "For over two centuries, corporations were viewed as fairly benign servants of the public good. But they are no longer our servants, and they are very often not benign."[1] Individuals, families, communities and governments have become the servants of corporations.

The foundational premises of neoclassical economics are based, not on data but on the quasi-religious beliefs of those who most benefit from this system. Markets don't operate as advertised. People are not motivated as claimed. All too often profit is made by externalizing costs, causing human suffering and destroying the natural world. Wealth trickles up, it turns out, not down. The cold hard reality is that this capital-driven economy cannot be excused by its faltering explanations. The internal contradictions of capitalism are as profound as those of totalitarian communism. More and more angry and dispossessed groups are emerging. Environmental degradation is increasingly becoming a string of environmental catastrophes. No economy can survive when the bees are gone, when the rivers are all polluted, when the oceans are dead and when the air is poisoned. No economy can survive the battering of runaway climate change. Disdain for life on the planet in order to preserve a failing capitalism is disdain for human life as well. An economy that increasingly serves the super-rich and their corporations and is losing its ability to meet human need cannot endure. Like a cancer, out-of-control capitalism is destroying its host — nature, and that includes us.

These conclusions are not a source of comfort. Communism did not collapse without its secret police, massive pollution and massacres. It is hard to imagine those currently enjoying tremendous privilege surrendering it without a struggle. But for those seeking to shift to a co-operative economy, it must be a peaceful struggle! There are two compelling reasons. First, and less importantly, the ability to command violence is much greater for those with economic power. Of much more importance, the use of violence to create the changes needed to shift from capitalism to a co-operative socialist alternative is a non-starter. Violence is abhorrent to co-operative values and principles. Violence is a "power over" action while co-operation is a "power to" action. Violence produces more violence and repression. War does not produce co-operation. The rich elite often uses violence to prevent change, but it is not an option for co-operators. Violence destroys solidarity, caring, sharing, honesty, democracy, openness, mutual self-help — almost every value and principle of co-operation. It is the antithesis of co-operation. The means destroys the end.

A peaceful, non-violent promotion of co-operation will not be a smooth ride. The collapse of capitalism, even over decades, will produce dislocations for civil society. The Great Recession of 2008 was an episode in the long painful demise of capitalism. The 2008 Recession needs to be analyzed for its impact on mortality rates as a result of suicide among the unemployed and malnourished.[2] With unemployment rates increasing around the world, those least able to feed their children are becoming even less able.to so. We need to understand the link between the 2008 corporate crimes and mortalities and suffering. The victims were almost all from the poorest segments of humanity. The cost of bailing out the wealthiest 20 percent of humanity and their failed financial institutions were borne, through austerity programs, on the less affluent 80 percent of humanity. It is austerity for the poor and socialism for the rich.[3] The true reforms called for after the collapse never happened. Capitalism, comprised of its business model and theoretical foundation, is in decline and its nature is to resist change and reform. Its theoretical foundation, neoclassical economics is also in denial and resistant to reform. In spite of the failure of structural adjustment programs in the last century and the abject failure of the austerity solution in countries where it has been tried, including most recently Greece, it continues to be trumpeted by the economic elite.

THERE IS AN ALTERNATIVE

The promoters of capitalism who reluctantly admit its serious problems, fall back on the lame TINA defence — There Is No Alternative. If you suggest the co-operative business model and a co-operative economy as an alternative, they quickly ignore the hundreds of thousands of examples of IOC failures with their disastrous results and want to talk about some co-operative failures. Yet the rate of co-operative failure is nothing compared to the incredibly worse failures of capitalism. Critics of co-operatives produce no examples of a co-operative failure on the scale of Lehman's, WorldCom, GM, Bophal, Love Canal, Rana Plaza, etc., etc.

If you suggest that co-operatives are consistent with human nature and that a co-operative culture brings out the best in people, they claim that hyper individualism, competition and greed are the most powerful motivators and that we must rely on them to achieve an abundant society. They minimize the terrible damage done to society and our natural world by their preferred motivators. They ignore the enormous potential of nurturing a co-operative culture. They ignore the facts: one billion people around the globe use co-operation to improve their lives; the output from all the world's co-operatives, if they were all in their own country, would give them a seat at the G7; more than 250 million people work in co-operatives.

Co-operation is the foundation of life on the planet, from cell level to country level. All living organisms use co-operation during their life spans. Informal co-operatives and co-operation have existed among people from the dawn of humanity. The current co-operative business model has roots back almost 200 years. From its inception, it drew on the resources of ordinary people who lacked pools of wealth to drive its growth and expansion. Co-operatives grew slowly but surely, both in spite of and because of corporate predatory activity, and always with much less access to capital. Their success rests more on the indomitable human spirit rather than the raw power of great wealth or the driving force of competition.

The following list outlines some of the enormous benefits to be had from a shift from corporate globalization to global co-operation:

- The purpose, values and principles of co-operatives encourage the best and discourage the worst in humanity. Co-operatives' operational performance is a systematic push-back against the major negative trends that have dominated the past two centuries.
- Co-operatives are centred on respecting nature while meeting human need rather than forcing nature and humanity to serve the economy and capital. The greater flexibility of the co-operative model allows, and co-operative principles encourage, environmental responsibility and respect for nature.
- Co-operatives nurture individuality in the context of mutual self-help, reflecting the dual aspects of humanity.
- The democratic structure of co-operatives allows workers, consumers, communities and society greater access to information and greater ability to influence decisions. This means, for example, that co-operatives are less likely to externalize costs on workers, consumers, communities, society and the environment.
- Co-operatives combat income inequality, and their very existence serves as a check on price gouging and unfair consumer practices. The impact is to increase people's buying power not just for co-operative members but for non-members as well. Co-operatives also operate with a far smaller income gap between highest and lowest paid workers.
- Co-operatives contribute to stabilizing family farm incomes and rural communities, slowing urbanization as well as providing a tool to urban slum dwellers to lift their oppression.
- Co-operatives promote food sovereignty, security and quality.
- The bottom-up and user ownership of co-operatives provides an alternative to dysfunctional global corporate concentration.
- A co-operative economy discourages unproductive, galloping financialization. Using capital as a tool to meet member and community need changes the financial dynamics of the economy in a fundamental way.
- Co-operatives are more stable than investor-owned businesses, and a co-operative economy, not dependent on quarterly growth, will be more resilient and free from predatory speculators.
- Economic democracy fosters a democratic culture and teaches practical

democratic skills. Everyone has the right to express themselves and have input into decisions.

- Co-operatives are focused meeting needs rather than on creating wants. Thus, the development of technology will become "need focused" rather than "profit focused." With the age of "intelligent robots" upon us, co-operatives will use technology to reduce work weeks and free people to more meaningful human work.

- Co-operatives will continue to allow people to solve the problems resulting from market failure. Co-operatives have historically been created to protect people when markets do not function well, for example, in the case of farmers getting gouged on the cost of farm inputs or receiving artificially low prices for their products.

This book suggests that we can build a better world for our children and future generations by shifting our economic activity to co-operation using the very flexible co-operative business model. We can adopt the most successful form of economic democracy. But how is this to happen? Is such fundamental change possible? When and how will capitalism die? In her 2014 novel, *Station 11*, Emily St. John Mandel makes interesting observations about change. "I wanted to write a love letter to this incredible world in which we find ourselves, this place where water comes out of taps, lighting up a room requires nothing more complicated than flicking a switch on the wall, and talking to someone on the far side of the world is as simple as entering a sequence of numbers into a device that fits into the palm of your hand."[4] Some of these changes my parents would have marvelled at; all would have astounded my grandfather in his youth. Deeply rooted and profound changes have characterized human history. The world of the 1500s is gone. The worlds of the Industrial Revolution and sailing ships are gone. The age of corporations serving the public purpose is gone. Better ideas drive change. The shift from capitalism to global co-operation is simply a better idea.

Many variables will shape the transition from the collapse of capitalism, and no outcome is inevitable. Let us imagine two strikingly different scenarios ones for a dying capitalism:

- The super-rich would wall themselves off in gated communities; commandeer the world's resources and surround themselves with protective armies; have more and more work done by robots; make co-operatives illegal; use force where they feel it necessary to suppress the majority of humanity; and hoard a larger and larger share of global production. As nature's ability to sustain life diminishes, more resources would be required to provide a comfortable healthy life for a declining elite. Punishments could be meted out for countries like Greece who defy the neo-classical economic line. The gap between rich and poor would deepen.

- Equally possible, and much more desirable, a series of peaceful transitions could gather steam. The super-rich, or many of them, may well see the wisdom of change and use their power to facilitate the shift; those with far more wealth than they need could sell their productive assets to their workers at a fraction of the real worth on condition that the resulting business be set up as solidarity co-operatives; people would stop using businesses that refused to change; economic democracy could grow and prevail, creating a more peaceful and open society; diminished consumerism and a fairer distribution of resources could support the current or even a slightly larger population, in harmony with the natural world; the gap between the rich and poor would not disappear but greatly diminish, as would abject poverty; technologies and human knowledge would be more commonly shared; work would become more meaningful and productive; consumerism would ebb, and an age of relationships would flourish.

Many other scenarios can be imagined and are possible. Transitions will be varied. It will not happen the same way in every country. In our global era, the progress and process in each country will impact others. The transition to a post-capitalism world will be complex and difficult to predict. In the face of this uncertainty what can be done to make a better world scenario more likely? The first and most important strategy is non-violence. Fanny's mother, a character of novelist Alice Walker, tells us: "Forgiveness is the true foundation of health and happiness, just as it is for any lasting progress. Without forgiveness there is no forgetfulness of evil; without forgetfulness there remains the threat of violence. Violence does not solve anything; it only prolongs itself."[5]

Many thoughtful people believe, with evidence to support their contention, that people can drive change, especially when they act in concert with others. Robert F Kennedy expressed it this way: "Each time a man stands for an ideal, or acts to improve the lot of others, or strikes out against injustice, he sends a tiny ripple of hope, and crossing each other from a million different centers of energy and daring, those ripples build a current which can sweep down the mightiest walls of oppression and resistance."[6] And Margaret Mead, who studied people around the world, observed: "Never doubt that a small group of thoughtful, committed citizens can change the world; indeed, it's the only thing that ever has."[7]

So what are the strategies possible? Broad public strategies can include systematically promoting "power to" organizations that will reduce apathy and the sense of powerlessness; stepping up research on the persistent and growing global problems fueled by our current economic system; growing the shift to control by users of economic institutions — through co-operatives, credit unions and other forms of social enterprise; shifting education programs so they help us understand our world and how to build healthy families and communities rather than preparing us for jobs; and shrugging off apathy and using every possible democratic lever still available to us to shift the direction of our world. People can move their money out of banks and into credit unions and demand that the credit unions they own operate in line with their purpose, values and principles. They can buy smaller quantities of more nutritious food at farmers' markets and food co-operatives. They can slowly shift their lives to build a better world.

CHALLENGE AND OPPORTUNITY FOR CO-OPERATIVES

"From those to whom much has been given, much is expected."[8] Co-operative leaders and co-operative organizations are uniquely positioned to play a positive role in shaping human history. The list of things co-operatives can do is almost limitless, but it includes:

- Refine and deepen the vision so that it has the power to stir the human soul, and that means a vision that is clear about our relationship to nature.
- Have the wisdom to co-exist with capitalist firms and co-operate with them without being co-opted. That means judging actions and structures, but not people, and accepting that some may not wish to co-operate.
- Develop appropriate education programs for workers, managers, boards, members and the community. The most powerful education is through living the values and principles in the day-to-day operations of the business and ensuring everyone understands why the co-operative operates as it does.
- Co-operate with nature rather than fighting nature. For example, co-operatives focused on food should have as models the agroecology co-operatives in Cuba and the food co-operatives in the U.S.
- Use the principle of co-operation among co-operatives to grow the co-operative movement by constantly seeking out business opportunities that can be developed into new co-operatives with which to network.
- Ensure the creation of strong co-operative development mechanisms capable of supplying a full range of co-operative friendly business development expertise, with or without the support of public policy.
- Promote conversions of family-owned firms lacking successors and firms being closed because they did not generate a maximum profit as investor-owned companies.[9]

- Help those developing curricula and doing research in publicly funded education systems, and develop a network of co-operative schools, as has happened in the U.K.[10]
- Work with governments to prevent hostile public policy development and promote co-operative-friendly public policy. When governments adopt hostile policies, as did the Canada during the International Year of Co-operatives in 2012, co-operatives need to use their "people power." One billion co-operative members, 250 million workers in co-operatives and 2.6 million co-operatives generate significant revenues. In most countries, Canada being a stark example, the government revenues generated by co-operative members, workers and co-operatives are far in excess of the value of government services they receive.
- Take a leadership role in seeking solutions to, and pressuring governments about, social and environmental problems and democratic reform.
- Insist governments allow them to create powerful pools of co-operative capital.

Co-operatives and co-operative leaders have in their hands the most powerful tools available to humanity to fuel the transition to a better world. Will they have the courage, wisdom and strength to play that important role? I have met many over the years who do have that courage and wisdom. Alas, a number do not, and they will act as a drag on the efforts co-operatives need to make in the decades ahead. Some people, infected not with optimism but with the curse of positive thinking, ignore negative information and events and assure us that everything will turn out okay.

Reality demands that we keep our eyes on both the positive and the negative. It is possible for unbridled self-interest to destroy our grandchildren's future. We need to be balanced — examining the negative forces in our world to gain understanding, and celebrating positive and progressive actions and structures. Nothing is inevitable. Nothing comes without effort. Nothing comes without planning and hard work. We will not get to a better world for our children and grandchildren and generations to come unless we know where we are going and are relentless in pursuit of it. Nothing is inevitable, but everything is possible.

Co-operatives are simply a tool, and co-operation is a way of thinking and a state of mind to get us to a better world. Co-operation is going back to the essence of being part of life on a beautiful planet. It is reclaiming and harnessing the most powerful force driving the evolution of life on Earth. The goal is a world where the joyful laughter of children has replaced the listlessness of malnutrition. It is a world where people are valued for who they are rather than how much they make, the colour of their skin or their gender. It is a world where everyone's contribution is valued, not as a commodity, but as a source of meaning. It is a world where a dew drop sparkling on a flower brings more joy than material consumption. It is a world where learning does not produce intellectual commodities but sharing. It is a world where the satisfaction of co-operation outweighs, but does not eliminate, healthy competition. It is a world of more and more winners and fewer and fewer losers. It is a world where healthy communities and families are more important than labour mobility. It is a world where music, art and literature are available to all, in balance with meaningful work. It is a world where humanity is more and more in harmony with the infinite beauty of nature, and where that beauty lifts our souls with joy. It is a world where love overshadows its opposites — apathy, fear and hatred.

Co-operation is a tool to build that world.

NOTES

1　Estes (1996: Chapter 1). See also Klein (2007).
2　Barr et al. (2012).
3　Stiglitz (2009).
4　Globe and Mail (2014).
5　Walker (1989: 308).
6　Kennedy (1966).
7　Margaret Mead <goodreads.com/author/quotes/61107.Margaret_Mead>.
8　Luke 12:35–48.
9　Such co-operatives include Best Western Hotels, Capricorn (garage owners) in Australia and New Zealand, Home Hardware in Canada and True Value hardware in the U.S.
10　<co-operativeschools.coop/about_us>.

BIBLIOGRAPHY

Adams, Walter, and James Brock. 2004. *The Bigness Complex: Industry, Labor, and Government in the American Economy*. Stanford, CA: Stanford University Press.

AFL-CIO. 2014. "CEO-to-Worker Pay Ratios Around the World." <aflcio.org/Corporate-Watch/ Paywatch-Archive/CEO-Pay-and-You/CEO-to-Worker-Pay-Gap-in-the-United-States/ Pay-Gaps-in-the-World>.

August, Arnold. 2013. *Cuba and Its Neighbours: Democracy in Motion*. Halifax: Fernwood Publishing.

Azurmendi, Joxe (ed.). 2004. "Reflections, A Translation of '*Pensamientos de Don Jose Maria Arizmendiarrieta*.'" Otalora Management Education Center, Mondragon Co-operative Corporation, Bº Aozaraza, 2, 20550 Aretxabaleta, Gipuzkoa, Spain.

Bahandri, Ravi. 2011. *Real World Globalization: A Reader in Economics, Business and Politics*. Boston: Economic Affairs Bureau, Dollars and Sense Collective.

Baken Joel. 2004. *The Corporation: The Pathological Pursuit of Profit and Power*. Penguin

Barbarini, Ivano. 2009. *How the Bumblebee Flies: Cooperation, Ethics and Development*. Italy: Baldini Castoldi Dalai.

Barr, B., D. Taylor-Robinson, A. Scott-Samuel, M. McKee and D. Stuckler. 2012. "Suicides Associated with the 2008–10 Economic Recession in England: Time Trend Analysis." *British Medical Journal* 345:e5142.

Bartl, Mariia. 2015. "TTIP's Regulatory Cooperation and the Politics of 'Learning.'" *Journal Social Europe*, November <socialeurope.eu/2015/11/ ttips-regulatory-cooperation-and-the-politics-of-learning/>.

Bayerl, Frank. 2014. "How a Corporate Agent Helped the U.S. Exploit Poor Countries." *CCPA Monitor* 20, 8 (February): 31.

BBC Horizons. 1980. "The Mondragon Experiment." 17 Nov. <youtube.com/ watch?v=2zMvktpKDmo>.

Bibby, Andrew. 2014. "Co-operatives Are an Inherently More Sustainable Form of Business." *Guardian*, March 11. <theguardian.com/social-enterprise-network/2014/mar/11/ co-op-business-sustainability>.

Birchall, Johnston. 2013. *Resilience in a Downturn: The Power of Financial Cooperatives*.

Geneva: ILO.

Bloomberg View. 2014. "The World Economy Is Far From Fixed." December 10. <bloombergview. com/articles/2014-12-10/china-greece-show-that-world-economy-isnt-fixed-yet>.

Blyth, Mark. 2013. "The Austerity Delusion." Foreign Affairs, Council on Foreign Relations, May-June issue. <foreignaffairs.com/articles/139105/mark-blyth/the-austerity-delusion>.

Borzaga, C., S. Depedri and E. Tortia. 2009. "The Role of Co-operative and Social Enterprises: A Multifaceted Approach for an Economic Pleuralism." Euricse Working Papers, N000/09.

Boseley, Sarah. 2015. "Experts call for global research fund for antibiotics, Ebola and other neglected diseases." <theguardian.com/society/sarah-boseley-global-health/2015/may/11/experts-call-for-global-research-fund-for-antibiotics-ebola-and-other-neglected-diseases>.

Boulding, Dr. Elise. 1978. "The Family as a Way Into the Future." Pendle Hill Pamphlet 222, Wallingford, PA.

Bradley, Keith. 1980. "A Comparative Analysis of Producer Co-operatives: Some Theoretical and Empirical Implications." *British Journal of Industrial Relations* 18 (July): 155–168.

Bradley, Keith, and Alan Gelb. 1982. "The Mondragon Co-operatives: Guidelines for a Co-operative Economy." In D.K. Jones and J. Svejnar (eds.), *Participatory and Self-Managed Firms*. Lexington, MA: Heath.

Brennan, Jordan. 2015. "Do Corporate Tax Rate Reductions Accelerate Growth?" <policyalternatives.ca/publications/reports/do-corporate-income-tax-rate-reductions-accelerate-growth>.

Brock, James. 2005. "Merger Mania and Its Discontents: The Price of Corporate Consolidation." *Multinational Monitor* 26, 7 (Jul/Aug).

Brown, Lester. 2011. *World on the Edge*. London, UK: Earthscan Ltd.

Bruni, Luigino, and Stefano Zamagni. 2007. *The Civil Economy – Efficiency, Equity and Public Happiness*. Oxford, UK: Peter Lang Press.

Capital Institute. 2012. "Economics, Finance, Governance for the Anthropocene: A Working Paper of the Third Millennium Economy Project." June.

Cato, Molly. 2006. Market Schmarket. New Clarion Press, UK

____. 2009. *Green Economics: An Introduction to the Theory, Policy and Practice*. London: Earthscan.

CBC (Canadian Broadcasting Corporation). 2014. *World's Oceans Threatened by Floating Trash*. April 1. <cbc.ca/news2/interactives/ocean-garbage/?mkt_tok=3RkMMJWW fF9wsRols6%2FLZKXonjHpfsX57%2B4kWaWwlMI%2F0ER3fOvrPUfGjI4ES8Rn I%2BSLDwEYGJlv6SgFS7jNMbZkz7gOXRE%3D>.

Centre for Corporate Policy. 2015. "Corporate Accountability: Addressing Concentrated Economic Power." <corporatepolicy.org/topics/sizematters.htm>.

Cevik, Serhan, and Carolina Correa-Caro. 2015. "Growing (Un)equal: Fiscal Policy and Income Inequality in China and BRIC+." Imf working paper WP/15/68. March. <imf. org/external/pubs/ft/wp/2015/wp1568.pdf>.

Chamard, John. 2003. "Education for Management of Co-operatives and Credit Unions." Las Vegas, NV: ASBBS Conference.

Chang, Ha-Joon. 2010. *23 Things They Did Not Tell You about Capitalism*. New York:

Bloomsbury Press.

____. 2014. *Economics: The Users Guide*. London: Penguin Books.

Chefurka, Paul. 2007. "Population, The Elephant in the Room." <paulchefurka.ca/Population.html>.

Clark, Neil. 2003. "NS Profile — George Soros." *New Statesman*, June. <newstatesman.com/economics/economics/2014/04/ns-profile-george-soros>.

Coady, David, Ian Parry, Louis Sears and Baoping Shang. 2015. "How Large Are Global Energy Subsidies?" IMF Working Paper WP/15/105, May. <imf.org/external/pubs/ft/wp/2015/wp15105.pdf>.

Cohen Theodore H. 2005. *Global Political Economy: Theory and Practice*. New York: Pearson Longman.

Consumer Federation of America. 2013. "Public Perceptions of Co-operatives." Survey carried out for the National Co-operative Business Association, Washington, D.C.

Corcoran, H., and G. O'Neil. 2013. "Social Enterprise that Empowers: The Co-operative Model." Paper presented at the Social Enterprise World Forum, Calgary, Alberta, 2–4 Oct. 2013. <socialenterpriseworldforum.org/blog/2013/10/01/social-enterprise-that-empowers-the-co-operative-model/>.

Côté, D. 2008. "Bests Practices and Cooperative Development: Lessons from the Quebec Experience." In Joy Emmanuel and Lyn Cayo (eds.), *Effective Practices in Starting Co-operatives: The Voice of Canadian Co-op Developers*. Victoria, BC: New Rochdale Press: 97–116.

____. 2009. "Managing Co-operative Equilibrium: A Theorical Framework." In Ian Macpherson and Erin Mcglaughlin-Jenkins (eds.), *Integrating Diversities within a Complex Heritage: Essays in the Field of Co-operative Studies*. Victoria, BC, New Rochdale Press: 3–40.

____. 2013. *Patronage, Loyalty, and Credit Unions' Shared Surplus*. Filene Research Institute Report, Publication #304 (7/13). Madison, WI: Filene Research Institute.

Cox, Michael. 2015. "Greece Surrendered, But the Real Defeat Was for Europe." *Social Europe* 16 (July). <socialeurope.eu/2015/07/greece-surrendered-but-the-real-defeat-was-for-europe/>.

Cypher, J., S. Rao and C. Sturr. 2011. *Current Economic Issues: Readings in Economics, Politics and Social Issues*. Boston: Economics Affairs Bureau, Dollars and Sense.

Dahl, Robert. 1985. *A Preface to Economic Democracy*. Los Angeles: University of California Press.

Dalberg, John Emerich Edward. 1887. "Lord Acton, Letter to Archbishop Mandell Creighton, Apr. 5, 1887." <history.hanover.edu/courses/excerpts/165acton.html>.

Damon, Andre. 2014. "Goldman Sachs Involved in Fraudulent Activities in Toxic Mortgage-Backed Securities." Centre for Research on Globalization. <globalresearch.ca/former-goldman-trader-involved-in-fraudulent-activities-says-8-million-bonus-too-low/5387990>.

Dauncey, Guy. 2014. "Sixteen Building Blocks for a Green, Entrepreneurial, Cooperative Economy." CCPA Goods Jobs Economy in BC Conference, November 21. <policyalternatives.ca/sites/default/files/uploads/publications/WorkingPaper_GuyDauncey_GoodJobsConf.pdf>.

Davis D.R., M.D. Epp and H.D. Riordan. 2004. "Changes in USDA Food Composition

Data for 43 Garden Crops, 1950 to 1999." *Journal of the American College of Nutrition* 23, 6 (Dec.): 669_82.

Davis, Fania, and Sarah van Gelder. 2015. "Can America Heal After Ferguson? We Asked Desmond Tutu and His Daughter." *Yes! Magazine* Summer. <yesmagazine.org/issues/make-it-right/can-america-heal-after-ferguson-we-asked-desmond-tutu-and-his-daughter?utm_source=YTW&utm_medium=Email&utm_campaign=20150529>.

Davis, Mike. 2006. *Planet of Slums*. London: Verso.

Deal, Jennifer J. 2013. "Welcome to the 72 Hour Work Week." *Harvard Business Review* 12 September. <hbr.org/2013/09/welcome-to-the-72-hour-work-we/>.

Delong, J Bradford. 2014. "Jobs and the Rise of the Robots." *Social Europe Journal* 30 September <socialeurope.eu/2014/09/rise-of-the-robots/>.

De Schutter, Olivier. 2011. "Agroecology and the Right to Food." Report presented at the 16th Session of the United Nations Human Rights Council [A/HRC/16/49], 8 March.

Devadhar, Y.C. 1971. "Alfred Marshall on Cooperation." *Annals of Public and Cooperative Economics* Volume 42, Issue 4 (Oct 1971.): 285–301. Wiley On line Library

Diamond, Dan. 2015. "Martin Shkreli Admits He Messed Up: He Should've Raised Prices Even Higher." <forbes.com/sites/dandiamond/2015/12/03/what-martin-shkreli-says-now-i-shouldve-raised-prices-higher/>.

Draperi, Jean-Francois. 2005. *Making Another World Possible: Social Ecnomy, Cooperatives and Sustainable Development*. Montreuil, France: Presses de L'Economie Sociale.

DuRand, Cliff. 2015. "Co-operative Cuba." Center for Global Justice. <globaljusticecenter.org/cooperative_cuba>.

Easterlin, Richard A., and Laura Angelescu. 2009. "Happiness and Growth the World Over: Time Series Evidence on the Happiness-Income Paradox." Discussion Paper No. 4060, March, IZA (Institute for Labour Study). <ftp.iza.org/dp4060.pdf>.

Edmonds, Tim. 2015. "Social Enterprise, House of Commons Library Standard Note." 28 January, Standard notes SN07089.

Eisenstein, Charles. 2011. *Sacred Economics: Money, Gift and Society in the Age of Transition*. Berkeley, CA: Evolver Books.

Elgar, Frank J. 2014. "Equality, Social Cohesion and Wellbeing." *Journal for a Progressive Economy* 2 (March).

Elliott, Larry. 2016. "Richest 62 People as Wealthy as Half of World's Population, Says Oxfam." *Guardian*, Monday, January 18. <theguardian.com/business/2016/jan/18/richest-62-billionaires-wealthy-half-world-population-combined>.

____. 2012. "Employee Ownership Is Good for Your Health: People Thrive in a Social Environment Characterised by Employee Ownership." Job Ownership Ltd., Draft report for the European Parliament (2012), On the Contribution of Cooperatives to Overcoming the Crisis, (2012/2321(INI)).

Estes, Ralph. 1996. *The Tyranny of the Bottom Line: Why Corporations Make Good People Do Bad Things*. San Francisco: Berrett-Kochler Publishers.

ETC Group. 2013. "Putting the Cartel before the Horse … and Farm, Seeds, Soil, Peasants, etc." Who Will Control Agricultural Inputs, Comunique 111, September. <etcgroup.org/sites/www.etcgroup.org/files/Communique%CC%81%20111%204%20sep%203%20pm.pdf>.

Eur-Lex, Access to European Union Law. 2015. "The Principle of Subsidiarity." <eur-lex.

europa.eu/legal-content/EN/TXT/?uri=URISERV:ai0017>.

European Parliament. 2012. "Report: On the Contribution of Cooperatives to Overcoming the Crisis." (2012/2321(INI)), Committee on Industry, Research and Energy, Rapporteur: Patrizia Toia.

European Trade Union Institute. 2015. Benchmarking Working Europe 2015. Brussels <etui.org/Publications2/Books/Benchmarking-Working-Europe-2015>.

Fair Shares. 2015. "Democratic Control: The Case for Fair Shares." <createspace. com/5522383?mc_cid=c9be79a867&mc_eid=4a4187df1b>.

Fazi, Thomas. 2016. "How Austerity Has Crippled the European Economy – In Numbers." *Journal of Social Europe,* 31 March. <socialeurope.eu/2016/03/austerity-crippled-european-economy-numbers/>.

Felicio, João Antonio. 2014. "There Are Alternatives to the Neoliberal Blind Alley!" *Social Europe Journal,* 24 June.

Ferri, Giovanni. 2012. "Credit Cooperatives: Challengs and Opportunitiesin the New Global Scenario." Euricse, Working Paper N. 031-12. Trento, Italy: University of Trento.

Fitousi, J-P., and Frencesco Saraceno. 2014. "Drivers of Inequality Past and Present: Challenges for Europe." *Journal for a Progressive Economy* 2 March.

Fontanilla, D., and C. Wright. 2015. "Keeping Food Security on the Table at U.N. Climate Talks." Inter Press Service News Agency. <ipsnews.net/2015/02/keeping-food-security-on-the-table-at-u-n-climate-talks/>.

Fox, Justin. 2009. *The Myth of the Rational Market: A History of Risk, Reward and Delusion on Wall Street.* New York: Harper Collins.

Frankl, Viktor. 1946. *Man's Search for Meaning.* Boston: Beacon Press.

Frayssinet, Fabiana. 2009. "Brazil: Agribusiness Driving Land Concentration." Inter Press Service News Agency. <ipsnews.net/2009/10/brazil-agribusiness-driving-land-concentration/>.

Freeman, Richard. 1995. "Control by the Food Cartel Companies: Profiles and Histories." Originally published in *Executive Intelligence Review.* <larouchepub.com/other/1995/2249_cartel_companies.html>.

Frey, Benedikt, and Michael A. Osbourne. 2013. "The Future of Employment: How Susceptible Are Jobs to Computerization?" Oxford Martin School, University of Oxford. <oxfordmartin.ox.ac.uk/downloads/academic/The_Future_of_Employment.pdf>.

Fullerton, John. 2014. "Finance for the Anthropocene." In S. Novković and T. Webb (eds.), *Co-operatives in a Post Growth Era: Creating Co-operative Economics.* UK: Zed Books.

____. 2015. "Is There Anyone's Money Harvard Woudn't Take?" 29 June. <capitalinstitute. org/blog/anyones-money-harvard-take/>.

Galbraith, J.K. 2012. *Inequality and Instability: A Study of the World Economy Just Before the Great Crisis.* Oxford University Press.

Gasaway, Diane. 2012. *Cascadia Regional Co-op Resource Survey: A Report Submitted on Behalf of the Cascadia Cooperative Network, a Project of Strengthening Local Independent Cooperatives Everywhere (SLICE).* Olympia, Washington: Northwest Cooperative Development Center.

Gaughan, Patrick A. 2011. *Mergers, Acquisitions and Corporate Restructuring,* fifth edition. New Jersey: John Wiley and Sons.

Gavett, Gretchen. 2014. "CEOs Get Paid Too Much, According to Pretty Much Everyone in the World." *Harvard Business Review* on line, 23 September. <hbr.org/2014/09/ceos-get-paid-too-much-according-to-pretty-much-everyone-in-the-world/>.

Gechert, Sebastian, and Rannenberg Ansgar. 2015. "The Costs of Greece's Fiscal Consolidation." Policy Brief, March. Duesseldorf, Germany: Macroeconomic Policy Institute, Hans-Böckler-Foundation.

Gibbs, T., and G. Leech. 2009. *The Failure of Global Capitalism*. Sydney, NS: Cape Breton University Press.

Glasbeek, Harry. 2002. *Wealth by Stealth: Corporate Crime, Corporate Law and the Perversion of Democracy*. Toronto: Between the Lines Press.

Gleick, P.H., et al. 2011. *The World's Water, Vol. 7. The Biennial Report on Freshwater Resources*. Washington, D.C.: Island Press.

Global Sustainable Investment Alliance. 2015. "2014 Global Sustainable Investment Review." <gsi-alliance.org/wp-content/uploads/2015/02/GSIA_Review_download.pdf>.

Globe and Mail. 2014. "Why Emily St. John Mandel's Wrote Her New Book: 'I Think of It as a Love Letter in the Form of a Requiem." 5 December. <theglobeandmail.com/arts/books-and-media/why-emily-st-john-mandels-wrote-her-new-book-i-think-of-it-as-a-love-letter-in-the-form-of-a-requiem/article21971241/>.

Goldenberg, Suzanne. 2015. "Exxon Knew of Climate Change in 1981, Email Says – But It Funded Deniers for 27 More Years." *Manchester Guardian*, 8 July. <theguardian.com/environment/2015/jul/08/exxon-climate-change-1981-climate-denier-funding>.

Grace, Dave, and Associates. 2014. "Measuring the Size and Scope of the Cooperative Economy: Results of the 2014 Global Census on Co-operatives." For the United Nation's Secretariat, Department of Economic and Social Affairs, Division for Social Policy and Development.

Greenspan, Alan. 2008. Former chairman of the U.S. Federal Reserve, the U.S. Committee of Government Oversight. Oct. 23.

Greenwood, R., and D. Scharfstein. 2012. "The Growth of Modern Finance." <people.hbs.edu/dscharfstein/growth_of_modern_finance.pdf>.

Greider, William. 1997. *One World Ready or Not*. Simon and Schuster.

Gutknecht, Dave. 2015. "Growth Stories and Quandaries." *Co-operative Grocer* #176 (Jan–Feb).

Gutstein, Donald. 2014. *Harperism: How Stephen Harper and His Think Tank Colleagues Have Transformed Canada*. Toronto: Lorimer.

Harding, Kevin. 2014. "Building Good Jobs: Cooperatively." A Good Jobs Economy in BC Conference (Nov. 21). <policyalternatives.ca/sites/default/files/uploads/publications/WorkingPaper_KevinHarding_GoodJobsConf.pdf>.

Hawken, Paul. 1993. *The Ecology of Commerce: A Declaration of Sustainability*. New York: Harper Business/Harper Collins.

_____. 2007. *Blessed Unrest: How the Largest Social Movement in History Is Restoring Grace, Justice and Beauty to the World*. Penguin Books.

Heilbroner, Robert L. et al. 1972. *In the Name of Profit*. Garden City, NY: Doubleday.

Helliwell, John F., and Robert D. Putman. 2004. *The Social Context of Well-Being*. London:

The Royal Society Publishing.

Hennessy, Trish. 2015. "Hennessy's Index." CCPA *Monitor* 21, 8 (February).

Hersh, Adam, and Jennifer Erickson. 2013. "5 Reasons the World Is Catching on to the Financial Transaction Tax." February 25. <americanprogress.org/issues/economy/news/2013/02/25/54503/5-reasons-the-world-is-catching-on-to-the-financial-transaction-tax/>.

Hiemstra, Glenn. 2015. "What Is the Global Future of Agriculture?" 26 Feb. <futurist.com/articles-archive/future-of-agriculture/>.

Hill, Roderick. 2000. "The Case of the Missing Organizations: Co-operatives and the Textbooks." *Journal of Economic Education* (Summer).

Hodgson, Paul. 2014. "Target CEO's Gold Parachute: $61 Million." *Fortune*, on line. <fortune.com/2014/05/21/target-ceos-golden-parachute-61-million/>.

Homer-Dixon, Thomas. 2014. "Complexity: Shock. Innovation and Resilience." In S. Novković and T. Webb (eds.), *Co-operatives in a Post Growth Era: Creating Co-operative Economics*. Zed Books.

Human Rights Watch. 1992. "Human Rights in Guatemala During President Leon De Carpio's First Year." <hrw.org/reports/pdfs/g/guatemla/guatemal946.pdf>.

Hussman, Rebecca. 2015. "The War on Water in Harrietsfield, Nova Scotia, Parts 1–3." Halifax Media Co-operative, Spring <halifax.mediacoop.ca/harrietsfieldtoxicwater>.

IMF. 2013. "Energy Subsidy Reform: Lessons and Implications." International Monetary Fund, 28 January.

____. 2015. "Global Growth Revised Down, Despite Cheaper Oil, Faster U.S. Growth." World Economic Outlook. <imf.org/external/pubs/ft/survey/so/2015/NEW012015A.htm>.

International Co-operative Alliance. 2013. "Co-operatives and Sustainability: An Investigation into the Relationship." <ica.coop/sites/default/files/attachments/Sustainability%20Scan%202013-12-17%20EN.pdf>.

____. 2015. "Facts and Figures." <ica.coop/en/facts-and-figures>.

Institute for Local Self Reliance. 2015. "Investment Cooperatives." <ilsr.org/rule/community-ownership-commercial-spaces/investment-cooperatives/>.

Institute of International Finance. 2014. "IIF: Emerging Growth Picks Up, Remains Fragile." 7 November. <iif.com/press/iif-emerging-growth-picks-remains-fragile>.

IPSOS Reid. 2013. "Co-operative Tracking Study." Ottawa: Ipsos Reid Inc.

Islam, Iyanatul. 2015. "Technology and the Future of Work in Advanced Economies." *Journal Social Europe* 23 April.

Ismi, Asad. 2014. "Western Companies Responsible for Deaths of Garment Workers." CCPA *Monitor* 20, 8: 32–34.

Jamison, D.T., J.G. Breman, A.R. Measham, et al., editors. 2015 [2006]. *Disease Control Priorities in Developing Countries*. 2nd edition, Washington, DC: World Bank. <ncbi.nlm.nih.gov/books/NBK11751/>.

Jambec, J., R. Geyer, C. Wilcox, T. Seiger, M. Peryman, A. Andrady, R. Naryan and K.L. Law. 2015. "Plastic Waste Inputs from Land into the Ocean." *Science* 347, 6223 (13 February): 768–771. DOI: 10.1126/science.1260352.

Jones, Owen. 2014. "Grotesque Inequality Is Not a Natural Part of Being Human." *Manchester Guardian*, 24 November. <theguardian.com/commentisfree/2014/nov/24/

grotesque-inequality-greed-human-nature-capitalism>.

____. 2015. *The Establishment: And How They Get Away with It.* UK: Penguin Random House.

Joyce, Frank. 2013. "How Successful Cooperative Economic Models Can Work Wonderfully ... Somewhere Else." Alternet July 23. <alternet.org/economy/how-successful-cooperative-economic-models-can-work-wonderfully-somewhere-else?akid=10739.1084026.kQ8kSt>.

Kagawa, Tpyohiko. 1937. "Brotherhood Economics, Student Christian Movement Press." London: 18 Bloomsbury Street.

Kay, John. 2015. *Other People's Money: Masters of the Universe or Servants of the People?* London, UK: Profile Books.

Kennedy, Robert F. 1966. "Day of Affirmation." Speech June 6 at the University of Cape Town, South Africa N.U.S.A.S. <rfksafilm.org/html/speeches/unicape.php>.

____. 1968. Speech at Unversity of Kansas. <jfklibrary.org/Research/Research-Aids/Ready-Reference/RFK-Speeches/Remarks-of-Robert-F-Kennedy-at-the-University-of-Kansas-March-18-1968.aspx>.

Ketilson Lou Hammond, and Johnston Birchall. 2009. *Resilience of the Cooperative Business Model in Times of Crisis.* Geneva: International Labor Organization.

Keynes, John Maynard. 1936. *The General Theory of Employment, Interest and Money.* Chapter 12, VI, first paragraph. <marxists.org/reference/subject/economics/keynes/general-theory/ch12.htm>.

Khandhar, Parag Rajendra. 2015. "REI Will #OptOutside on Black Friday. Can It Change Retail (and the Economy)?" *Yes Magazine,* 27 November <yesmagazine.org/new-economy/rei-will-optoutside-on-black-friday-can-it-change-retail-and-the-economy-20151124?utm_source=YTW&utm_medium=Email&utm_campaign=20151127>.

Kidder, Tracy. 2003. *Mountains Beyond Mountains: The Quest of Dr. Paul Farmer, a Man Who Would Cure the World.* New York: Random House.

Klein, Naomi. 2007. *The Shock Doctrine: The Rise of Disaster Capitalism.* London, UK: Allen Lane, Penguin.

____. 2014. *This Changes Everything: Capitalism vs The Climate.* Toronto: Alfred A Knopf.

Korten, David. 2015a. "Obama's Push for Corporate Rule: A Moment of Opportunity." *Yes Magazine,* 25 June. <yesmagazine.org/obamas-push-for-corporate-rule-a-moment-of-opportunity?utm_source=YTW&utm_medium=Email&utm_campaign=20150626>.

____. 2015b. "A Trade Rule that Makes It Illegal to Favor Local Business? Newest Leak Shows TPP Would Do That and More." *Yes Magazine* on line, 15 April. <yesmagazine.org/new-economy/trade-rule-illegal-favor-local-business-tpp-leak-wikileaks?utm_source=YTW&utm_medium=Email&utm_campaign=20150417>.

Kowalski, Wolfgang. 2015. "Understanding the European Union's Façade Democracy." *Social Europe Journal.* <socialeurope.eu/2015/04/understanding-the-european-unions-facade-democracy/>.

Krugman, Paul. 2015. "What You Need to Know About the Eurozone Crisis." <socialeurope.eu/2015/03/what-you-need-to-know-about-the-eurozone-crisis/>.

Landy, Benjamin. 2013. *Graph: How the Financial Sector Consumed America's Economic Growth.* Century Foundation website, February 25. <tcf.org/blog/detail/graph-how-the-financial-sector-consumed-americas-economic-growth>.

Lardy, Nicholas R. 2014. *Markets over Mao: The Rise of Private Business in China*. Washington: Peterson Institute for International Economics.

Leonard, Christopher. 2014. *The Meat Racket: The Secret Takeover of America's Food Business*. Simon Schuster.

Lehndorff, Steffen. 2015. *Divisive Integration: The Triumph of Failed Ideas in Europe Revisited*, European Trade Union Institute, Brussels

Levitt, Kari. 2013. *From the Great Transformation to the Great Financialization*. Halifax, NS: Fernwood Publishing.

Lewis, Michael. 2011. *The Big Short: Inside the Doomsday Machine*. New York: W.W. Norton.

Lincoln, Abraham. 1863. *Gettysburg Address*. <abrahamlincolnonline.org/lincoln/speeches/gettysburg.htm>.

Lipsey, R.G., and C. Ragan. 2010. *Introduction to Microeconomics*, 11th edition. Toronto: Pearson.

Logue, John, and Jacquelyn Yates. 2005. "Ownership and Participation Make a Difference." Ohio Employee Productivity in Co-operatives and Worker Owned Enterprises, Employee Ownership Center, Kent State University. Prepared for Employment Sector, International Labour Office, Geneva.

Loomis, Erik. 2015. *Out of Sight: The Long and Disturbing Story of Corporations Outsourcing Catastrophe*. New York: The New Press.

Lynch, Lori, Marilee Urban and Robert Sommer. 1989. "De-Emphasis on Cooperatives in Introductory Economics Textbooks." *Journal of Agricultural Cooperation* 4.

Mac Cormac, Susan H. 2011. "New Corporate Forms: Flexible Purpose Corporations, Benefit Corporations, and L3Cs." Berkeley Law, University of California. <law.berkeley.edu/files/bclbe/Berkeley_Handout_1182011_-_1.pdf>. Accessed 18 April 2015.

Mackensie, Hugh. 2015. "Glory Days Are Back for Canada's CEOs." *CCPA Monitor* 21, 8 (February).

Macleans Magazine. 2014. "Who Earns What: Global CEO-to-Worker Pay Ratios." 27 September. <macleans.ca/economy/money-economy/global-ceo-to-worker-pay-ratios/>.

MacPherson, Ian, and Joy Emmanuel (eds.). 2007. *Co-operatives and the Pursuit of Peace*. Victoria, BC: British Columbia Institute for Co-operative Studies, University of Victoria.

MacPherson, Ian. 2009 *A Century of Co-operation*, (Ottawa: the Canadian Co-operative Association)

Macrotrends. <http://www.macrotrends.net/chart/1369/crude-oil-price-history-chart>.

Madeley, John. 1999. *Big Business Poor Peoples: The Impact of Transnational Corporations on the World's Poor*. London: Zed Books.

Mandel, Emily St. John. 2014. *Station 11*. Toronto: Penguin Random House.

Mander, Jerry. 1991. *In the Absence of the Sacred: The Failure of Technology and the Survival of the Indian Nations*. San Francisco: Sierra Club Books.

Marshall, Alfred. 1920 [1890]. *Principles of Economics*, 8th edition. London: Macmillan and Company.

Mason, Paul. 2015. "The End of Capitalism Has Begun." *The Guardian*, 17 July. <theguardian.com/books/2015/jul/17/postcapitalism-end-of-capitalism-begun>.

Mayer, Ann-Marie. 1997. "Historical Changes in the Mineral Content of Fruits and Vegetables." *British Food Journal* 99/6 [1997] 207–211, MCB University Press.

McMurtry, J. 2013. *The Cancer Stage of Capitalism*. London: Pluto Press.

Mendel, Marguerite (ed.). 2005. *Reclaiming Democracy: The Social Justice in the Political Economy of Gregory Baum and Kari Levitt.* Montreal: McGill-Queens Press.

Menzani, Tito, and Vera Zamagni. 2010. "Cooperative Networks in the Italian Economy." *Enterprise & Society* 11, 1 (March): 98–127. Oxford University Press.

Meyer, Henning. 2014. "If You Look at One Graph About Inequality Look at This!" *Social Europe,* 29 September <socialeurope.eu/2014/09/look-one-graph-inequality-look/>.

Milanovic, Branko. 2011. *The Haves and the Have-Nots: A Brief and Idiosyncratic History of Global Inequality.* New York: Basic Books.

Mill, John Stuart. 1987 [1848]. Principles of Political Economy. Fairfield, NJ: A.M. Kelley.

Ministry of Economic Development, Innovation and Export in Québec. 2008. *Survival Rate of Co-operatives in Québec.* <file:///C:/Users/acer/Desktop/Documents/Co-op%20 Library/Capitalism%20in%20Crisis%20vs%20Co-ops/Co-op%20Survival%20 Rate%20in%20Qu%C3%A9bec,%202008%20_%20The%20On%20Co-op%20Blog. htm>.

Mintz, Morton. 1985. *At Any Cost: Corporate Greed, Women, and the Dalkon Shield.* New York: Pantheon Books.

Mintzberg, Henry. 2013. "Rebuilding American Enterprise." Author's Website, 14 May. <mintzberg.org/enterprise>.

Mitchell, Alanna. 2009. *Sea Sick: The Global Ocean in Crisis.* Toronto: McClelland and Stewart.

Mokhiber, Russell. 1988. *Corporate Crime and Violence.* San Francisco: Sierra Club Books.

Morell, Virginia. 1999. "The Sixth Extinction." *National Geographic Magazine.* 2004. Vol 195, No. 2, February 1999: 49.

Morell, Virginia. 2015. "Feeding Frenzy: Orcas Show Their Smarts by Working Together to Whip Up a Meal." *National Geographic,* July.

Moss, Michael. 2013. *Salt, Sugar, Fat: How the Food Giants Hooked Us.* Toronto: McClelland and Stewart.

Murphy, Raymond. 2009. "Leadership in Disaster: Learning for a Future with Global Climate Change." Montreal: McGill-Queens University Press.

Murray, Carole. 2011. *Co-op Survival Rates in British Columbia.* BC-Aberta Social Economy Research Alliance, Canadian Centre for Community Renewal (CCCR).

Nachtergaele, F., J. Bruinsma, J. Valbo-Jorgensen and D. Bartley. 2010. *Anticipated Trends in the Use of Global Land and Water Resources.* FAO, Solaw Background Thematic Report TR01

Nadeau, Rober. 2008. "The Economist Has No Clothes." *Scientific American,* April. <scientificamerican.com/article/the-economist-has-no-clothes/>.

New Economy Coalition. n.d. "There Are Many Alternatives — It's Time for a New Economy."<neweconomy.net/>.

Nickerson, Mike. 2009. *Life, Money and Illusion.* Gabriola Island, BC: New Society Publishers.

Novković, Sonja, and Leslie Brown. 2012. *Social Economy: Communities, Economies and Solidarity in Atlantic Canada.* Sydney, NS: Cape Breton University Press.

Novković, Sonja, and Tom Webb (eds.). 2014. *Co-operatives in a Post Growth Era: Creating Co-operative Economics.* London, UK: Zed Books,

Nowak, Martin A. 2012. *Super Cooperators: Altruism, Evolution and Why We Need Each*

Other to Succeed. New York: Simon and Schuster.

____. 2012b. "Why We Help." *Scientific American* 307, 1: 34–39. <scientificamerican.com/article/why-we-help-evolution-cooperation/?responsive=false>.

Nowak, Peter. 2006. "Gattung Admits Telcos Not Being Straight." *New Zealand Herald*, Monday, May 8. <nzherald.co.nz/business/news/article.cfm?c_id=3&objectid=10380894>.

O'Heagan, Eia Mae, and Nicholas Shaxon. 2013. "Heard that Countries Should 'Compete' on Tax? Wrong." *Guardian*, 18 April.

OAS, IACHR (Inter-American Commission on Human Rights). 1992. "Report N° 26/92, Case 10.287." September 24. El Salvador.

Oberai, A.S. 1993. *Population Growth Employment and Poverty in Third World Mega-Cities.* The ILO Studies Series.

Opinion Research Corporation. 2003. "Perceptions of Co-operatives." Survey carried out for the National Co-operative Business Association and the Consumer Federation of America. Washington, D.C.

Oreskes, Naomi, and Erik M. Conway. 2010. *Merchants of Doubt: How a Handful of Scientists Obscured the Truth on Issues from Tobacco to Global Warming.* New York: Bloomsbury Press.

Ormaechea, Jose Maria. 1993. *The Mondragon Co-operative Experience.* Basque Country, Spain: Otalora, Mondragon Co-operative Corporation.

Ostrom, Elinor. 1990. *Governing the Commons: The Evolution of Institutions for Collective Action.* Cambridge, UK: Cambridge University Press.

____. 2012. "The Future of the Commons: Beyond Market Failure and Government Regulation." London, UK: Institute of Economic Affairs. <iea.org.uk/sites/default/files/publications/files/IEA%20Future%20of%20the%20Commons%20web%20 29-1.10.12.pdf>.

Oxfam. 2013a. "The Cost of Inequality: How Wealth and Income Extremes Hurt Us All." <oxfam.org/sites/www.oxfam.org/files/cost-of-inequality-oxfam-mb180113.pdf>.

____. 2013b. "Behind the Brands: Food Justice and the Big 10 Food and Beverage Companies." <oxfam.org/sites/www.oxfam.org/files/bp166-behind-the-brands-260213-en.pdf>.

____. 2014. *Even It Up: Time to End Extreme Inequality.* Oxfam UK for Oxfam International.

Page, Antony, and Robert A. Katz. 2012. "The Truth About Ben and Jerry's." *Stanford Social Innovation Review* 10, 4 (Fall).

Patel, Raj. 2009. *The Value of Nothing: How to Reshape Market Society and Redefine Democracy.* New York: Picador, Saint Martin's Press, Pan Books.

Patterson, Scott. 2012a. *Dark Pools: High Speed Traders, AI Bandits and the Threat to the Global Financial System.* New York: Crown Business, Random House.

____. 2012b. "Breakdown: A Glimpse Inside the 'Flash Crash.'" *Wall Street Journal*, 10 June. <wsj.com/articles/SB10001424052702303296604577454330066039896>.

Pawlick, Thomas F. 2006. *The End of Food: How the Food Industry Is Destroying Our Food Supply and What You Can Do About It.* Vancouver: Greystone Books.

Peck, M. Scott. 1987. *The Different Drum: Community Making and Peace.* New York: Simon and Schuster.

Pelling, M., D. Manuel-Navarrete and M. Redclift. 2012. *Climate Change and the Crisis of Capitalism: A Chance to Reclaim Self, Society and Nature.* Abingdon, UK: Routledge.

Perkins, John. 2006. *Confessions of an Economic Hit Man.* New York: Penguin Books.

Piketty, Thomas. 2011. "Top Incomes in the Long Run of History." *Journal of Economic Literature* 49: 3–17.

____. 2014. *Capital in the Twenty First Century.* Boston: Harvard University Press.

Pimentel, David. 2006. "Soil Erosion: A Food and Environmental Threat." *Journal of Environment, Development and Sustainability* 8, 1 (February): 119–137.

Pink, Daniel. 2010. *Drive: The Surprising Truth about What Motivates Us.* London: Penguin.

Pobihushchy, Sidney. 2003. "Establishing a Co-operative Economy." Co-op Life Conference, Montpelier, VT, November 13–14.

Polanyi, Karl. 1944. *The Great Transformation: The Political and Economic Origins of Our Time.* Boston: Beacon Press.

Press Progress. 2015a. "Canada's CEO-to-Worker Pay Gap Among the Worst in the World." Ottawa: Broadbent Institute. <pressprogress.ca/en/post/canadas-ceo-worker-pay-gap-among-worst-western-world>.

Press Progress. 2015b. "Target Comes to Canada — Ruins Thousands of Lives — Goes Back to America." 15 January. <pressprogress.ca/en/post/video-target-comes-canada-ruins-thousands-lives-goes-back-america.

Proto, E., and A. Rustichini. 2014a. "GDP and Life Satisfaction: New Evidence." Center for Economic Policy Research, 11 January. <voxeu.org/article/gdp-and-life-satisfaction-new-evidence>.

____. 2013. "A Reassessment of the Relationship Between GDP and Life Satisfaction." <journals.plos.org/plosone/article?id=10.1371/journal.pone.0079358>

Rees, William E. 2014. Are Prosperity and Sustainability Compatible? In Novkvic, S, and Webb, T. Eds. Co-operatives in a Post Growth Era: Creating Co-operative Economics, Zed Books, London. 2014.

Reich, Robert B. 2015. *Saving Capitalism: For the Many Not the Few.* New York: Penguin Random House.

Restakis, John. 2010. *Humanizing the Economy: Co-operatives in the Age of Capital,* New Society Publishers, Gabriola Island, BC, Canada

____. 2013. "Social Co-ops and Social Care: An Emerging Role for Civil Society." <bcca.coop/sites/bcca.coop/files/u2/Social_Co-ops_Social_Care.pdf>.

____. 2015. "Civil Power and the Partner State: A Social Solidarity Economy Response to Austerity in Greece." Keynote address, Good Economy Conference, Zagreb. *Co-operative Grocer* 178 (May/June). <grocer.coop/articles/civil-power-and-partner-state>.

Ridley, D., H. Grabowski and J. Moe. 2006. "Developing Drugs for Developing Countries." *Health Affairs* 25, 2 (March): 313–324. <content.healthaffairs.org/content/25/2/313.full>.

Ridley, Mark. 2001. *The Cooperative Gene: How Mendel's Demon Explains the Evolution of Complex Beings.* New York: The Free Press, Simon and Schuster.

Robb, Alan, James Smith and Tom Webb. 2010. "Co-operative Capital: What It Is and Why Our World Needs It." Presented the Euricse conference on Financial Co-operative Approaches to Local Development Through Sustainable Innovation, 10–11 June, Trento, Italy.

Rodrik, Dani. 2015a. "TTIP and the War of Trade Models." *Social Europe Journal,* 6 May. <socialeurope.eu/2015/05/ttip-and-the-war-of-trade-models/>.

____. 2015b. "The Muddled Case for Trade Agreements." *Social Europe*, 17 June. <socialeurope.eu/2015/06/the-muddled-case-for-trade-agreements/>.

Rogers, Stan. 1976. "Make and Break Harbour." <lyricsfreak.com/s/stan+rogers/make+and+break+harbour_20255111.html>.

Roubini, Nouriel. 2015. "Will Technology Destroy Jobs?" *Social Europe*, 14 January. <socialeurope.eu/2015/01/technology-2/>.

Rudolph, L., S. Gould and J. Berko. 2015. *Climate Change, Health, and Equity: Opportunities for Action*. Oakland, CA: Public Health Institute.

Sachs, Wolfgang. 1993. *Global Ecology: A New Arena of Political Conflict*. UK: Zed Books; Halifax, NS: Fernwood Publishing.

Saney, Issac. 2004. *Cuba: A Revolution in Motion*. Halifax, NS: Fernwood Publishing.

Schatzker, Mark. 2015. *The Dorito Effect: The Surprising New Truth About Food and Flavor*. Toronto: Simon and Schuster.

Schneider, Nathan, and Trebor Scholz. 2015. "The Internet Needs a New Economy." The Next System Project. <thenextsystem.org/the-internet-needs-a-new-economy/?mc_cid=ac5b406e9b&mc_eid=fb8f82f85f>.

Schweickart, David. 2002. *After Capitalism*. Lanham, MD: Rowman and Littlefield Publishers.

Schweickart, David, and James Lawler. 1998. *Market Socialism: The Debate among Socialists*. New York: Routledge.

Scientific American. 2007. "Dirt Poor: Have Fruits and Vegetables Become Less Nutritious?" <scientificamerican.com/article/soil-depletion-and-nutrition-loss/>.

Senate of Canada. 1984. "Soil at Risk: Canada's Eroding Future." The Senate, Parliament Buildings.

Shabecoff, Phillip. 1988. "Global Warming Has Begun, Expert Tells Senate." *New York Times*, 24 June. <nytimes.com/1988/06/24/us/global-warming-has-begun-expert-tells-senate.html?mkt_tok=3RkMMJWWfF9wsRoiua3LZKXonjHpfsX57%2B4kWaWwlMI%2F0ER3fOvrPUfGjI4GTMdnI%2BSLDwEYGJlv6SgFS7jNMbZkz7gOXRE%3D>.

Sherman, Zoe. 2014. "Are We Better Off Than We Were 40 Years Ago? Weighing Increased Per Capita Income Against Rising Inequality, Insecurity, Burdens of Work, and Environmental Degradation." *Dollars and Sense*, November/December <dollarsandsense.org/archives/2014/1114sherman.html>.

Smelling, T., S. Morelli and J. Thompson. 2014. "Recent Trends in Income Inequality in the Developed Countries." *Journal for a Progressive Economy* 2 (March).

Smith, Adam. 2009 [1776]. *The Wealth of Nations*. Blacksberg, VA: Thrifty Books.

Smith, Phillip, and Manfred Max-Neef. 2011. *Economics Unmasked: From Power and Greed to Compassion and the Common Good*. Cambridge, UK: Green Books.

Snider, Laureen. 2015. *Corporate Crime*. Black Point, NS: Fernwood Publishing.

Social Europe Report. 2015. "After Rana Plaza." <socialeurope.eu/wp-content/uploads/2015/01/SER-RanaPlaza.pdf>.

Sommer, Michael. 2014. "After Rana Plaza: Business as Usual?" *Social Europe Journal*. <socialeurope.eu/2014/11/rana-plaza-business-usual/>.

Stanford, Jim. 2008. *Economics for Everyone: A Short Guide to the Economics of Capitalism*. Halifax, NS: Fernwood Publishing.

Statistics Portal. n.d. "Insured losses caused by natural disasters worldwide from

1995 to 2015 (in billion U.S. dollars)." <statista.com/statistics/281052/insured-losses-from-natural-disasters-worldwide/>.

Stiglitz, Joseph. 2003. *Globalization and Its Discontents*. New York: WW Norton and Company.

_____. 2009. "America's Socialism for the Rich." *Guardian*, 12 June. <theguardian.com/commentisfree/2009/jun/12/america-corporate-banking-welfare>.

_____. 2012. "The Price of Inequality." <nytimes.com/2012/08/05/books/review/the-price-of-inequality-by-joseph-e-stiglitz.html?pagewanted=all>.

_____. 2013. *The Price of Inequality: How Today's Divided Society Endangers Our Future*. New York: Norton and Company.

_____. 2015a. "Rewriting the Rules of the American Economy: An Agenda for Growth and Shared Prosperity." Roosevelt Institute. <rewritetherules.org/>.

_____. 2015b. "Investor Protection: The Secret Corporate Takeover." *Social Europe*, 14 May. <socialeurope.eu/2015/05/investor-protection-the-secret-corporate-takeover/>.

Stringham, Richard, and Celia Lee. 2011. "Co-op Survival Rates in Alberta." Alberta Community and Co-operative Association and BC-Alberta Social Economy Research Alliance, Port Alberni, BC. <uwcc.wisc.edu/pdf/BALTA%20A11%20Report%20-%20Alberta%20Co-op%20Survival.pdf>.

Stuckler, D., S. Basu, M. Suhrcke, A. Coutts and M. McKee. 2011. "Effects of the 2008 Recession on Health: A First Look at European Data." *Lancet* 378, 9786 (9 July): 124–125.

SustainAbility. 2014. "Model Behavior: 20 Business Model Innovations for Sustainability." <sustainability.com/library/model-behavior#.VWv_wkarEqk>.

Swiss Re. 2015. "Insured Losses from Disasters below Average in 2014 Despite Record Number of Natural Catastrophe Events, Says Swiss Re Sigma Study." <swissre.com/media/news_releases/Insured_losses_from_disasters_below_average_in_2014.html>.

Talley, Ian. 2015. "China Is One of the Most Unequal Countries in the World, IMF Paper Says." *Wall Street Journal*, 26 March. <blogs.wsj.com/economics/2015/03/26/china-is-one-of-most-unequal-countries-in-the-world-imf-paper-says/>.

Tcherneva, Pavlina R. 2014. "Reorienting Fiscal Policy: A Bottom-up Approach." *Journal of Post Keynesian Economics* 37, 1 (Fall): 43–66.

Thatcher, Margaret. 1987. Interview for *Women's Own*, Sept. 23, Margaret Thatcher Foundation. <margaretthatcher.org/document/106689>.

Todaro, M and Smith S. 2003. *Economic Development*, 8th edition. New York: Pearson Education Press.

Tran, Mark. 2013. "Malnutrition Identified as Root Cause of 3.1 Million Deaths Among Children." *The Guardian*, 6 June. <theguardian.com/global-development/2013/jun/06/malnutrition-3-million-deaths-children>.

Tutu, Desmond. 2000. "Bishop Romney Memorial Lecture." Toronto: Trinity College, February 16.

United Nations. 1948. "The Universal Declaration of Human Rights." <un.org/en/documents/udhr/>

_____. 2010. *Report Submitted by the Special Rapporteur on the Right to Food*. Olivier De Schutter, Human Rights Council, Sixteenth session, Agenda item 3, 20 December.

____. 2014. *World Urbanization Prospects.* Department of Economic and Social Affairs, Population Division. World Urbanization Prospects: The 2014 Revision, Highlights (ST/ESA/SER.A/352).

____. 2015. "Hunger Vital Statistics: Global Hunger." <un.org/en/globalissues/ briefingpapers/food/vitalstats.shtml>.

United States, Congress, House. 1973. "Energy Reorganization Act of 1973: Hearings." Ninety-third Congress, first session, on H.R. 11510. p. 248.

United States Department of Agriculture. 2005. "Agricultural Concentration." Farm Bill Forums. <www.usda.gov/oce/newsroom/archives/testimony/2005-1997files/051701co.html>.

van Gelder, Sarah. 2015. "Rev. Sekou on Today's Civil Rights Leaders: 'I Take My Orders From 23-Year-Old Queer Women.'" Interview with Rev. Osagyefo Uhuru Sekou, *Yes Magazine* on line, 22 July. <yesmagazine.org/peace-justice/black-lives-matter-s-favorite-minister-reverend-sekou-young-queer?utm_source=YTW&utm_medium=Email&utm_campaign=20150724>.

Victor, Peter. 2014. "Living Well: Explorations Into the End of Growth." In S. Novković and T. Webb, *Co-operatives in a Post Growth Era: Creating Co-operative Economics.* London: Zed Books.

Vionea, Anca. 2014. "France Is Witnessing a Growth in Worker Co-Operatives." *Co-operative News*, 14 July, Manchester, UK.

Viswanathan, Balaji. 2013. "Why Is Apple Stock Falling Down?" *Forbes* Online, 13 February. <forbes.com/sites/quora/2013/02/13/why-is-apple-stock-falling-down/>.

Vitali, S., J.B. Glattfelder and S. Battiston. 2011. "The Network of Global Corporate Control." <arxiv.org/PS_cache/arxiv/pdf/1107/1107.5728v2.pdf>.

Wackernagel, Mathis, and W. Rees. 1996. *Our Ecological Footprint.* Gabriola Island, BC: New Society Publishers.

Walker, Alice. 1989. *The Temple of My Familiar.* New York: Pocket Books, Washington Square Books.

Webb, T., L. Benander, L. Cirillo, C. Laier and S. Aljuwani. 2005. "Marketing Our Co-operative Advantage." Cooperative Development Institute, Greenfield, MA. A report prepared for the National Co-operative Bank, Washington. <cdi.coop/wp-content/uploads/2014/06/ncbsmall2.pdf>.

Weeks, John. 2014. "Inequality Is Falling Globally! (And Similar Nonsense)." *Social Europe Journal* 23/07.

West, Darrell E. 2014. *Billionaires: Reflections on the Upper Crust.* Washington: Brookings Institution Press.

Whyte, W.F., and K.K. Whyte. 1991. *Making Mondragon: The Growth and Dynamics of the Worker Cooperative Complex.* Ithica, NY: Cornell University Press.

Wilkinson, Richard, and Kate Pickett. 2011. *Spirit Level: Why Greater Equality Makes Societies Stronger.* UK: Bloomsbury Press.

World Bank. 2014. "Climate Smart Development: Adding Up the Benefits of Actions That Help Build Prosperity, End Poverty and Combat Climate Change." Washington and San Francisco: 2014 International Bank for Reconstruction and Development/The World Bank and Climate Works Foundation.

____. 2015. "Global Economic Prospects to Improve in 2015, But Divergent Trends Pose

Downside Risks, Says WB." <worldbank.org/en/news/press-release/2015/01/13/global-economic-prospects-improve-2015-divergent-trends-pose-downside-risks>.

World Water Organization. 2010a. "Total Renewable Fresh Water Supply by Country." <worldwater.org/data20082009/Table1.pdf>.

____. 2010b. "Fresh Water Withdrawal by County and Sector (2009)." <worldwater.org/data20082009/Table2.pdf>.

Williams, Robert Gregory. 1986. *Export Agriculture and the Crisis in Latin America*. University of North Carolina Press.

Zamagni, Stefano, and Vera Zamagni. 2010. *Co-operative Enterprise: Facing the Challenge of Globalization*. Cheltenham, UK: Edward Elgar

Zamagni, V., P. Battilani and A. Casali. 2004. *La cooperazione di consumo in Italia*. Il Mulino, Italy.

Zucman, Gabriel. 2015. *The Hidden Wealth of Nations: The Scourge of Tax Havens*. University of Chicago.

WEBSITES OF SOME ORGANIZATIONS EXPLORING ECONOMIC ALTERNATIVES

Broadbent Institute, Canada <broadbentinstitute.ca>

Canadian Centre for Policy Alternatives, Canada

Capital Institute, U.S.

Center for Corporate Policy, U.S. <corporatepolicy.org/issues/crimedata.htm>

Center for Global Justice, U.S.

Carey Center for Democratic Capitalism, U.S.

Council of Canadians, Canada

Democracy Collaborative, U.S.

EURICSE (European Research Institute on Cooperative and Social Enterprises), Italy

FairShares, U.K.

Foundation on Economic Trends

Future of Humanity Institute <fhi.ox.ac.uk/research/research-areas/>

Green Worker Cooperatives, U.S.

The Guardian Co-operative Hub: <theguardian.com/sustainable-business/series/co-operatives-and-mutuals>.

New Economics Foundation, U.K.

New Economy Coalition, U.S. and Canada

Institute for New Economic Thinking International <ineteconomics.org/er>

International Co-operative Alliance, Global

P2P Foundation, International <p2pfoundation.net/Main_Page?mc_cid=8c8cc279f6&mc_eid=fb8f82f85f>

Progressive Economics Forum, Canada <progressive-economics.ca>

Schumacher Center for a New Economics

The Working World, New York <theworkingworld.org/us/>

The Next System Project, U.S.

United States Federation of Worker Cooperatives, U.S.

Yes Magazine, U.S.

INDEX